Contents

List of tables

SOCIAL WORK AND CHILD WELFARE POLITICS

Through Nordic lenses

Edited by Hannele Forsberg and Teppo Kröger

First published in Great Britain in 2011 by

The Policy Press
University of Bristol
Fourth Floor
Beacon House
Queen's Road
Bristol BS8 1QU
UK

t: +44 (0)117 331 4054
f: +44 (0)117 331 4093
e: tpp-info@bristol.ac.uk
www.policypress.co.uk

North American office:
The Policy Press
c/o International Specialized Books Services
920 NE 58th Avenue, Suite 300
Portland, OR 97213-3786, USA
t: +1 503 287 3093
f: +1 503 280 8832
e: info@isbs.com

British Library Cataloguing in Publication Data
A catalogue record for this book is available from the British Library.

Library of Congress Cataloging-in-Publication Data
A catalog record for this book has been requested.

ISBN 978 1 84742 900 1 paperback
ISBN 978 1 84742 406 8 hardback

The right of Hannele Forsberg and Teppo Kröger to be identified as editors of this work
has been asserted by them in accordance with the 1988 Copyright, Designs and Patents Act.

Cover design by The Policy Press
Front cover: image kindly supplied by www.istock.com
Printed and bound in Great Britain by Marston Book Services, Oxford.

Notes on contributors

Helena Blomberg is Professor of Social Policy, especially social work, at the University of Helsinki, Finland. Her major fields of research concern policy changes in, and the legitimacy of, the Nordic welfare state model and comparative social work. She participates in a Nordic research project focusing on the conditions and circumstances of social work practice in child welfare.

Clary Corander is a researcher at Folkhälsan Research Center in Helsinki, Finland. She has an MSocSc in social policy from Åbo Akademi and an MSocSc in social work from the University of Helsinki. In 2005-08 she worked as a research assistant at the Swedish School of Social Science, University of Helsinki, and participated in a Nordic research project focusing on the conditions and circumstances of social work practice in child welfare.

Tuija Eronen is a researcher and PhD student of social work at the University of Tampere, Finland. Her ongoing PhD research is based on the narrative inquiry of children's homes as a part of the life stories and personal lives of current and former residents. She has extensive practical experience in child welfare.

Guðný Björk Eydal is Associate Professor in the Faculty of Social Work at the University of Iceland. Her main research topics include the welfare state and policies on families and children, in particular childcare policies. She participates in the Nordic REASSESS Centre of Excellence in welfare research. Among her recent publications are articles on childcare policies in the Nordic countries, Icelandic family policy and children and the Nordic welfare states.

Reidun Folleso is Associate Professor in the Department of Social Sciences, Bodø University College, Norway. Her main field of research is user participation in child protection services.

Hannele Forsberg is Professor of Social Work in the Department of Social Work Research at the University of Tampere, Finland. Her main research fields are family and childhood research and social work practices. Her ongoing research project concerns contested family practices and moral reasoning.

Margareta Hydén is Professor of Social Work at Linköping University, Sweden. She has written extensively in the fields of family violence, gender studies, narrative social work and the methodological aspects of research, including children and researching sensitive topics.

Sigrun Júlíusdóttir is Professor of Social Work and chair for the Research Centre of Family Relations, University of Iceland, and formerly a chief social worker at the Icelandic University Psychiatric Hospital. She runs a part-time private practice and has extensive experience of family research, supervising, teaching and writing on family matters and professional development of social work.

Christian Kroll is a lecturer in social work and social policy at the University of Helsinki, Finland. His research interests include normative bases of welfare policy, welfare policy discourses and comparative social policy and social work. He participates in a Nordic research project focusing on the conditions and circumstances of social work practice in child welfare.

Teppo Kröger is Academy Research Fellow, working at the University of Jyväskylä, Finland. Formerly a social worker and lecturer in social work, his main research interests focus on comparative research on social care, including childcare, care for disabled people and care for older people. He is the founder and coordinator of the Nordic network 'Nordfaso: Family-oriented social work in the Nordic countries', whose members have collaborated in writing this book.

Marjo Kuronen is a senior lecturer in social work at the University of Jyväskylä, Finland. Her research interests include gendered practices of parenting and post-divorce family relations, feminist social work and qualitative cross-cultural research methodology. She is currently the chief editor of the Finnish *Journal of Social Policy and Social Work Research*.

Riitta Laakso is a PhD student of social work at the University of Tampere, Finland. Her ongoing PhD research is focused on child protection in a children's home. She is a lecturer in social services and education at the Lahti University of Applied Sciences.

Pia Lahtinen is Manager of Merikratos Child Welfare Ltd, Central Finland. She has worked as a social worker, as a lecturer at the Jyväskylä University of Applied Sciences and as a project manager in the Development Unit in Central Finland. She has recently accomplished her licentiate degree specialising in social work with children and young people.

Anna Meeuwisse is Professor of Social Work at Lund University, Sweden. Her major fields of research concern the history of social work, comparative social work, voluntary organisations and the welfare state. She participates in a Nordic research project focusing on the conditions and circumstances of social work practice in child welfare.

Kate Mevik is Associate Professor in the Department of Social Sciences, Bodø University College, Norway. She has published a number of books and articles on the needs and rights of children whose parents are suffering from mental illness.

Keith Pringle is Professor in Sociology with a specialism in social work at Uppsala University, Sweden, Research Professor in Social Work and Social Policy at London Metropolitan University, UK, and Honorary Professor at both Aalborg and Warwick Universities, Denmark and UK. His research fields include comparative welfare analysis and intersectionality where he has published widely, including five books as author or co-author and six as co-editor. He is also a qualified social worker with 10 years' practice experience.

Tarja Pösö is Professor of Social Work in the Department of Social Work Research at the University of Tampere, Finland. Her research interests include: the social problems of children, young people and families; institutional practices, especially child protection; and qualitative inquiry.

Aino Ritala-Koskinen is Assistant Professor of Social Work in the Department of Social Work Research at the University of Tampere, Finland. Her research interests include child welfare, childhood studies and changing family structures.

Roberto Scaramuzzino is a PhD student at Malmö University, Sweden. His fields of research concern comparative social work, immigrant organisations and the welfare state. He participates in a Nordic research project focusing on the conditions and circumstances of social work practice in child welfare.

Hans Swärd is Professor of Social Work at Lund University, Sweden. His major fields of research concern child welfare, homelessness and social work. He participates in a Nordic research project focusing on the conditions and circumstances of social work practice in child welfare.

Inger Marii Tronvoll is Associate Professor in the Department of Social Work and Health Science at the Norwegian University of Science and Technology, and formerly a researcher at the Norwegian Centre for Child Research, Trondheim, Norway. Her research experience includes issues concerning children and social work.

ONE

Introduction

Hannele Forsberg and Teppo Kröger

Social work within 'a welfare paradise'

In international comparisons the Nordic countries – Sweden, Norway, Finland, Denmark and Iceland – are often described as child-centred welfare paradises for children (see, for example, Haavind and Magnusson, 2005; James and James, 2008, pp 1-2). Researchers have pointed out that there is a specific tradition of welfare state support for families with children in this region, which is characterised by comprehensiveness, generosity, universalism, gender equality and egalitarianism (for example, Björnberg, 1999; Sainsbury, 1999; Hiilamo, 2002, 2007; Ellingsæter and Leira, 2006). The paradise image is strengthened by empirical findings from international studies that have shown, for example, child poverty to be rare and children's well-being and health to be relatively high in the Nordic countries (for example, UNICEF, 2007; Hiilamo, 2008). Seeing the Nordic region as an ideal place for children's welfare has also been further supported by the emphasis of the Nordic societies on the individuality of children; in these societies, children are regularly seen as individuals with rights of their own, whether the question is of children's relations to families, welfare institutions or policy (see Millar and Warman, 1996, p 46; Brembeck et al, 2004).

If the Nordic countries really form a specific paradisiacal sociocultural context for childhood, what does this mean for social work with children and families? The basic understanding of social work is that it exists to provide remedies of some kind to people who experience social threats, problems or risks in the area of welfare. Does the Nordic welfare context make a difference to the nature of child welfare social work? These are the basic questions that this volume and its chapters aim to address, making both public discussions and everyday child welfare practices from the Nordic countries available for English-speaking readers. Until now Nordic perspectives have been rather rare in the body of English-language social research on child welfare and child protection, even though the Nordic welfare states and their child welfare are, because of their international 'top position' ranking, objects of large international interest.

The paradise image needs immediate specification in three respects. First, the Nordic welfare states are not immune to strong global and local pressures to reinterpret and change their welfare model. The economic recession of the early 1990s hit especially Finland and Sweden and the current recession is affecting most strongly Iceland. More generally, there are continuous international pressures for governments to lower their tax rates and limit their welfare programmes. Within welfare services, outsourcing and privatisation have entered the Nordic region also, reducing public provision and bringing a more mixed economy of welfare. Furthermore, new public management is a global trend that has influenced also the Nordic countries, bringing market-oriented approaches and practices within the field of welfare. As well, globalisation of the economy and European integration are affecting the Nordic welfare model and social work with children and families.

Second, there are snakes in the paradise; the utterly positive general image of children's welfare in the Nordic countries is not the whole story. Social exclusion and poverty do exist also in the Nordic region. Lone mothers and people from minority ethnic communities are particularly at risk, facing barriers to achieve economic and social well-being for their children. Youth unemployment has become a lasting phenomenon. Divorce rates are high and the Nordic countries have been rather slow to recognise and address the prevalence of violence that children and women are facing inside the family home. Thus, the broad scale of welfare programmes provided for families with children in the Nordic countries does not mean that these countries will be free from social problems or that there will be no more need for social work with families with children.

Third, the Nordic region is not just one entity; it consists of five separate and independent nation states. Close historical and cultural bonds bring the five countries together, and a continuous and extensive interaction between the countries has been a trademark of the Nordic region for a long time. However, their 20th century histories are partly dissimilar and even today EU membership divides the Nordic countries into two groups: Norway and Iceland have preferred to stay outside whereas Denmark, Sweden and Finland are member states. Finland, nevertheless, is the only Nordic country that has adopted the Euro as its currency. Saying that all the Nordic countries belong to the 'social democratic welfare regime' is also an oversimplification as right-wing parties have participated in the construction of their welfare states, in particular in Iceland and Finland. The scant comparisons that have been made so far show that there are national differences within the Nordic cluster that also concern child welfare social work practices (see Forsberg and Vagli, 2006; Grinde, 2007).

Children and families are at the heart of social work all over the world. Currently the field is in the process of reform in many national contexts. This volume aims to offer a Nordic contribution to the international discussion on the changing field of child welfare. Even if the Nordic countries do not fully live up to their remarkably positive image and if the individual Nordic countries are dissimilar in many respects, they fare exceptionally well in international comparisons on children's welfare and form a distinctly close-knit 'family of nations' (Castles, 1993). It is thus worth looking at what kind of context the Nordic welfare model provides for social work with families with children and some of the special features it offers. This book presents examples and critical interpretations of social work and child welfare politics from Nordic perspectives.

The background and aims of the volume

The idea for this book arose during the meetings of a Nordic network of social work researchers and teachers focusing on social work with children and families (funded by the NORDPLUS programme 2004-08). The principal aim of the network has been to promote development in teaching and research in family-focused social work in the Nordic region. The network has included members from eight Nordic social work schools from all the five countries: from Iceland the University of Iceland in Reykjavík; from Finland the Universities of Tampere and Jyväskylä (which has coordinated the network); from Norway the Norwegian University of Science and Technology in Trondheim and the Bodø University College; from Sweden the Universities of Linköping and Lund; and from Denmark the University of Aalborg. The collection of articles that we have here is a result of a five-year-long collaboration of social work researchers from these eight universities.

The aim of the volume is to address questions of the impact of the Nordic sociocultural context for child welfare and social work with children and families. Being critically aware that the international discussion on social work with children and families is mostly dominated by experiences and perspectives from English-speaking countries, the network members have wished to make Nordic social work research available in English, to promote cultural sensitivity in the debate around child welfare social work and to reflect on whether there are particular Nordic aspects that could add to the understanding concerning the current challenges of social work with children and families in other parts of the world.

The contributors shed light on some of the ongoing debates within research on social work and child welfare politics in the Nordic countries, including the changing character of relations between welfare professionals, parents and children, and the growing variation of family forms. In particular, emerging new understanding on children's rights has started a reorientation process within Nordic child welfare practices and a quest for new approaches and methods in supporting families with children. The tendency to individualise children and childhood has been particularly strong in the Nordic countries and this has brought new ideological, practical and structural dilemmas to child welfare. How to balance children's and their parents' interests and rights? Should social work focus more on working with the children or with the parents? Which formal institution can best protect the needs of children – social welfare or the judicial system?

Another influential trend in the Nordic region has been to emphasise prevention instead of taking children into care and separating them from their parents. New methods like 'family work' have been developed for this but their aims and features remain partly unclear. Even when placements of children take place, they are almost always defined as temporary and attention is given to keeping a close contact between children and their parents. On the other hand, this dominant preventive tendency has made the roles of child protection, control and substitute care – which unavoidably remain an essential part of child welfare in every country – ambivalent. When child welfare is defined as prevention and support for families with children, control and protection of children vanishes out of sight. Taking children into care as well as foster care and institutional care of children become issues that are difficult to discuss openly; as they do not fit in with the dominant child welfare ideology, they become surrounded by an atmosphere of discomfort and uneasiness. As a consequence, problems that require direct intervention and even control, like violence in families and close relations, also become difficult to raise and address.

This book will consider and critically examine the impact of these features – coming from both the Nordic welfare model and current understanding on childhood, as well as from prevailing welfare ideology – on child welfare practices of the Nordic countries. Drawing on contemporary research and debates from Finland, Iceland, Norway and Sweden the book considers how social work and child welfare politics are produced and challenged as global and local ideas and practices.

Nordicness, child welfare and welfare politics

The starting point of this volume has been mostly thematic, explorative and eclectic – aiming to cover different topical discussions and ongoing transformations within Nordic child welfare – instead of following a single theoretical or methodological approach when analysing Nordic welfare policies and practices. Nevertheless, in the course of the working process, we have become aware of certain common analytical dimensions that are important across the chapters.

The first of these dimensions is the concept of Nordicness. What is Nordicness and how does it affect child welfare? On the one hand Nordicness can be argued to have a genuine historic-material basis in the social and political organisation of the five Nordic countries (Brembeck et al, 2004, p 11). As already emphasised, the Nordic countries have long been seen as very close to each other, as a lot of their past is a shared history and they have very close cultural and – concerning the three Scandinavian nations (Sweden, Norway and Denmark) – even linguistic connections. At the turn of the 15th century all five countries even formed a union, as the monarchies of Denmark, Sweden and Norway had an alliance, Finland was under the rule of Sweden and Iceland had recently been handed over from Norway to Denmark. This unique historical Nordic union did not last for long but close relations have remained. Since World War II the Nordic region has consisted of five countries. During the post-war period, Nordic cooperation has taken many institutionalised forms. For example, the Nordic Council was established in 1952 as a consultative and advisory forum for interparliamentary cooperation of the five Nordic parliaments. Also the Nordic Council of Ministers, the forum for Nordic governmental cooperation, was formed in 1971 (Arter, 1999.) Family and child policies are among those whose convergence these collaboration organisations have promoted during the post-war period.

On the other hand Nordicness can be seen as a fluid rhetorical resource that is activated from time to time in certain situations to serve the interests of its advocates. Equality (upheld by a strong society with collective responsibility) and individual freedom (originating from the Nordic peasant society) are brought out as the fundamental ideas of Nordicness and as the basic values of the Nordic welfare state. (Brembeck et al, 2004, pp 11-15.) The idea of Nordicness has been used as a building block for national identities in the region as well as a buffer in the face of perceived foreign threat – like the EU and its conservatism 'destroying the good old Nordic values'. These values are understood to concern children as well. In this book we investigate the possible implications of these general ideas of Nordicness on one particular field, that is, social work with families and children.

The second dimension is the way we approach and examine childcare social work. Most of the authors in this volume use the concepts of 'child welfare' or 'social work with children and families' instead of 'child protection' (for a cultural focus on these concepts, see Hearn et al, 2004). By this conceptual choice we want to underline one essential aspect of Nordic child welfare social work practices. Nordic countries tend to take a broad view of child welfare, emphasising the importance of preventive measures (various social services and social security schemes) to support families with children. The Nordic societies offer families psychosocial services like maternity and childcare clinics, home help, day care, family guidance clinics, school health care, as well as financial support. These services are also often the first arena where concern for a child's well-being is raised. On the other hand, these general services form an important support resource for child protection social workers dealing with child welfare/protection needs that have already been identified.

The Nordic countries have been understood – in particular when compared with English-speaking countries – to base child welfare social work on the so called 'welfare or family service model' instead of a legalistic justice model, which is a more typical feature in English-speaking countries (more detailed discussion on this in Chapter Three). Nevertheless, a few authors do use the concept of child protection here (for example in Chapter Ten). They do that deliberately in order to underline the specific character of their subject, child protection work, in relation to more general childhood politics and discussion on children's well-being.

Third, throughout the book we use the concept of 'welfare politics' in addition to that of social work in order to emphasise the broad welfare orientation that is characteristic of Nordic child welfare. With this choice we wish to stress the interrelated nature of wider welfare policy and child welfare practices in the Nordic countries. Welfare is defined comprehensively in the Nordic countries and promoting the welfare of children is a publicly expressed objective for a large number of welfare policies. Compared with many other countries, welfare politics concern larger parts of everyday life and family policies give more long-lasting financial support to families with children (Haavind and Magnusson, 2005, p 228).

With welfare politics, we are also referring to a widened understanding of politics. In this respect our approach is close to 'cultural politics of childhood', a concept offered by James and James (2008, pp 37–40) in their analysis of similarities and differences in social policies and practices of EU countries. Cultural politics of childhood focus on how cultural determinants, political mechanisms and the discourses they produce construct and define childhood and, thereby, what children can actually do in any given society. The approach looks at political mechanisms and processes, such as framing social policy and subsequent legislation, but also at the cultural factors that determine the different images and understandings of childhood, including the collective and individual influence of children themselves. For us, child welfare politics include not just political decision making and the resulting policies but also cultural processes and discourses, as well as the roles and spaces that are given to children, parents and social workers.

Finally, in line with these broad understandings of child welfare and welfare politics, we speak about 'Nordic lenses', referring to a multiplicity of themes and approaches included in this volume. The view is kaleidoscopic, offering glimpses of child welfare politics and practices of different Nordic countries. Different authors focus on different issues using different theoretical and methodological approaches in their analyses. This kind of perspective does not offer a final truth of its subject but is appropriate for dicussing a topic that is complex and for offering alternative resources for interpretation and further research and debate. Nordic social work and child welfare is multifaceted and this multiplicity is reflected in the composition of this volume.

The contents of the chapters

It is difficult to understand Nordic child welfare social work without clarification of the Nordic welfare state model – without general knowledge of its family policies and family legislation. Family policies form the context in which social work with children and families is practised as social work is faced with the positive and negative outcomes of social security and childcare policies. Chapter Two, written by Guðný Björk Eydal from Iceland and Teppo Kröger from Finland, gives a policy background of the main features of family law and family benefits and services in the five Nordic countries. It also provides an overview of the changing family structures and of the general economic and social situation of families with children in the Nordic region. A question addressed by the chapter is to what extent are the societal and policy contexts similar in the five Nordic countries, that is, to what extent can we say that the starting points for social work with children and families are the same all over the Nordic region?

Chapter Three presents results from an ongoing comparative Nordic research project in the field of child welfare social work. It is written by a Finnish and Swedish author group including Helena Blomberg, Clary Corander, Christian

Kroll, Anna Meeuwisse, Roberto Scaramuzzino and Hans Swärd, and it focuses on the conditions and circumstances of social work practice being linked to the current scholarly discussion about the development of social work in Europe and Scandinavia. The chapter is based on results from a study of child welfare referrals in four Nordic capitals. The empirical findings are discussed in the light of earlier studies conducted in countries belonging to other welfare models. The chapter provides new perspectives on the relevance and productiveness of welfare model thinking and comparative research in the case of child welfare services. Special attention is given to the question of how child welfare problems are understood and handled within the 'family service oriented' Nordic model.

Chapter Four focuses on changing cultural ideas of the quality of childhood in one Nordic national case context, Finland. By examining the emergence of a new concept, 'illfare of children', in the public discussion of child welfare politics, the traditional structural and institutional levels of analysis of welfare models, policies and practices are complemented by an analysis of dominant ideas/discourses. Hannele Forsberg and Aino Ritala-Koskinen ask whether the emergence of the illfare discourse is a sign of the erosion of the Nordic welfare universalism. One of the most circulated pieces of evidence for the increasing illfare of children has been the growing number of child welfare clients in Finland. This kind of use of statistics will be considered, besides the grass-roots experiences of child welfare social workers, in reflecting whether the growing public concern on children's illfare is justified. The chapter argues that the increased focus on children and childhood is part of a broader ongoing cultural trend, a change in attitudes towards childhood that is present also in many other late-modern societies. The overall aim of the chapter is to call for more critical awareness of the way public concern over childhood is shaping both the identification and solution of children's problems.

Concern about increasing and more complex problems of children and their families has caused a demand for targeted support for parenting and family life. In Finland new forms of services and methods of working with families and even a new particular professional group have emerged to meet this demand. However, the current field of this 'family work' has been criticised for being confusing and indefinite because of its various definitions, forms and activities. For 'family workers' the crucial question is finding a balance between helping parents and protecting children, and drawing the delicate line between control and support. Chapter Five, written by Marjo Kuronen and Pia Lahtinen from Finland, aims to clarify the character of this new type of working with families in the field of child welfare, which is targeted on families and children assessed to be in need of corrective and more intensive interventions in their everyday life. Critical discussion is raised concerning the objectives, targets, methods and effectiveness of this work.

Chapter Six is written by Sigrún Júlíusdóttir from a historical and professional perspective on the development of 'family social work'. Although based mainly on studying, working with and teaching about families in Iceland, the perspectives are integrated and stimulated by intertwined experiences from the other Nordic countries and the US. The chapter looks at the ideological roots of social work with families and child welfare, and it highlights the relevance of preserving the original holistic approach. On the other hand, postmodern thinking and values together with increased democratisation and revised ideas about the nature and function of power have radically influenced social work and changed the conditions, definitions and meanings of its position and role. The methodological shift from corrective interventions towards partnership and conferencing in family-focused social work is analysed as part of a paradigm shift concomitant with the professionalisation of social work. It is argued that the reflexive effects of postmodern processes are essential for the emerging reconstructions of families and family relationships, and theoretical skills and contextual understanding are needed to handle these transformations.

Chapter Seven, written by Reidun Follesø and Kate Mevik from Norway, examines critically three recent trends within the Norwegian Child Welfare Services. First, children are increasingly seen to have their own independent rights. Second, the family and the local social environment are more and more expected to be involved in decisions about which child welfare measures should be taken. Third, Norway aims currently for child welfare services that are knowledge-based. The chapter highlights some possible tensions between these trends and discusses what kind of implications there might be for a child in a situation where the three perspectives are in conflict with one another. The paper is written from the Norwegian context, but the questions raised have relevance for all of the Nordic countries as well as for other societies.

Child poverty has become a topic even in advanced welfare states. Chapter Eight, written by Inger Marii Tronvoll from Norway, discusses how social workers from social welfare and child protection services can contribute more actively towards helping children in families who face poverty. The theme is discussed from a discourse analytical approach, identifying the relevance of three different discourses: first, children's rights as parents' responsibilities; second, case processing rules guiding the practice in relation to children; and, third, children as subjects in their own life. These discourses are examined here from the point of view of Norwegian social work practices, looking at how they influence the practice of workers but also social work practice more generally. The connections presented in the chapter contribute to the more general ongoing debate on child poverty. Adult responsibility for children's rights and specific rules to ensure equal and fair case processing for all citizens are necessary principles in child welfare. The chapter argues for supplementing these two ways of thinking with the idea of understanding the child as an active subject.

The idea that it is harmful for children to be exposed to violence by growing up in a family where the mother is subjected to violence has received increased attention during the last few years. This has happened even in the Nordic countries where the established ideologies on consensus and gender neutrality have made age- and gender-based power asymmetries within families largely invisible.

Taking the child's perspective on 'mum's getting beaten' is the core of Chapter Nine, written by Margareta Hydén from Sweden. This means more than simply listening to the voices of children. It also implies acknowledging the kind of spaces that must be offered for children and discussing what analytical steps need to be taken in order to understand the children's experiences. The chapter directs attention to these methodological concerns. First, it aims to find a useful way of conceptualising the child's experience. Second, it discusses research strategies that will serve the purpose of gaining knowledge about the children's experiences told in a group therapy session.

Chapter Ten, written by Tuija Eronen, Riitta Laakso and Tarja Pösö, looks at Finnish residential childcare, which has a long history but which is not an issue that is high on the agenda of social policy debate, research or development. The chapter is based on reports, statistics and studies on residential childcare in Finland, and the material is interpreted from the perspectives of culture and child protection policy. In comparison with other countries, Finland is usually seen as having a high number of children and young people in residential care. Several structural changes are currently taking place within institutional service provision, including a growing number of private institutions. However, very little is known about these changes and their influences on the actual quality of care or on the rights of children and young people. The basic ambivalence concerning institutions for children and young people – 'Now you see them – now you don't' – is examined in the chapter from the point of view of a cultural silence. Three waves of silences and forgetting are located in Finnish national history.

Chapter Eleven is an epilogue that brings the book to its close. It is written by Keith Pringle, who is not a member of the original Nordic network of social work researchers. Inspired by the major themes of the other chapters the epilogue critically reflects on and outlines future challenges in the Nordic and international child welfare social work debate. Having a special experience in child welfare and social work research and practice from both Britain and the Nordic countries, the author raises some important points to learn from and for further discussion. He argues that, even though the welfare achievements of the Nordic countries have not been as comprehensive as the world might have wanted to believe, if any place in the world has a chance of developing what might be regarded as a genuinely empowering welfare system then it is probably still one of the Nordic countries.

TWO

Nordic family policies: constructing contexts for social work with families

Guðný Björk Eydal and Teppo Kröger

Introduction

The aim of this chapter is to provide a context for the other chapters of this book – to give a policy background for detailed analysis of Nordic child welfare social work practices. Social work is not practised in a societal vacuum. In order to understand social work practices, it is useful to know the main features of family law and family structures in the five countries as well as the general economic and social situation of families with children. Furthermore, family policies – which we understand here to include policies on childhood – form the context where social work is practised; social work is faced with the positive and negative outcomes of social security and childcare policies. To what extent is this societal and policy context similar in the five Nordic countries, to what extent can we say that the starting points for social work with children and families are the same all over the Nordic region?

The chapter starts with a brief description of the development and main features of Nordic family laws. In family legislation we include here also laws that are focused specifically on children and childhood. This is followed by an overview of family structures and of the economic labour market and social conditions of families with children in the five Nordic countries. A profile of the main outlines of family policies in the countries is provided as well, covering social security as well as childcare policies. The chapter concludes with a discussion about the basic situation of Nordic families with children, taking the existence of rather developed family policies into account, focusing on the similarities and dissimilarities between the five countries.

Family law in the Nordic countries

Legislation reflects prevailing normative understandings of a society and this goes also for family law. On the other hand, family legislation also structures family life, making certain family forms and lifestyles easier to realise than others. As in most nations, in the Nordic countries the 20th century was marked by radical changes in the understanding of a family.

Already during the 1910s and 1920s, the Nordic countries had joined forces in organising a special family law committee, which led all five countries to revise their family legislation. These two decades saw reforms in all Nordic marriage legislations (Bradley, 1996; Melby et al, 1999). According to Göran Therborn (1993, p 258), the reformed legislation "declared an explicit basic equality between husband and wife, father and mother, provided for no-fault divorce (after a procedure of separation) and established the principle of the best interests of the child as the main criterion for deciding issues of custody". During the same period, Nordic laws in respect of children were also changed. The revised laws provided children born out of marriage with the rights to an inheritance from their father. However, the timing of the implementation of these ideas was not identical in all Nordic countries. For example, in Finland, non-fault divorce became possible only in 1948 (and without joint application only from 1988) (Litmala, 2001).

These reforms were important milestones, indicating society's changing attitudes towards diversifying family forms (Therborn, 1993.) They also exemplify Nordic cooperation and exchange of information and experience, which has continued to the present day (Danielsen, 2005). Hence, similar main trends can be observed in the development of family legislation over the last decades. These trends include: first, increasing legal rights of children; second, a growing concern for the right of children to receive care from both parents, regardless of the parental relationship; and, third, a gradual legalisation of rights for same-sex couples.

All of the Nordic countries have ratified the Child Convention of the UN. In order to strengthen children's legal rights each Nordic country has also founded the office of an ombudsman of children. While the provision of care and the protection of children have been seen as essential parts of the Nordic welfare system for decades, the principle of participation has been emphasised more recently in line with the Child Convention (Eydal and Satka, 2006). Thus, children and young people are regarded as competent social actors with their own rights to influence their daily lives and society – for example, through participation in planning, politics and decision-making processes in families and schools (Kjørholt and Lidén, 2004).

Part of the change towards the increased rights of children has been the emphasis put on the right of the child to receive care from both parents. While it has been put forward in a gender-neutral tone, this change is mainly to ensure that fathers have the same opportunities as mothers to care for their children. Ever since the 1920s, Nordic law has emphasised that the children's best interests need be the decisive factor when decisions about their custody are being made (Therborn, 1993). Previously legal custody could be given to only one of the parents if they were not married. Even though the letter of the law was gender-neutral, it was highly unusual to give the legal custody to the father after divorce. In the case of Sweden, Bergman and Hobson (2002) have come to the conclusion that, until 1977, divorced men were granted the legal custody only when the mother could be proven to be an unsuitable parent. Furthermore, they point out that there was no legal principle favouring the mother in custody cases, but it was considered 'natural' that children remain with their mother (Bergman and Hobson, 2002, p 100).

The legal changes that took place in the Nordic countries in the 1970s and early 1980s changed the situation and have been of major importance for fathers (Table 2.1). The reforms introduced joint legal custody and emphasised children's access to both parents, regardless of how the relationship between the parents developed (Bergman and Hobson, 2002; Björnberg and Dahlgren, 2003; Forssén et al, 2003). All Nordic countries have adopted joint legal custody as the main rule after divorce or separation, Iceland last in 2006 (Danielsen, 2005; Ólafsson and Eydal, 2008).

Table 2.1: The timing of the first legislation on joint legal custody in the Nordic countries

	Denmark	Finland	Iceland	Norway	Sweden
First law on joint legal custody	1985	1983	1992	1981	1976
Courts can order joint legal custody	2007	1983	–	1981	1988

Sources: Júlíusdóttir and Sigurðardóttir (2000); Bergman and Hobson (2002); Lodrup et al (2003)

The rules on how to proceed if the parents are not in agreement on their children's custody differ somewhat between the countries (Table 2.1). Gradually the Nordic countries have given the courts the right to order joint legal custody despite disagreements between parents, with the exception of Iceland (Nielsen, 1997; Júlíusdóttir and Sigurðardóttir, 2005). According to Björnberg and Dahlgren (2003), the main argument for giving the authorities this right is to prevent one parent from being able to exclude the other parent from having custody.

Nevertheless, even after joint legal custody has become the main rule, most children remain living with their mothers after divorce or separation (for example, Júlíusdóttir and Sigurðardóttir, 2005; Ottosen, 2006) and the majority of lone-parent families are lone-mother families (NOSOSCO, 2007). Consequently, the right of the child to meet the non-residential parent has been regarded as an important part of policies that define fatherhood.

During the last decades of the 20th century, the Nordic countries emphasised the importance of the child to have access to both parents and to their care (Lodrup et al, 2003). The increase in joint legal custody has not made these arrangements less important. In all five Nordic countries some children do live with both parents after divorce, but because of a lack of comparable statistics on the living arrangements of children it is not possible to tell how many children do spend the same amount of time with both parents.

All the Nordic countries have enacted laws on public services to parents in order to support parents in their roles and to support families in crisis. The institutional setting varies between the countries but Hiilamo (2007) points out a common characteristic for all the Nordic countries: an unmet demand for parenting support services and family counselling, which further increases the demand for social work. Social workers also provide a wide range of services within the child protection systems. All the Nordic countries have a special law on child and youth welfare, covering general measures as well as individual cases where children are believed to be at risk. In all the countries children may be placed outside their home without the consent of their parents. In Finland and Sweden such decisions are made by the courts; in Denmark and Iceland they are decided by a special municipal child and youth committee (and can take up to two months in Iceland); and in Norway they are under the jursidiction of a government committee (NOSOSCO, 2007; see other chapters of this book).

The third major change in family law in the Nordic countries over recent decades is the increase of legal rights for same-sex couples and their families. All the Nordic countries have provided same-sex couples with a legal right to enter a registered partnership, which has in most respects the same legal status as marriage. However, the original laws on registered partnerships did not address parenthood or parental rights of same-sex couples, but such rights have been expanded gradually (Waaldijk, 2005).

Family structures in the Nordic countries

Despite a gradual decline in fertility rates over time, the current fertility rates in the Nordic countries do surpass the OECD average (Table 2.2). There are slight differences among the Nordic countries, Iceland having the highest fertility rate. The mean age of the mother at first birth has increased, but teenage births have remained marginal in the Nordic countries, Iceland making a slight exception. The number of children born out of marriage is relatively high in the Nordic countries. Already by 1980, 40% of all children born in Iceland and Sweden (and a third in Denmark) were born to unmarried parents and by 2004 less than half of children were born to married parents in these two countries (see Table 2.2).

Table 2.2: Birth statistics, 1970 and 2004/05

	Total fertility rate (average number of children)		Mean age of women at first birth (years)		Births out of marriage (% of all children)		Teenage birth rate (per 1,000 women aged 15-19)
	1970	2005	1970	2004	1980	2004	2004
Denmark	1.95	1.80	23.8	28.4	33.2	45.4	6.8
Finland	1.83	1.80	24.4	27.8	13.1	40.8	10.0
Iceland	2.83	2.05	21.3	26.2	39.7	63.7	17.6
Norway	2.50	1.84	..	27.6	14.5	51.4	9.6
Sweden	1.92	1.77	25.9	28.6	39.7	55.4	6.9
OECD	2.70	1.63	24.2	27.5	11.2	30.9	15.8

Source: OECD (2007a, p 31)

The same trend has taken place in other OECD countries, including Finland and Norway, but at a later time.

However, it is necessary to remember that only a proportion of children who are born out of marriage are born to lone mothers. Often the parents are living together but they have not formalised their relationship by getting married. The growth of cohabitation is a trend that has characterised the change of family forms in the Nordic countries (Björnberg, 2001). Sometimes parents wed after having children, sometimes they don't. In 2005, 17-22% of all families with children were cohabiting couples in Denmark, Finland, Iceland and Norway (Table 2.3). In Sweden, cohabitation is so much the norm that recent family statistics do not differentiate between cohabiting and married parents. Another family form that is seen as a rather normal family arrangement is lone-parent families who make up a fifth of all families with children in each Nordic country.

Table 2.3: Families with children in the Nordic countries (%), 2005

	Married couples	Cohabiting couples	Lone parents	Total
Denmark	62	17	20	100
Finland	62	18	20	100
Iceland	57	21	21	100
Norway	57	22	21	100
Sweden	79		21	100

Source: Nordic Statistical Yearbook 2007, p 79

Families also change and among indicators of family change the proportions of couples who marry and divorce each year are defined (Table 2.4). In Denmark there are relatively many divorces, but equally many marriages. In Finland, Norway and Sweden there are more divorces than marriages per year. Iceland is an exception here with the lowest number of divorces, being the only country where marriages are more common than divorces. It is important to note that these statistics do not include cohabiting couples, thus the changes between different family forms are only partially represented by these figures.

Table 2.4: Marriages and divorces in the Nordic countries, per 1,000 mean population, 2006

	Marriages	Divorces
Denmark	6.7	6.6
Finland	5.4	6.7
Iceland	5.5	4.8
Norway	4.7	6.1
Sweden	5.0	6.5

Source: Nordic Statistical Yearbook 2007, p 77

Concerning the number of children, Icelandic families are again slightly different, having more children per family than is the case in the other Nordic countries. The average number of persons in a family is 2.6 in Iceland. The next country by the size of its families is Norway (2.2) while in the other three countries the average number of family members remains below 2 (NOSOSCO, 2007, p 281).

Overall, family structures have experienced significant changes in the Nordic countries during the last decades. The number of children has decreased, but not as dramatically as, for example, in Southern Europe. Cohabitation, lone-parent and same-sex families have all become common and normatively accepted family forms.

Labour market and economic conditions of families in Nordic countries

Active participation of women in paid employment has been characteristic of the Nordic societies for several decades. Recently the female employment rate has risen in many countries but still there is a considerable difference between the Nordic countries and the OECD average in this respect (Table 2.5). If only the core period of the working career is taken into account, excluding under 25s when many are still studying as well as over 54s when several have already retired because of health problems, four out of every five women in the Nordic countries are in paid work. However, whether their work is part-time or full-time differs between the five countries. Foremost in Norway but also in Denmark and Iceland a significant proportion of women are in part-time employment. In Finland and Sweden, on the other hand, women in part-time work are more rare than in most OECD countries.

It is not just Nordic women in general who take part in the labour market; it is also mothers of children (Table 2.6). In Iceland as many as 84% of mothers

Table 2.5: Female employment, age 25-54, 2000/06

	Female employment rate, 2006	Share of part-time employment in total female employment, 2006	Share of temporary employment in female employment, 2006	Proportion of managers who are female, 2000
Denmark	81.7	25.6	11.2	23.4
Finland	79.7	14.9	20.0	29.8
Iceland	83.8	26.0	9.7	31.1
Norway	81.0	32.9	12.6	26.6
Sweden	81.5	19.0	18.7	31.6
OECD	65.7	26.4	14.0	..

Source: OECD (2007a, p 45)

of children under six years old are in paid work and other Nordic countries are not far from this figure. The difference from other countries becomes even more definitive when the focus is on the mothers of the youngest children. Finland makes an exception from the Nordic rule; there, many women stay out of paid work while their children are under the age of three. Not even when having more than two children do the majority of women of the Nordic countries stay away from work, as is usually the case in the OECD countries.

Table 2.6: Maternal employment rates, age 15-64, 1999-2005*

	By age of youngest child			By number of children under 15		
	0–2	3–5	6–16	One child	Two children	Three children
Denmark	71.4	77.8	77.5	..	..	..
Finland	52.1	80.7	84.2	71.2	70.9	60.1
Iceland	83.6		86.5	88.5	82.3	
Sweden	71.9	81.3	76.1	80.6	84.7	75.6
OECD	51.9	61.3	66.3	60.6	57.0	44.0

Note: *Denmark: 1999, Finland: 2002, Iceland: 2002 for women aged 25-54, Sweden: 2005.
Source: OECD (2007a, p 46)

During the economic recession of the 1990s, the unemployment rate reached 10% in Sweden and Denmark and 16% in Finland, but the employment situation had improved by the end of the decade. Iceland has had the lowest unemployment rate, followed by Norway and Denmark (Table 2.7). The most recent economic crisis in 2008 hit Iceland most severely, but unemployment figures have been rising also in the other Nordic countries. There are some gender differences in unemployment: in Denmark, Finland and Iceland it has been slightly more difficult for women to find work, while the situation is the opposite in Sweden. In Norway, there is practically no difference between women and men in this respect.

An issue that is closely connected to poverty and other social problems is long-term unemployment. A considerable proportion of unemployed people have been without work for over a year in the Nordic countries also. According to the results from the Labour Force Study of EU member states conducted

Table 2.7: Unemployment rates in the Nordic countries, age 16-64, 2006

	Women	Men	Total
Denmark	4.7	3.5	4.0
Finland	8.2	7.5	7.8
Iceland	3.1	2.8	2.9
Norway	3.4	3.5	3.5
Sweden	5.2	5.5	5.4

Source: Nordic Statistical Yearbook 2007, p 144

in 2000, 20% of all unemployed people in Denmark have been unemployed for over a year. In Finland the figure was 25% and in Sweden 31%. Overall, a high general unemployment rate indicates a high proportion of long-term unemployment and, thus, it affects Finland and Sweden in particular. However, long-term unemployment figures from the Nordic countries are still considerably lower than figures from Southern Europe, Greece with 56% having the highest rate. These differences are explained by active labour market measures by which the Nordic countries have been able to cut the length of unemployment for many individuals (Statistics Finland, 2006). Nevertheless, for those families who are affected, long-term unemployment brings considerable financial and social difficulties, some needing the services of social workers.

However, when it comes to child poverty rates the Nordic countries generally fare better when compared with other countries (for example, OECD, 2007c). A recent example is the EU–SILC measurement of poverty in Europe that uses the term 'at risk of poverty' (families below 60% of the median) (Table 2.8). The at–risk–of–poverty rates are lower for all family types for the Nordic countries than for the EU 25 countries. The Nordic countries have quite similar figures in most cases. When the number of children at risk of poverty before and after social benefits is compared, all the countries make a considerable effort towards reducing poverty. However, around one child out of 10 is still living at risk of poverty in every Nordic country.

Table 2.8: At risk of poverty* by family type, 2005

	Denmark	Finland	Iceland	Norway	Sweden	EU 25 countries
Total	12	12	10	11	9	16
Lone parent with 0-15-year-old children	21	20	14	19	18	32
Two adults with one child	4	7	8	4	4	12
Two adults with two children	5	5	8	4	5	14
Two adults with three or more children	14	12	10	10	9	24
Children at risk of poverty before social benefits	26	32	26	32	36	..
Children at risk of poverty after social benefits	10	10	10	9	8	19

Note: *The share of persons with an equivalised disposable income below the risk of poverty threshold, which is set at 60% of the national median equivalised disposable income (after social transfers)
Source: Eurostat (2008)

An agreement on how child poverty should be measured does not exist and one criticism of traditional poverty measurements is that a measurement of parents' incomes does not necessarily provide a clear picture of the living standards of children (for example, Ridge, 2002; Bradshaw et al, 2007; Salonen, 2007). However, these results show that the Nordic countries compare promisingly and other research shows that they are doing better than most countries in regard to supporting families with children (for example, Vleminckx and Smeeding, 2001; Adamson, 2007). The literature corroborates that, beyond the support of the welfare state, the key to this success is the active labour market policy and the public support given to working parents (Sinfield and West Pedersen, 2006; Whiteford and Adema, 2006; Flaquer, 2007). At the same time, poverty research confirms that, despite the support of the Nordic welfare systems, they have not managed to eliminate child poverty and this fact is gaining increased attention in the Nordic countries (see *Velstandens paradoks*, 2007). Social workers meet the families at risk of poverty in their work, in different institutional settings, and work with the complicated situations that poor families with children have to face in these affluent societies.

Family social security policies in the Nordic countries

The Nordic countries are known for having developed various transfer payments to support families with children. These payments move many, but not all, families above the poverty line. Essential for family incomes are the tax systems and general benefit schemes like unemployment and sickness benefits, as well as disability pensions, but here we touch mainly on those benefits that are expressly meant for families with children. These include child allowances and maintenance payments. Housing benefits and social assistance are mentioned because they are important for families with low incomes, even though they are available also for people without children.

It may come as a surprise that public spending on cash payments for families is not exceptionally high in the Nordic countries in international comparison (Table 2.9). Furthermore, tax breaks for families are nowadays an almost unknown phenomenon in all five countries. It is only when spending on services is taken into account that Nordic family policies can be seen as particularly generous or widespread. From the year 2000 the Nordic countries, in particular Norway and Sweden, have actually decreased their spending on families, as the latest figures from 2005 show that four of the five countries are spending only 2.8-3.0% of GDP on family policies, Denmark being the exception with more spending (3.8 %) (*Nordic Statistical Yearbook 2007*, p 102). When spending on families is viewed, Iceland seems to spend a lot on families when looking at its share of total social expenditure, but social expenditure in its entirety makes up a considerably smaller part of GDP there than in Denmark or Sweden.

Universal child allowance is a basic family benefit in every Nordic country. It is tax free and independent of parents' income, with the exception of Iceland

Table 2.9: Public spending on family policies, 2000/04

	Spending on cash benefits (% of GDP, 2000)	Spending on services (% of GDP, 2000)	Spending on tax breaks for families (% of GDP, 2000)	Total spending on families (% of GDP, 2000)	Total spending on families (% of social expenditure, 2004)
Denmark	1.6	2.3	0.0	3.9	13.0
Finland	1.6	1.4	0.0	3.0	11.5
Iceland	1.5	1.7	0.0	3.2	14.0
Norway	1.9	1.5	0.1	3.6	11.9
Sweden	1.6	1.9	0.0	3.5	9.6
OECD	1.3	0.9	0.2	2.4	..

Sources: OECD (2007b); NOSOSCO (2007, p 39)

where the major part of the child allowance is means-tested. All countries except Sweden provide a supplement for lone parents and Norway and Denmark are the only ones that do not pay extra for additional children. There is some variation between the countries concerning how long the benefit is paid. In Denmark, Norway and Iceland it is payable until a child reaches the age of 18, in Finland until the age of 17 and in Sweden until 16-20 years of age, depending on whether the child is still receiving an education (NOSOSCO, 2007, pp 54-5).

For children whose parents do not live together, the parent who is not living with the child usually pays a maintenance payment. The amount of the payment is decided during divorce proceedings or in connection with the birth of a child out of marriage, either through mutual agreement or through a decision from the court or local authorities. In all the Nordic countries public authorities guarantee that the child receives a minimum maintenance payment, mostly in cases where the non-resident parent for some reason fails to pay (NOSOSCO, 2007). The latest policy arrangements, made to further ensure the possibilities of both parents caring for the child, have brought some changes in the maintenance duties of the non-resident parent. Finland, Sweden and Norway have reorganised their systems of child support in order to emphasise that, "fathers should not be socially excluded from families because of high child support payments" (Bergman and Hobson, 2002, p 119). One effect of this policy is that the maintenance payments of a parent can be reduced on account of visitation with the child (Björnberg and Dahlgren, 2003).

All Nordic countries have schemes of housing benefits for families with and without children. All five countries pay a tax-free, means-tested benefit to families living in rented accommodation and also to families in owner-occupied housing in Finland, Norway and Sweden. The family size and housing costs are taken into consideration when the housing benefit is calculated (NOSOSCO, 2007, pp 174-6.)

An important component of support to families with children is state support to students with families. All the Nordic countries provide students who are in higher education and have started a family of their own with support in the form of extra student loans or grants, as well as an offer of subsidised housing (Björnberg et al, 2006). All the countries have benefit schemes for parents of children with an illness or a disability and there are various benefit schemes that are country specific – for further information, please see NOSOSCO, 2007).

All the Nordic countries also provide a scheme of means-tested social assistance (Bradshaw and Terum, 1997; Sipilä, 1997). Social assistance is provided by local authorities and it is thought to be the last resort, which should be paid only if all other possibilities have been exhausted. What makes these schemes exceptional in the Nordic context is that they do not follow the logic of social security systems, which for most part in these countries is based on the rights of the individual. On the contrary, in social assistance it is the family (household) income that is means-tested (Bradshaw and Terum, 1997; NOSOSCO, 2007). Local authorities administer the scheme but national minimum guidelines have been set by central authorities. The number of families receiving social assistance varies from one family with children out of 10 in Denmark to one out of 20 in Iceland (Table 2.10).

Table 2.10: Families with children who received social assistance (%), 2005

	Denmark	Finland	Iceland	Norway	Sweden
Single men	9.5	17.4	21.1	7.7	7.3
Single women	19.0	26.3	14.3	15.8	20.8
Married/cohabiting couples	8.3	4.9	0.9	3.8	2.9
Families with children	10.2	9.0	4.6	5.0	6.2

Source: NOSOCO (2007, p 190)

The system of paid benefits is composed of different schemes throughout the Nordic countries and only the major schemes that are found in all the countries have been discussed here briefly. The expenditure figures on cash benefits for families are an indicator of the size of support in the Nordic countries. When measured by public spending on family benefits in PPP (purchasing power parities[1]) per a 0–17-year-old child, Norway has the highest figure and Iceland the lowest (NOSOSCO, 2007). If and how these schemes meet the needs of the families is difficult to say, but an indicator showing that the systems are to a certain extent successful in supporting families with children is the fact that the Nordic countries have relatively low at-risk-of-poverty rates for families with children (Table 2.8).

Childcare policies in the Nordic countries

The development of public childcare policies is one of the main characteristics of family policies in the Nordic countries. The division of labour between the state and the families in childcare has been a central issue in all the Nordic countries since the 1970s. There have been two main arguments for an active state intervention and support for families. The first argument has emphasised that the state needs to safeguard the interests of children, whereas the second has stressed the importance of facilitating gender equality (Rostgaard and Fridberg, 1998; Ellingsæter and Leira, 2006).

Parental leave

In the late 1970s and early 1980s all the Nordic countries expanded their parental-leave policy, periods of paid parental leave were extended and the right of fathers to a specific parental leave slowly started to gain acceptance both in the public and the private sphere. Statistics showed that, despite the fact that legislation in the Nordic countries had to a varying degree given fathers the opportunity to share the parental leave with mothers, the participation ratio of fathers in most cases had remained low (for example, Leira, 1999. This also applied to Sweden, where fathers have been encouraged since 1974 to share the relatively long parental leave with mothers. Haas and Hwang (1999) argued that the main reasons why it proved to be so difficult to generate a major change in the traditional gender roles were to be found in the organisational context in the labour market and the gendered patterns of breadwinner and carer roles.

The disappointing results gave rise to attempts in some of the Nordic countries to implement new policies meant to encourage increased parental choice and a more active childcare role for fathers (Björnberg and Kollind, 1996; Moss and Deven, 1999). Norway was the first Nordic country in 1992 to introduce a special independent right of fathers to a one-month parental leave, sometimes referred to as 'daddy quota' or 'use or lose' since the fathers could not assign their right to the mothers. According to Leira (1999, p 275), the "introduction of a daddy quota in the parental leave scheme shows an interesting development in political thinking concerning the relationship between parents, children and the state. Instituting a right of fathers to care for their children signals a new approach to fatherhood and gender equality".

Sweden reserved one month of parental leave for fathers in 1996 and extended their right to two months in 2002 (Table 2.11) (Finch, 2006). In Iceland, new laws on parental leave came into force in 2000, which stipulated that mothers and fathers should have equal rights to parental leave, both having a three-month leave. So far the Icelandic parental leave scheme is the only one in the world to give both parents fully equal individual rights, providing the most comprehensive support to fathers in their caring role (OECD, 2007c). Neither Denmark nor Finland has implemented special parental leave quotas for fathers but, if a Finnish

Table 2.11: Parental leave schemes in the Nordic countries, 2006

	Denmark	Finland	Iceland	Norway	Sweden
Maximum number of weeks in which maternity/paternity/parental leave benefits are payable	50-64	44	39	42-52	69
Of which (weeks): Only mother	18	18	13	9	8
Only father	None	2 (if also the 2 last weeks of the parental leave period are used by the father)	13	6	8
Additionally: father together with mother	2	3	None	2	2
Per cent of total number of benefit days used by fathers in the event of pregnancy, childbirth and adoption in 2005	6	5	33	9	20
Per cent of previous income in 2005*	**100	70	80	100/80	80***
Income ceiling per week for full compensation in PPP-Euros	340	596	1193	619	513

Notes: * Parents who have not been gainfully employed – for example, students and unemployed – are entitled to a certain minimum benefit, its amount being different in each Nordic country
** When the common leave period of 32 weeks is extended to 40 or 46 weeks, the daily cash benefit will be reduced accordingly, so that it corresponds to 80% for the 40 weeks and to about 70 per cent for the 46 weeks
*** From 1 July 2008, Swedish parents who share the parental leave equally will receive a bonus of 3000 SEK per month (Westlund, 2007)
Source: NOSOSCO (2007)

father uses the two last weeks of the parental allowance period, he is entitled to a paid leave of two more bonus weeks that cannot be transferred to the mother.

In summary, all the Nordic countries place an emphasis on parents being ensured financial support so that they can be absent from the labour market and care for their children during a certain period after birth. However, the length and the flexibility of the schemes vary, as well as the individual entitlements of each parent.

Home care allowance

In addition to the schemes of paid parental leave, some of the Nordic countries have established national schemes of cash allowances for daily care of young children, usually organised in their home.

In Finland parents of children under three have been entitled to a payment since 1985 if their child is not enrolled in public day care. In 1997, the payment was divided into three separate benefits. If the family is using a private day care provider, a private day care centre or a registered childminder, they will receive a Private Day Care Allowance (€137 per month in 2008 plus a possible means-tested supplement). On the other hand, if a parent wishes to shorten his/her working hours, some loss of income will be covered by Partial Care Allowance (€70 per month). Finally, the family will receive a Child Home Care Allowance if their child is cared for at home (€294 per month plus a possible means-tested supplement). Many municipalities pay also their own local supplements to these allowances in order to reduce the demand for public childcare services. Of the three benefits, the last one is by far the most popular and almost always it is the mother of the child who stays at home and provides the childcare. In 2005, 61% of all Finnish children under three were covered by these three benefits (NOSOSCO, 2007.)

Also, Norway adopted into its legislation in 1998 the entitlement of a cash benefit (*kontantstøtte*) for care of children under three, if their children were not placed in a day care institution. If the child attends formal childcare part-time, the parents are entitled to a proportion of the grant in accordance with the quantity of hours. The allowance can be used to pay for childcare and was introduced as a policy to increase parents' choices (Morgan and Zippel, 2003). The Norwegian scheme has been heavily criticised and Leira (2006, p 41), for example, has pointed out that, "interpreted as supporting the traditional male-breadwinner family and as a backlash to gender equality, cash grants also had their antagonists. Regarded by some as undermining the right of children to attend state-sponsored day care, cash grant schemes met with opposition on these grounds, too."

In Denmark it is possible for parents of children who were born prior to the introduction of the new maternity leave scheme in 2002 to go on childminding leave for up to 52 weeks. The payment is 60% of daily cash benefits, but local authorities can grant a supplementary benefit (NOSOSCO, 2007). From 1 July 2008 local governments in Sweden have been able to decide whether to introduce home care allowance scheme for parents of children under three (worth €323) (Westlund, 2007). The Icelandic parliament has not enacted such a law, but some local authorities have nevertheless established different child home care or private day care allowance schemes (Einarsdóttir and Ólafsdóttir, 2007).

Day care institutions and family day care

From the late 1960s to the 1980s, the campaign for gender equality called for support for women's active participation in the labour market and all the Nordic countries adopted a new set of policies to promote gender equality. These included offering a wider range of day care services (Sipilä, 1997). However, it is important to keep in mind that these services were not only promoted as an answer to women's demands to better access to the labour market; an emphasis was also placed on the child's entitlement to public care for the child's own benefit. All the Nordic countries have constructed formal child day care systems where the service is, at least in principle, available to every family with children. The services are heavily subsidised by the public sector and user fees paid by parents cover only a part of the cost (NOSOSCO, 2007). Finland, Sweden and Denmark – and from autumn 2008, Norway also – have formulated the access to publicly provided childcare formally as a legal right for families (Eydal, 2005).

The volumes of day care for children aged three to five are quite similar for all five countries with the exception of Finland, which has lower volumes (Table 2.12), but there are greater differences regarding the younger children. Finland has the lowest take-up rate followed by Norway, but the usage of the home care allowance schemes would explain these differences. Denmark has by far the highest coverage followed by Iceland and Sweden, despite the relatively long parental leave in Sweden. In Finland, since 2000, practically all six year olds are attending a new half-day preschool; two thirds are also using additional day care. In Sweden and Denmark, the volumes of day care for six year olds and after-school care for older children are considerably higher. In Norway and Iceland this information is missing.

Table 2.12: Children enrolled in day care institutions and other publicly financed day care (% by age), 2005

	1–2 years	3–5 years	6 years	7–10 years
Denmark	85	95	88	63
Finland	37	69	67	28
Iceland	76	94	..	..
Norway	54	91	..	..
Sweden	67	95	84	61

Source: NOSOSCO (2007, p 62)

In all the Nordic countries there has been a political emphasis on providing public childcare and increasing fathers' rights to paid paternity and parental leaves. But, despite these basic similarities, these aims have been fulfilled in different ways and with different results. High volumes of public childcare and long, flexible parental leaves have characterised the Swedish childcare model. Denmark also offers high volume of public childcare, but a slightly shorter parental leave. Norway provides extensive paid parental leave but its system of public childcare has a less extensive volume of day care than is found in either Sweden or Denmark. Norway is closest to Finland, where the take-up rate of day care is the lowest in the Nordic countries.

On the other hand, Finland and Norway have developed childcare allowance schemes, which give parents a right to receive a home care allowance, supporting childcare at home until children reach the age of three. In these two countries the cash for care schemes obviously influence the demand for day care. Iceland has provided fewer rights for paid parental leave and still provides shorter total periods of paid care leaves than the other Nordic countries. The provision of public day care increased rapidly in Iceland in the 1990s and is now second highest in the region. Norway, Iceland and Sweden have all promoted policies on individual rights of fathers to paternity leave. All the Nordic countries have developed childcare policies that emphasise promoting good circumstances for young children and support to their parents in their parenting roles. The policies also aim to secure that both parents have realistic chances of combining care and participation in the labour market. However, they have chosen somewhat different paths when developing their childcare and parental leave policies.

Conclusions

The image of a unified Nordic welfare model mostly prevails when looking at the structures of families as well as family policies in the five countries. The countries share the same main features and trends even though there are numerous differences of detail between the countries. Family forms in all of the five countries have become more diversified as cohabitation and divorces along with lone-parent and same-sex families have become more usual, socially accepted and legally recognised. On the other hand, Nordic families are also characterised by a lack of change in the respect that the number of children per family has not dropped dramatically like it has done in many other countries.

Nordic countries have been among the first ones to modernise their family legislation, making non-fault divorce and joint legal custody possible, though the timing of these legal reforms has been partly dissimilar in the five countries. The economic and social position of families with children is also relatively good in all Nordic countries, compared with other nations, because of welfare state family benefits and the prevailing dual-earner family model. However, the other side of the coin is that there are a number of families facing long-term unemployment and poverty within these affluent societies. It is largely these families that social workers encounter in their daily work.

Developed childcare and parental leave policies have been seen as a specific feature of Nordic family policies (for example, Bradshaw and Hatland, 2006; Ellingsæter and Leira, 2006). All of the five countries provide rather long and generously paid parental leave and, at the same time, childcare services that are universally available to all families with children under school age. There are national differences in the flexibility of the entitlements and in the strength of the emphasis on promoting men's participation in childcare; Iceland, Norway and Sweden are in this respect the most ambitious with their specific 'daddy quotas' of parental leave. On the other hand, Finland and Norway offer childcare leave benefits that are said to reproduce traditional gender roles, keeping women longer at home with their children. However, in general terms, women, including mothers of young children, participate in paid work in all the Nordic countries more regularly than in most other nations and all the five countries represent the dual-earner model.

Conclusively it can be said that the main features of family structures, family legislation and family policy are relatively similar in the five Nordic countries and, thus, they provide a largely uniform context for social work with families. There are some country-specific particularities if we examine the institutional settings more closely in detail. However, in general, a shared cultural heritage, common values, continuous formal and informal Nordic cooperation together with similarities in policies set a scene for social work with children and their families that is broadly the same across the Nordic region.

Note

[1] Purchasing power parities (PPP) are defined as the currency conversion factor corresponding to the purchasing power of the individual currencies. This means that a certain amount, when converted from different currencies by means of PPP factors, will buy the same amount ('basket') of goods and services in all the countries. The PPP calculations in the present report are in PPP-Euro (EU25=1) in respect of private consumption. 2005-estimates were used. The estimates for the individual countries are as follows: Denmark 10.48; Finland 1.21; Iceland 116.09; Norway 11.31 and Sweden 11.05 (NOSOSCO, 2007 p 220).

THREE

A Nordic model in child welfare?

*Helena Blomberg, Clary Corander, Christian Kroll, Anna Meeuwisse,
Roberto Scaramuzzino and Hans Swärd*

Introduction

The aim of this chapter is to capture similarities and variations in the performance of child welfare through a comparative Nordic approach. Child welfare is chosen because it is historically one of the core areas of social work and because the work presupposes considerations of a wide range of problems: for example, family relations, abuse, poverty, addiction and 'immigrant problems'.

The chapter will provide new perspectives on the discussion on whether the welfare model thinking is producing good results in the case of child welfare services in the Nordic countries, as well as general reflections on methodological issues in comparative research on personal welfare services. Welfare model research often departs from a 'macro top-down' perspective. What happens if you change the point of departure in favour of a 'meso from-below' perspective? Special attention will be paid to the question of how child welfare problems are understood and handled in what is sometimes referred to as the 'family service oriented' Nordic countries, based on results from a study of all the referrals that four child welfare offices in four Nordic capital areas received during the three to six first months of the year 2006.

Welfare state models and models of social work

Walter Lorenz, in his book *Social work in a changing Europe* (1994), claims that there are clear correlations between different types of welfare state models and ways of solving social problems. Lorenz puts forward the idea that the welfare state typologies described by theorists such as Titmuss (1974) and Esping-Andersen (1990) can be used for the analysis of different countries' ways of organising social work.

The basis for Lorenz's application of models of social policy to social work rests on the assumption that *underlying ideologies*, such as a liberal or a social democratic standpoint, also pervade the practice of social work. This determines, for example, whether social work is regarded as a task for voluntary organisations, as a public duty or as something based on market solutions. The responsibility of the state varies in different systems, as do tax resources and the degree to which different systems are effective in protecting children or in combating poverty.

One of the four models in social work sketched by Lorenz is 'the Scandinavian model'. Unlike the 'residual', the 'corporative' and the 'rudimentary' models, this is characterised by an *all-embracing social service*. In this model, general social policy programmes guarantee people a relatively high standard of living, and the civil and social rights of all citizens are emphasised. Instead of the market, the family, voluntary organisations and local authorities play a central role as producers of welfare services and as organisers of comprehensive social work (Meeuwisse and Swärd, 2007). The position of the *municipalities* as organisers and providers of social services within the welfare system has been unique by international standards, and social workers are mainly employed by the *public sector*.

As a result of this, unlike, for example in the American system, social work is performed within the general Scandinavian-type administrative system, and is based on case management and on the application of the law. Thus, social workers acquire a dual role as both helpers and controllers. When Nordic social work is compared with that of other countries it is further emphasised that it contains not only work with obvious social problems, as in some other countries, but also *preventive measures*. The preventive orientation is particularly expressed in child welfare (Lorenz, 1994; Fox Harding, 1996).

There is often an, at least implicit, assumption of common Nordic features in social work. This is also the case in more critical comments expressed on some aspects of social work in the Nordic countries. It has, for instance, been pointed out that there is a Nordic tradition of coercive care for children and for adult substance abusers (Pettersson, 2001). The large proportion of qualified social workers and their collaboration with other experts is seen as another distinctive feature, as is the fact that social workers have relatively high status and power compared with those in other systems (Meeuwisse and Swärd, 2007). Further, since the Second World War, a large number of Nordic organisations have emerged to ensure cooperation in social work, stressing the geographical proximity, a partially shared history and the similar languages, which enable communication and facilitate inter-Nordic exchange (Larsson, 2000).

While the many considerations referred to speak in favour of the assumption of the existence of a Nordic social work model parallel to, or even as an 'integral part' of, the general Nordic welfare state model, there are also various factors that, directly or indirectly, can be put forward against such assumptions. In what follows, some arguments pointing in the latter direction are presented, before moving on to a further discussion of possible Nordic features in the specific field of child welfare.

One line of argument against a common model in Nordic social work is related to the general critique often presented against the relatively 'static' perspective behind theories of welfare state models. One line of thought, which assumes an increasing convergence of welfare states and welfare policies, claims that increased globalisation, internationalisation and market thinking is erasing national differences (Khan and Dominelli, 2000; Penna et al, 2000; Pugh and Gould, 2000). Trends of convergence at a general societal and policy level could, however, also be assumed to result in a growing divergence in service provision within (and thereby perhaps also between) the Nordic countries. There is research (for example, Trydegård, 2000; also Huhtanen et al, 2005) that shows that people are treated differently depending on which municipality they live in, which raises the question of whether people really are equal and whether everyone has the same right to care in practice at the local level. Although this is not a new question, the complex dialectic between the Nordic traditions of local responsibility for social services on the one hand and the universal character of their social policies on the other is probably being affected by changes presently under way in national social policies.

But there are also other types of arguments questioning the idea, if not of a Nordic social work model, then at least concerning the inclusion of social work in the Nordic welfare state model. Thus, for instance, Anttonen and Sipilä (1996) have questioned whether social work should be regarded as a social service in the same sense as other public social services, mainly with reference to the largely involuntary nature of the latter. In some researchers' view, at least some aspects of social work should, rather, be regarded as reminiscences of the tradition of local poor relief (cf Sunesson et al, 1998, pp 21-2).

Others, again, have pointed out circumstances that might be seen to speak against the view of specifically *Nordic* features, at least in social work *practices*. It has, for instance, been pointed out that, besides Nordic cooperation, social workers have for a long time been involved in powerful international professional organisations, and there has always been a wider international exchange through conferences, journals, books and so on (Larsson, 2000). There is a great deal to suggest that the Anglo-Saxon influence is greater than Nordic ideals and influences when it comes to figures of thought in social work (see, for example, Midgley, 1981; Brauns and Kramer, 1986; Lorentzen, 1994; Pettersson, 2001; see also Ejrnæs and Kristiansen, 2002).

Four levels of social work

Although the various types of critique against attempts at placing national (or local) policies into policy models, of which only a few perspectives have been hinted at here, reveal the limitations of the 'welfare modelling business' (Abrahamsson, 2000), in general, as well as within social work, the point of departure taken in this chapter is that policy models still provide a useful analytical tool when investigating social policy, as well as social work issues.

However, the issue of possible models should be made into an empirical question, with a focus on clearly enough defined variables. As the discussion on general welfare models has shown, a division, for analytical reasons, between different aspects or levels of social work seems to be a fruitful starting point. With reference also to the discussion above, one might make a division – for example, between the *normative level* (general values guiding social work, that is the 'social [work] policy goals' in the respective countries), the *structural level* (including the specific organisational conditions affecting social work and the role of social work in relation to other social policy measures), the level of *social work practices* (including professional ideology, theories and information guiding professional actions), as well as the level of *outcomes* of measures taken.

With such an approach, the question does not primarily concern the possible existence of *a* Nordic model in social work generally, or in child welfare, but *in what respects* there seems to exist such a *common* model and to what extent it, then, can be considered uniquely *Nordic*.

As pointed out in the introduction to this chapter, our study will investigate this question from a 'meso from-below' perspective within child welfare. This perspective is believed to be fruitful in a situation in which, not only the degree of common features between the countries, but also the question of the exact variables relevant in this context are not necessarily known beforehand. The assumption in this situation is that answers to some of the questions about similarities and differences in social work in different countries can only be obtained by investigating how social work is organised and worked out in practice.

Bearing the discussion in this present section in mind, we will now turn to previous attempts to identify common features in Nordic child welfare in general, which provide an additional perspective to the question of the existence of a Nordic model in child welfare as a sub-field within social work.

Common features in Nordic child welfare?

Scholars focusing on child welfare in a wide sense have, with more or less explicit reference to the discussion on general welfare state models, drawn attention to distinct Scandinavian features concerning this particular field (Gould, 1988; Gilbert, 1997; Hort and McMurphy, 1997; Hessle and Vinnerljung, 1999). Gilbert (1997) discusses the organisation of child welfare in various countries by comparing nine European and North American countries' child abuse reporting systems. Two ideal models are identified. A division is made between a 'child protection' and a 'family service' orientation respectively. The first model, regarded as typical of English-speaking countries, assumes an individualistic or moralistic approach to child abuse problems; the first intervention measures are legalistic in nature, the relationship between state and family is marked by conflict, and thus placements are made primarily against the will of the family. The latter model, to which the Nordic countries, but also countries in continental Europe are said to belong, is marked by a social or psychological approach to child abuse problems; the first intervention is focused on the needs of the family, the relation between family and state is characterised by cooperation and placements are mainly made with the family's consent.

As Hetherington (2002), who makes a distinction between various types of factors that shape the functioning of child welfare systems – namely, culture, structures and professional ideology (which thus bears resemblance to the division between levels of social work discussed in the previous section) – notes, there are countries both with and without mandatory reporting systems in both of Gilbert's models. This leads her to conclude that the characteristics of the models are not primarily tied to *structural* differences in the systems of the countries in the respective model. But, since the filing of mandatory reports seems to have different implications for further action in different types of countries, Hetherington (2002) instead argues that what she calls '*culture*', or the 'wider political philosophy of the country' (a concept fairly similar to what was called the normative level in the previous section), is the dominant factor for explaining the response of the respective national systems. This is, according to Hetherington, probable, since the third factor considered, '*professional ideology*' among social workers, is said to be very similar cross-nationally. Thus, the conclusion might be seen to support the view of Lorenz (1994).

With reference to Esping-Andersen (1990), who linked general welfare regimes and political philosophies, Hetherington (2002) further makes an attempt at combining Gilbert's model with Esping-Andersen's tricothomy of welfare states (see Table 3.1). While the (English-speaking) countries with a 'child protection orientation' also belong to Esping-Andersen's 'liberal' welfare state model, the Nordic and continental European countries with a 'family service orientation' in child welfare, which share similar values regarding preventive and supportive work, belong either to the 'social democratic' or 'conservative' model, depending on their views as regards the role of the state in delivering services. In the continental European countries with their idea of subsidiarity, which requires that all interventions take place at the least formal level feasible, it is expected that the delivery of services should primarily be organised within local communities,

Table 3.1: Hetherington's model on welfare regimes and child welfare systems

Welfare regime / Child welfare system		'Social democratic'	'Conservative'	'Liberal'
'Family service orientation'	State service delivery	Nordic countries		
	Subsidiarity		Continental European countries	
'Child protection orientation'				English-speaking countries

Source: Hetherington (2002)

although with state help if necessary. This has resulted in a large proportion of non-governmental agencies and gives families a choice about the source of help. Thus, voluntary engagement of the family is pivotal. Within this context, the absence of a mandatory reporting system seems easily explained. In the Nordic countries, again, the state is seen as representing the community of citizens and as the provider of social services in a broad sense. Families are thought to expect state help and to trust social workers, and within this context mandatory reporting can be seen as a means of ensuring that help is made available.

Gilbert's and Hetherington's attempts at combinations could be questioned on a number of points, some of which were touched on in the previous section and some of which concern, for instance, the justification for the (relative) emphasis on a common 'orientation' in child welfare systems between the Nordic and continental European countries. On the other hand, there sometimes seems to be a tendency among Nordic scholars to emphasise 'Nordic uniqueness'. In any case, the Finnish scholar Raunio (2004; see also Pösö, 1996), for instance, regards the possibilities within social work, in addition to reactive measures to make interventions to prevent the aggravation of problems and to improve the situation for people in difficult situations, as a specifically Nordic feature. According to Raunio, the ambition of social work to achieve 'normalisation' of the life situation of clients is unique to the Nordic countries, and he mentions child welfare social work as an example of this Nordic orientation in social work; in this connection, the possibilities for social workers to intervene in cases where there are problems within the child's *family* – for example, because of substance abuse – although there are no signs of maltreatment, abuse or neglect of the child – are emphasised. The setting is complicated even further by some estimates according to which cuts and reforms within the social services, in combination with growing social problems among some population groups, have resulted in a situation where preventive social work hardly exists any longer, since all resources have to be directed at more acute cases – although the formal aims of the system have not been altered.

Given the limited Nordic, as well as broader, international, comparative, empirical research on these matters to date, the question of similarities and differences in child welfare between countries is probably best regarded as an, at least partly, open question, to which the current chapter aims to provide some answers by studying child welfare mainly from the perspective of the work carried out at the social welfare office level. Obviously, the intra-Nordic perspective applied will not be able to address all the questions discussed directly. But providing knowledge of the 'degree of Nordicness' on various dimensions of child welfare work at the 'office level' in four Nordic countries is believed to be an important step on the way to an increased knowledge of the determinants of social work in an international perspective.

The four child welfare offices studied: legal and organisational frameworks

The research to which this chapter refers is based on case studies of municipal individually geared social work in four Nordic capital areas (Copenhagen, Helsinki, Oslo and Stockholm). The study focuses on small work units (11-14 social workers working with the investigation of referrals and interventions), in fairly similar districts (areas characterised by relatively widespread poverty and social problems), working with treatment and exercise of authority within the care of children and young people. A mixed method approach has been used for the data collection. It includes: statistical and descriptive data (including the legal framework, a description of the organisations, number of clients, different types of organisational plans, annual reports and so on); a systematic analysis of all incoming referrals to the child welfare office; vignette studies; personal interviews with social workers, managers and politicians; focus group interviews with teams of social workers; and participant observations.[1] The description is based on statistics, annual reports and strategic plans from the districts studied, as well as on interviews with leading civil servants at the offices.[2]

In this chapter, results from the first two parts of the study will be presented with the aim of highlighting some possible features of a Nordic model in child welfare. The comparison of legal and organisational frameworks will provide some information on the normative as well as structural levels, while the referral study will provide other perspectives on these dimensions by indicating what kind of problems are considered to be child welfare problems in the respective countries, as well as the resources in terms of personnel available at the offices. Analysis of the process of the work with the referrals within the agencies studied will provide some information about social work practices.

As a first step in the analysis, the formal conditions affecting the work at the four child welfare offices investigated will be charted in brief (in order to provide some information on the normative as well as the structural levels of social work). The focus in this brief description will be on the legal framework in each country as well as on the organisational framework for each office.

The Norwegian office studied is situated in the Grorud district (approximately 25,032 inhabitants) of Oslo. The Finnish office lies in the Vuosaari-Nordsjö district (approximately 32,000 inhabitants) of Helsinki-Helsingfors, while the Swedish office studied is located in the Skogås/Trångsund district (approximately 22,000 inhabitants) of the municipality of Huddinge, the second largest municipality in the county of Stockholm and adjacent in the south west to the City of Stockholm. In Denmark, Rødovre municipality, which is one of the municipalities belonging to the capital area of Copenhagen (36,500 inhabitants), was included in the study.

The *legal framework* regulating child welfare work in the four offices studied bears many similarities. Legislation in all countries stresses 'the best interest of the child' and the importance of early intervention and support to families. Some differences in the interpretation of these overarching principles can, however, also be found. For example, the 'biological principle' – that is, the principle that children should grow up with their biological parents (or relatives) – is stressed to a greater extent in Norwegian legislation than in the legislation of the other countries studied.

Although child welfare legislation is national, the local – municipal – level is responsible for providing/organising child welfare services.[3] Social services, including child welfare services, are subordinated to the municipal councils and boards, consisting of laymen elected through the local political process.

Thus, there are similar principles of democratic control and political steering of the work at the offices in the different Nordic countries. On the other hand, there are, again, also some differences in this respect between countries/offices studied. In Finland and Sweden, politically chosen laymen (in the municipal social welfare board) have a more central role in making 'first' decisions about taking children 'into care' than in Denmark and Norway.[4] Further, the possibility for inhabitants/clients to communicate with their 'political representatives' in the social welfare board or in other political bodies varies in practice. The most direct link between inhabitants and politicians seems to be found in the Danish municipality where, for example, the chair of the social welfare board is available for local citizens who wish to put forward complaints about the social services administration. All citizens also have the possibility to book a meeting with the elected municipal politicians (including the mayor) in order to put forward questions or complaints about the functioning of the local administration.

Concerning organisational framework and various agency procedures, one can detect both similarities and differences. The offices studied are all part of the respective municipal welfare services, the conditions of activities, including economic resources, of which are laid down by the respective local government. Concerning agency procedures, the division of labour and some differences could be detected. For example, while the Finnish, Swedish and Danish social workers seem to work in a rather integrated manner – that is, all social workers worked with investigations as well as interventions – the Norwegian office displayed a somewhat more specialised way of working, including four different steps of interventions. Services are divided into preventive work, referrals and the investigation of these referrals, voluntary and 'open care' measures, as well as long-term residential childcare, with different social workers responsible for each area. Another example is that other activities related to child welfare (such as family counselling services) in some municipalities belonged to the same office as the social workers working with investigations and interventions, while these services in some of the other offices studied were centralised.

Activities within all the offices studied have in common an emphasis on preventive measures in social work. The preventive approach was a leading key word in many of the plans and strategies of the offices (or the social welfare offices at large), although it was seldom given a very precise meaning. All offices were also engaged in different preventive projects, often aimed at supporting children at risk (usually together with the school authorities), couples expecting a child or couples who have recently become parents (usually together with health care personnel), as well as anonymous counselling.

The referral study: the number and nature of referrals

As a second step in the analysis, data on all referrals that the child welfare offices received during a selected period will be presented. In Norway and Denmark data was collected for a three-month period; in Finland and Sweden the period investigated covered six months. Thus, for practical reasons, the collected data for Norway and Denmark is more limited, something that should be kept in mind. The number and nature of the referrals are seen as an outcome of the interplay between the Nordic societies' views on child welfare problems and the Nordic social child welfare systems and their practices. Here, 'referrals' also include applications from the client and his/her family.

First, the report source and the type of conditions reported will be presented. Then, the inflow of referrals in the four child welfare offices studied will be investigated in relation to the number of social workers at the respective offices. Finally, some preliminary results concerning agency procedures (that is, interventions made) after the reception of referrals are presented. The respective findings could be summarised as follows:

As regards the nature of the referrals, the distribution by 'report source' can clearly be seen to reflect the 'mandatory reporting system' that exists in all four countries. The main report source consists of the group of 'mandated' actors, including, for example, the police, the schools, health care, childcare and social welfare.[5] Even if the general pattern is the same in all Nordic countries, there are also some differences between them; while the share of mandated sources is about 80 per cent in Sweden, Finland and Norway, it is only about 60 per cent in Denmark (Table 3.2). This trend also became clearly visible when interviewing the personnel at the Danish office. The social workers stressed that many clients seek help from the authorities on their own initiative. This was seen as both a positive and a negative phenomenon – positive as it showed the authorities were regarded as a 'partner' in child education, but negative in some cases as the social workers saw a risk of parents turning to the authorities as soon as problems occurred instead of first trying to utilise their existing own resources and social networks.

Table 3.2: Report source (%)

	Finland (Jan-June)	Sweden (Jan-June)	Norway (Jan-March)	Denmark (Jan-March)
Report source				
Mandate	74	85	78	62
Non-mandate	26	15	22	38
N	*311*	*243*	*71*	*67*

The predominant report source among the non-mandated sources is the client him/herself. Referrals from the public constitute only a small share of the non-mandated sources of referrals. This could perhaps be interpreted as being in concordance with the assumptions presented earlier, according to which families in the Nordic countries would expect state help and trust public social workers to act on their behalf.

Although over half of the referrals in all four offices concern children aged nought to 12 years, the remaining proportion concerning adolescents (13-17 years of age) seems rather high in a wider international perspective (Table 3.3). This may be partly due to the system, similar within the Nordic countries, where the police file a report to the social services in cases where an offender is a minor. Perhaps one could say that addressing delinquency is an integral part of the Nordic child welfare model. However, the number of referrals concerning adolescents remains high, even when police reports are excluded. Thus, there seems to be a common (Nordic?) view that 'childhood welfare' also includes the time of 'youth'. The data (Table 3.3) further reveals a fairly equal distribution of referrals by gender of the child in all four offices; to what extent this is specifically a 'Nordic' feature is still subject to investigation.

Table 3.3: Referrals by age and gender of the child (%)

	Finland (Jan-June)	Sweden (Jan-June)	Norway (Jan-March)	Denmark (Jan-March)
Age				
0-12	60	48	68	60
13-17	40	52	32	40
Gender				
Male	48	52	56	63
Female	52	48	44	37
N	311	243	71	67

Concerning 'conditions reported' the following findings can be mentioned (Tables 3.4 and 3.5).[6] First, if we study 'conditions reported' separately for young children and adolescents, strikingly different patterns emerge for the two groups. Referrals concerning the child's behaviour (behavioural problems, criminal behaviour and so on) account for a vast majority of the referrals within the age group 13-17, whereas these issues represent only a minority within the age group nought to 12 years. In the latter, referrals concerning 'harmful domestic conditions' (for example, deficiency in care, family violence and so on) dominate. There is, however, one office deviating from this pattern – in the Norwegian data, 50% of the referrals among adolescents concern the child's own behaviour and 50% are related to domestic conditions.

Table 3.4: Conditions reported for young (nought to 12 years) children (%)

	Finland (Jan-June)	Sweden (Jan-June)	Norway (Jan-March)	Denmark (Jan-March)
Problems related to the child's behaviour	19	18	17	23
Harmful domestic conditions				
Abuse	2	14	11	0
Neglect	5	17	9	8
Deficiencies in care	34	21	18	23
Parental problems	41	30	45	46
N	188	154	65	26

Several conditions per child may have been reported

Table 3.5: Conditions reported for adolescents (%)

	Finland (Jan-June)	Sweden (Jan-June)	Norway (Jan-March)	Denmark (Jan-March)
Problems related to the child's behaviour				
Behaviour problems	19	25	18	32
Criminal behaviour	12	29	10	37
Other	35	24	25	18
Harmful domestic conditions	34	21	47	14
N	142	160	40	24

Several conditions per child may have been reported

Second, concerning different harmful domestic conditions, 'abuse or physical neglect' is relatively uncommon as a reason within the younger age group (Table 3.4). One should, however, note that, in Sweden, 14% of the referrals concerned 'abuse'. A significant share of the referrals can be classified as rather vague 'deficiencies in the care of the child' (including, for example, 'a general concern for the child's well-being' or other, rather 'unspecified problems'). An even bigger share of the referrals concern 'domestic conditions', such as family violence, mental problems and alcohol abuse among the parents. The pattern, thus, seems to be in line with the assumptions of a preventive 'Nordic child welfare model' where (a concern about) unfavourable circumstances of the child is considered to be reason enough for involving the child welfare authorities.

Although the nature of referrals at the offices investigated reveals rather similar general 'Nordic' patterns, there are considerable differences regarding the situation at the respective offices in terms of referrals per social worker. While the Norwegian office received the least referrals (20) per social worker in the 'core work force',[7] the Finnish office received the largest (52) number of referrals per social worker, indicating differences in workload among social workers in the respective offices (Table 3.6).

Table 3.6: Referral rates and indicators for workload among social workers

	Finland	Sweden	Norway	Denmark
Number of social workers	12	12	14	11
Children in area (age group nought to 17)	7,850	6,010	5,700	7,700
Number of social workers per 1,000 children	1,5	2	2,5	1,4
Number of social workers	12	12	14	11
Referrals (per year)*	622	486	284	268
Number of referrals per social worker	52	40	20	24
Referrals in relation to the number of children living in the district (%)	8.0	8.1	5.0	3.5

Note: * Estimate based on the first three/six months of the year respectively

The Danish office had received the least referrals, while the Finnish and Swedish offices received most referrals in relation to *the number of children* living in the district (Table 3.6). Thus, the results indicate a rather extensive organisational and structural diversity, the effects of which, in terms of practices and outcomes, will be further investigated through other methods.

The referral study – the number and nature of interventions

In order to get a more comprehensive picture of procedures (that is, interventions made) *after* the reception of referrals, some additional analyses were conducted. Since this required a reading of all the personal files of clients that were reported during this time and, thus, was very time consuming, these analyses had, for practical reasons, to be limited to Finland and Sweden only. All referrals (and client files) that led to interventions during a time period from April to June 2006 were analysed.

First, some estimates on screening out – that is, referrals that did not result in any interventions/measures – are presented. Our data showed that about 40 per cent of the Swedish and the Finnish referrals were screened out. For Sweden, the findings are in line with fairly comparable data provided in a study by Wiklund (2006), in which respondents (middle managers within social services) made estimates on screening out. According to these results, 36 per cent of referrals did not lead to a formal investigation. Our results are also in line with another (local) Swedish study, which indicated that 41% of the referrals were screened out (Cocozza, 2003).

In this connection, it should be noted that both statutory referrals and applications from the client were classified as referrals (as was the case in Wiklund's study). Quite a few of the screened out referrals were client applications, which were passed on to other authorities (this was the case, for example, in matters related primarily to parental disputes over visiting rights and so on). Another group with a rather high rate of screening out was adolescents who were reported (by the police) for minor offences: In Sweden, only 25% of this type of referral resulted in interventions. Even regarding reports on 'behaviour problems' about half of the cases were screened out. In Finland about half of the reports concerning criminal behaviour and about half of the reports on 'behaviour problems' were screened out.

It is also interesting to note that, concerning a vast majority of reported cases, there had also been earlier referrals. In Sweden nearly half of the cases (48%) had also been referred earlier (at least once, but mostly several times); in Finland the corresponding share was two thirds (73%) of the cases.

Second, within a time period of six months (after the referral), the 'Swedish' social worker had been in contact with the client (family) once or twice in about one eighth of the cases, three to five times in almost one third of the cases and six times or more in 46% of the cases. The corresponding figures were nearly the same in Finland (Table 3.7). These numbers indicate the labour intensive (or client intensive?) nature of the child welfare system.

Table 3.7: Number of contacts between social worker and client(s) (%) during the six-month period following the referral

Number of contacts	Finland	Sweden
0	5	8
1-2	28	14
3-5	27	31
>5	41	46
N	108	83

Third, most interventions made had been characterised as 'counselling and guidance'. In both countries, over 90 per cent of clients had been taking part in this type of measure. Different (specific) community care interventions had been undertaken in about 50 per cent of cases in Sweden and in about 40 per cent of cases in Finland (Table 3.8).

Table 3.8: Type of intervention (%) during the six-month period following the referral

Type of intervention	Finland	Sweden
Counselling and guidance	92	98
Cooperation with other professional groups	57	76
Supporting measures in community care	36	51
Temporary custody	7	18
Non-voluntary care	2	1
N	110	83

Multiple alternatives possible

The need for collaboration between professional groups within social and health services is strongly emphasised in Nordic legal frameworks and administrative guidelines. This aim is also reflected in our empirical results, which show that collaboration with other experts is another frequently used type of measure (Table 3.8). Here, collaboration with school staff and personnel working within the child/youth mental health services are the most common partners in both countries studied. Collaboration with personnel working within day care institutions is, in turn, very rare, which appears somewhat surprising, given the official focus within the system on 'preventive social work'.

Further, in Sweden, the child/adolescent had been taken into temporary custody during the six-month period following the referral in 18% of cases. In Finland, the corresponding figure was 7%. In Sweden, 1% and, in Finland, 2% of the children/adolescents had been taken into non-voluntary care during the six-month period following the referral (Table 3.8).

Concluding discussion

What, then, can be said regarding the initial question of the possible existence of a common Nordic model in child welfare in the light of the findings on the performance of child welfare in the four offices studied?

The similarities at the normative level between the Nordic countries that were detected on the basis of a comparison of the legal frameworks seem to be present also in the light of the referral study, as shown by the kind of problems reported – problems that are thus considered to be child welfare problems in the respective countries. Typical features include a considerable number of referrals on the basis of what seems to be a more general concern about the child's living conditions and a rather low number of referrals concerning abuse and physical neglect; a high number of referrals concerning adolescents; and a fairly equal distribution of referrals by gender. The high number of referrals by mandatory reporters indicates that the legal requirements for other authorities are also followed in practice. These results are concordant with the few previous (national) empirical studies on these issues (see Wiklund, 2006; Cocozza et al, 2007 for Sweden; Laurila, 2008 for Finland).

These similarities at the normative level prevail alongside rather extensive structural differences between the countries studied. These include a varying extent of organisational specialisation – the Norwegian office being more specialised than the Finnish, Swedish and Danish ones. But our study also indicated rather considerable differences regarding the workload at the respective offices in terms of number of referrals per social worker.

An analysis of the process of work with the referrals within the agencies studied provided some initial information about the practices in two of the countries studied (namely Finland and Sweden). Here, we identified similarities in screening out policies, use of type of measures/interventions (including the use of compulsory measures) and contact frequency with clients.

Taken together, the results from our study seem to clearly reflect a family service oriented and preventive Nordic child welfare system. Since referrals concerning abuse or neglect of the child do not predominate, social work practices to a large extent focus on 'supervision, guidance and cooperation'.

Previous studies (see Gilbert, 1997; Wiklund, 2006) have indicated that, in a wider international perspective, the referral rates in the Nordic countries seem to be on an average level. Thus, the rate of referrals is not different in the Nordic countries than elsewhere, but, in the light of the above, the reasons for making referrals could be partially different when compared to other countries.

Our empirical results could be discussed in the light of two types of criticism that have been put forward regarding the preventive nature of child welfare in the Nordic countries. First, several non-Nordic researchers have claimed that the Nordic countries have a rather undifferentiated approach to child abuse. Social work practices in these countries are believed to focus mainly on family preservation, not on the child's situation and 'risk assessment', resulting in a risk of overlooking abuse at the referral stage or during an inquiry (Khoo, 2004; see also Barth, 1994).

Second, for example, Wiklund (2006, pp 19-20) has, with reference to Sweden, claimed that:

> ... if the low representation of abuse and neglect reflects actual conditions, the scope of the [Swedish] system may be interpreted in two ways. In a positive sense, it could be viewed as a strong system that is able to address family problems before they escalate. In a more critical sense, the system could be perceived as an obtrusive one, where the threshold for state intervention is set too low.

The fact that many of the referred families in our study had also been referred repeatedly before seems to speak against the assumption of the threshold being set too low. Instead, the results raise the question as to whether the actual approach in the Nordic countries perhaps prevents problems from escalating, but does not solve them.

In any case, at least in some respects, the results so far available from this study indicate that the Nordic model is more 'preventive' when the kind of problems considered to be child welfare problems that should be reported is used as a measure than when it comes to the level of social work practices, as reflected, for instance, in the very high screening out rates for adolescents reported (by the police) for minor offences as well as for behaviour problems. Here, except for a possible 'preventive' effect of a referral *per se*, the preventive intentions of the system seem to 'fade away' at the level of practices. Further in-depth analyses are needed in order to provide more comprehensive answers regarding the discussed issues, including, for example, the reasoning of social workers. To what extent, for instance, are these results connected to problems related to cuts in the system? One should also note that some researchers have raised the question of whether crime reports should automatically enter the mandated report process, as, if registered nationally, 'this could result in a deflation of mandatory reports' when the content of referrals ranges from child abuse to a youth pilfering a chocolate bar (Cocozza et al, 2007, pp 209-10). However, this following-up of cases of minor offences can be regarded as a direct consequence of the preventive ambitions of the Nordic social work model.

Finally, there is reason to note the obvious limitations connected to the generalisation of some of our results. Our case study has been aiming to compare previously developed theory with empirical results (Yin, 1994) – namely, to try to establish whether there are indications in support of the assumption of a common Nordic model (at different levels) in child welfare and whether such a common model is characterised by the features that have been regarded as typical of the 'Nordic' model. Taken together, our analyses, departing from a 'meso from below perspective', do point at a common model of child welfare in the selected welfare offices in the four countries. This common model also in many respects seems concordant with the features that are usually considered typically 'Nordic'. However, further international comparisons would be needed in order to establish whether these features are actually unique to Nordic child welfare.

Notes

[1] A Nordic reference group consisting of experts in the field of child welfare has taken part in the organisation and planning of the study. Pilot studies in Stockholm and Oslo have been conducted in 2005 (Bengtsson and Persson, 2005). In Finland some parts of the study (the so-called referral study) have been carried out, in addition to the child welfare office chosen for the study in Helsinki-Helsingfors (Vuosaari-Nordsjö), also in the child welfare office in adjoining Vantaa-Vanda (Koivukylä-Björkby), in order to obtain an additional comparative element in the study (see Laurila, 2008).

[2] **Sweden**: Handlingsplan 2006, Huddinge kommun, Socialförvaltningen, individ- och familjeomsorgen, barn och familj; Områdesplan för Skogås 2006; Huddinge kommun, Socialförvaltningen 2005; Statistik 2005, Huddinge kommun, socialförvaltningen, barn och familj, Skogås; Huddinge kommun, Socialförvaltningen, Verksamhetsplan 2006 i sammandrag; SOU 2000:77, *Omhändertagen*. **Denmark**: Børne- og familjeafdelingen (2006) Personal 1. Maj 2006; Rødovre Kommun, Fødelsesamarbejdet i Rødovre; Rødovre Kommun, Åben anonym rådgivning for familjer børn og unge; Rødovre Kommun (2003) Børn og unge politik, Internet www.rk.dk; Social- og sundhedsforvaltningen & Børne- og kulturforvaltningen (2004) Lokaliseringsprojekt till børn, unge og familjer med særlige behov – lokalt tværfagligt samarbejde, maj 2004; Socialudvalget (2006) Orientering om Børne- og Familieafdelingen 14. marts 2006; Styrelsen for Social Service, Håndbog om anbringelsereformen. **Norway**: Barne- og familieetaten, Oslo kommune (2005a) Årsberetning 2005; Barne- og familieetaten, Oslo kommune (2005b); Strategisk plan for Barne- og familieetaten 2005-2008; Bogen H. and Huser A. (2005) Evaluering av finansieringsordning i barnevernet i Oslo kommune, Fafo-rapport 483; Bydel Grorud, Oslo kommune (2005) Årsmelding for 2005 fra Bydel grorud; Bydel Grorud, Oslo kommune

(2006) Budsjett 2006 for Bydel Grorud, Sak BU 112/05; Byrådsavdelning for velferd og sosiale tjenester, Oslo kommune (2004) Strategisk plan 2004-2007, Strategidokument; Bystyrets sekretariat (2005) Slik styres Oslo; FAKS Bydel Grorud, Oslo kommune,Veiledning og kurs til minoritetsforeldre med barn/ungdom 10-14 år; FLIPOVER, Innføringsseminar i metoden Flipover for Grorud Barneverntjeneste 01.02.06; Fylkesmannen i Oslo og Akershus (2005) Årsrapport 2005 om tilsyn med barnevernet; Kommunrevisjonen, Oslo Kommune (2006) Bydelsbarnevernet i Oslo kommune – En undersøkelse av påstandene om at det tas utilbørlig hensyn til økonomi i bydelsbarnevernet, Foreløpig rapport; NOU 2000: 12, Barnevernet i Norge, Tilstandsvurderinger, nye perspektiver og forslag til reformer. **Finland**:Tilasto/Vuosaaren lastensuojelun budjetti 2006 ja 2007;Vuosaaren yhteistyökumppanit 2006; Tilasto/avohuollon asiakkaat 2006, Helsingin kaupunki; Tilasto: huostaan otetut ja sijoitetut asiakkaat 2006, Helsingin kaupunki; Sosiaalivirasto 2006 – kumppani asukkaiden arjessa. Annual Report 2006, Barnskyddslag 5.8.1983/683; Barnskyddslag 13.4.2007/417.

[3] Fairly recently there has been a reformation of the system of child protection in Norway, through which responsibility for a part of the tasks within child welfare services has been moved over to national authorities – with the exception of the City of Oslo, where the municipal level remains responsible also for the tasks in question.

[4] After the study was carried out, the Finnish Child Welfare Law was changed in this respect – the social welfare board is no longer involved in the process of taking children into care. In the case of voluntary care it is now the leading child welfare officer and in the case of compulsory care it is the administrative court.

[5] In Table 3.2, the source that actually made the referral is presented (this is in line with other studies in the field – see, for example, Heino, 2007). However, in some cases, the mandate actor (report source) had got his/her information from non-mandate sources (relatives, neighbours phoning the police and so on). If this fact is taken into account, the share of non-mandate actors is somewhat larger than the figures presented in Table 3.2 indicate.

[6] The main categories of 'Harmful domestic condition' and 'Problems related to the child's behaviour' were created by the authors. It should be noted that several referrals included many reported conditions. In Table 3.2, all types of conditions reported are presented and, thus, the number of conditions reported exceeds the number of referrals.

[7] Social workers working with the investigation of referrals and/or interventions.

FOUR

From welfare to illfare: public concern for Finnish childhood

Hannele Forsberg and Aino Ritala-Koskinen

Introduction

In this chapter attention is focused on *changing cultural ideas* and understandings of the quality of childhood in one Nordic national case context, Finland. By examining the emergence of a new concept, 'illfare of children', in the public discussion and child welfare politics, we complement the traditional structural and institutional levels of analysis of welfare models, policies and practices. The approach on studying ideas explaining how welfare politics change has grown in popularity in social sciences, especially during recent politically and financially volatile times (for example, Björklund, 2008). Analysing the dominant concepts, ideas or discourses of welfare debate in any society may offer a new kind of perspective to understand the dawning directions of welfare politics in uncertainty.

At the turn of the millennium, concern over the 'illfare'[1] of children became a central topic in the Finnish media. The debate had a completely new tone. Until then, we had been accustomed to hearing that our children are the healthiest in the world and that the welfare of our children is reasonably well safeguarded, thanks to the support, service and educational systems embedded in the Nordic welfare model (see, for example, Millar and Warman, 1996, p 46; also Eydal and Kröger in this book). Now, the concern over the increasing illfare of children was being debated with an unprecedented intensity. The collective awareness of Finnish childhood appeared to be undergoing a sea change, for according to the most pointed comments illfare was threatening nearly every child. Even children from 'normal' middle-class families seemed to be faring ill, so ill in fact that they were able to commit terrible crimes. Public concern over the illfare of children has been both widespread and of such a nature that it appeals strongly to the emotions. At the moment, the most heated public debate seems to have passed,[2] but the new concept that has been introduced – 'children's illfare', as opposed to welfare – still lives on in the talk of many professionals working with children, for example. The premise of increasing illfare is used to justify various administrative and political development projects aimed at solving social problem situations involving children. In social work with children, it is important to reflect critically on this 'illfare boom'. The public debate on illfare is a matter of a widely recognised and shared cultural way of constructing phenomena and assigning meanings to them. Such strong cultural interpretations that highlight problematic matters inevitably involve social work that deals with social problems. In this chapter, we focus on a discussion of the dominant features of the illfare talk and the embedded challenge for more critical and nuanced knowledge on the qualities of childhoods. In so doing we do not want to say that problems involving children should not be a cause of public concern or that public concern has not had any positive consequences for social work with children.

Thus, the aim of the chapter is to examine trends in the late-modern cultural politics of childhood (James and James, 2004, pp 1-2), more precisely, to consider the dominant framework of public debate on childhood in Finland at the turn of the millennium – the concern for children's illfare. In what follows, we refer to this phenomenon as 'the discourse on children's illfare'. By the concept of discourse we mean a kind of interpretation system, or a specific way of talking about, giving meanings to and understanding the world through social interaction. We are preoccupied by the sensational nature and prevalence of the illfare discourse and its resistance to challenges. We attempt to understand the logic of the activation and attraction of the illfare talk and to examine its implications for the framing of social problem situations involving children. Hence, our focus here is more in the meaning-making activities of childhood and social problems rather than in the 'factual conditions' of them, even though the two are intertwined.

We view the public illfare discourse as part of the social process of knowing through which childhood becomes communicated and known in a certain light. For this reason, our interest is in the use of evidence/knowledge when justifying social concern about illfare. One of the most disseminated pieces of evidence for increasing illfare has been the growing amount of child welfare clients in Finland. This selective aspect of the discourse gives us the opportunity to consider the most obvious of the social work related parts of the talk and a typical example of the (uncritical) way of using numbers when justifying public concern. A major issue in the illfare debate is that of what constitutes knowledge of the qualities of childhoods. We introduce some 'other knowledge' (Hänninen et al, 2005), the grass-roots-level experience of child welfare social workers with their clientele, to compare with the public illfare discourse in order to 'test' some of the claims of the public concern. In this section we base our discussion on the report of a recent research project (Heino, 2007), which we call 'the pilot'. One of the tasks of this project was to obtain grass-roots knowledge of who the new clients of municipal child welfare are.[3] Our overall aim is to call for a more critical view of how social concern over childhood is shaping the identification and solutions of problems that affect children.

Why is it important to reflect on the production and reproduction of childhood at this particular moment? Discussing children in terms of concern is not as such a new phenomenon. The phenomenon has been historically activated, particularly during periods of profound social change (Hendrick, 2003). We suggest that a specific change is currently taking place in the attitudes towards childhood and welfare in the Finnish context. As a result of social development, the (Nordic) welfare state and its social policy system is facing strong pressures to change. According to Raija Julkunen (2001), the ethos of the Finnish welfare state is transforming: universalism, humanism and solidarity, which have been the basic cornerstones of the welfare state, have had to give way to the principles of economic efficiency calculation, individual responsibility and means testing. Child welfare legislation has also just been amended. The need for new legislation is often seen as a manifestation of change in society. Hence child welfare practice and legislation are viewed as needing 'updating'. The 1983 Child Welfare Act, which was in force until the end of 2007, can be characterised as the law for *all* children, not only for vulnerable children, emphasising children's welfare and rights. The new 2007 Child Welfare Act, which came into force in 2008, is based on the 1983 Child Welfare Act in many ways. However, it emphasises anticipating individual problem situations and the protection of children even more than before.[4] We assume that at any historical moment both childhood and social problems that affect children will be constructed around a complex interplay of competing socioeconomic and political priorities (Goldson, 1997, p 4). A study of history shows that different eras favour different ways of knowing (see Hendrick, 2003). In this way we attempt to capture an image of the times.

The chapter proceeds as follows: We first describe a few brief observations on the public illfare discourse, in particular the ways in which childhood and children's problems have been debated. We highlight the dominant features in the discourse, especially the claim that children's illfare has increased and the way that this growing illfare has been explained. We also explore the logic or social function of this talk of public concern. So far, there is very little research data on this phenomenon (the public concern on illfare) that is specific to Finland. We therefore rely on existing secondary sources (research reports, statistics and information from various reports aiming to promote the welfare of children) and on our own contemporary observations as social scientists and members of Finnish culture. In the next section we narrow our examination and focus on the direction of municipal child welfare social work and related knowledge on child welfare clients and their problems. We are interested in how the client figures as indicators of the illfare of children are constructed. We also examine how the grass-roots knowledge of child welfare social workers resonates with the claims raised in the public illfare discourse. Finally, in the last section, we reflect on the implications of the observed processes of knowing for social work practices with children and families, and present some conclusions.

The public concern for Finnish children's illfare

Defining the problem

Without the media, public concern over the illfare of Finnish children would not have been so widely discussed or examined. Those who study the construction of social problems (for example, Spector and Kitsuse, 1987; Best, 1990) note that public labelling is an essential part of our becoming aware of social problems. Nowadays the media has a central role in this process. An Internet search with the two Finnish words, *'lasten pahoivointi'* ('children's illfare'), reveals numerically[5] how the debate heated at the turn of the millennium in the leading and most widely circulated daily newspaper in Finland, the *Helsingin Sanomat*,[6] during the decades of 1990-2007. The debate on children's illfare was also conducted in other media, as well as in seminars for professionals and politicians. Finland is such a small and homogeneous cultural landscape that it is easy to see the role of public discussion as important and extensive. However, it is often said that it is possible to have only one dominant public discussion at a time in Finland.

There have been some heavily publicised, unexpected and catastrophic incidents during the time period in question, which have probably shaken the conventional sense of social security and social order. The most sensational of these incidents, which we have presented in Table 4.1, also seem to have intensified the public concern on children's illfare.

Riitta Jallinoja's study (2006) on the debate on family issues in the *Helsingin Sanomat* during the period 1999-2003 shows the central place occupied by the 'illfare issue' in the paper at the turn of the millennium. Family problems took centre stage and children's illfare became one of the most common topics of discussion (Jallinoja, 2006, pp 23, 120-5; see also Sihvonen, 2005). Out of all the texts on family issues ($N = 1,539$), 41% spoke of the illfare of children and young people (Jallinoja, 2006, p 120). Other topics included parenthood (especially 'missing parenthood'), childcare and family policy (for more detail, see Jallinoja, 2006, p 23), of which the first is directly linked to the threatening image of children's increased illfare. The growing number of child welfare clients has been widely disseminated as a symptom of children's growing illfare in public discussion (see, for example, Jallinoja, 2006, p 120).

In the media, children's illfare has become a sort of *umbrella concept for a wide range of problems* affecting children, which are widely divergent with regard to their nature and seriousness. The same concept has been used to include both children's headaches and difficult family problems leading to taking into care measures. There has been little discussion on the criteria for defining children's illfare. At its most extreme, merely mentioning a problem has been interpreted as an alarming increase in illfare. For the most part, children's illfare has been based on a romanticised view of the past. The tone of the debate has resembled a panicked reaction to an active concern, accompanied by exaggeration and generalisations (compare the concept of moral panic – for example, Cohen, 1972).

Table 4.1: Timeline of incidents regarding children's illfare in *Helsingin Sanomat*, 1990-2007

Year	Number of items	Some heavily publicised catastrophic incidents
1990	8	
1991	5	Economic recession
1992	5	Economic recession
1993	7	Economic recession
1994	4	Economic recession
1995	4	
1996	8	
1997	7	
1998	23	A dismemberment murder by young Satanists in Hyvinkää
1999	27	
2000	44	Murder of Elina Lappalainen by her schoolmate
2001	63	World Trade Centre attack in USA Murder of the Heino couple by young people
2002	51	Bomb attack by a youth at the Myyrmanni shopping center
2003	33	
2004	26	Tsunami in South East Asia
2005	24	
2006	35	
2007	26	School shooting in Jokela high school

At the same time, the concern over illfare grew into such a strong collective attitude that it has been difficult to call for or accept critical or alternative interpretations. When considering more closely the content of the previously mentioned incidents discussed in the *Helsingin Sanomat* it is possible to see that, at the beginning of the 20th century, the concept was used more precisely to refer either to the physical ill-being of children (like vomiting, headache), mental health problems or more generally to the illfare of the whole society or families. As the millennium approached, the concept became a more vague phenomenon, which is, nevertheless, widely shared – a 'true fact' that 'everybody knows'. According to Riitta Jallinoja (2006), media writing on children's illfare has been characterised by a particular ethos and the interweaving of a particular attitude, emotional pessimism and dramatisation with information on the phenomenon. In order to be received by the general public, the attitude required an audience that had internalised a similar ethos (Jallinoja, 2006). Thus, there was something 'in the times' that nurtured and supported this type of debate.

The way in which children's illfare was presented in the Finnish media was at times not consistent with the neutral provision of information, which is what we have been accustomed to look for in an informative media. For example, issues dealing with few children may have been quoted under a heading that labels them as representative of the whole child population. Traditionally, when summarising information for the media, journalists reporting on research findings have been careful not to distort the original research design and the conclusions derived from it. It is assumed that the pressing need to do well financially contributes to the drive to make the media more entertaining, as this will guarantee a wide public appeal. In this situation, dramatisation, the use of clichés and repetition may be consciously selected as rhetorical devices (for example, Best, 2004, p 3; Frankfurt, 2005; Luostarinen and Uskali, 2006; Raittila et al, 2008) The media is interested in newsworthy incidents, but "for today's media, a dramatic event can become a news story in its own right", writes American sociologist Joel Best (2004, p 4).

As far as we are aware, the concern over children's increased illfare in the other Nordic countries has not been as obvious, or at least it has not become a discourse that obsesses the whole nation. What actually lies behind the activation of talk on children's illfare in Finland? Concern for children made the headlines at the same time as the nation grew more prosperous than ever before. The assertion of the increasing illfare of all children preoccupies us because it conflicts with the lived experiences of many Finnish people. Moreover, the existing research knowledge on the qualities of Finnish childhood is scant and contradictory. There are also indicators that show that children's well-being has been developing in a positive direction (for example, in the recent comparison of children's well-being in OECD countries, Finland is ranked in the fourth position just after the Netherlands, Sweden and Denmark – see UNICEF, 2007, p 2). At the same time, we do not ignore the possibility that more and more children and their families may face difficult life situations. What is an issue for us here, instead, is to resist reducing a complicated social condition to a simple melodramatic format.

The function of the illfare discourse

It is possible to discern certain remarkable processes and events in the background of the illfare discourse, which apparently made a crack in the collective consciousness of social order and childhood in Finland. These phenomena paved the way for the actualisation of the discourse.

First, the debate is situated in the context of a post-industrial society undergoing several profound changes. Among the important changes that took place during the last decade were the deep economic stagnation in Finland (1991-94), the subsequent unprecedented economic growth, globalisation, the integration into the information society and the levelling out of strong economic growth – despite which the Finnish economy has grown the fastest of all OECD countries since 1994. During the second half of the 1990s income inequality and relative poverty increased due to the fact that high-income groups received a great deal of income from assets as well as the decline in the redistributive effect of the welfare state (Uusitalo, 2000). The public welfare system is affected by the wide-ranging social transformations based on the ideas of new economy. These changes affect not only the parents of many children, but also the children themselves. The increasing mobility of financial capital and the consequent strengthening of the market forces are challenging the basic ethos of the welfare society (Bardy, 2006, p 140). At the same time, debate on the increasingly rapid changes in working life, the hectic pace of life and their eroding impact on family life has intensified. At the turn of the millennium, Finland existed in an era termed the late modern. This era has been described in international literature as a context of childhood characterised by the diversification of family structures (divorces, lone parents and stepfamilies) that is embedded in an increasing cultural emphasis on love in intimate relationships, changes in the nature of the parents' paid work (the pervasiveness of short-term jobs, increased pace and mobility, information work, the blurring of boundaries between work and home), a higher education level and the prevalence of gainful employment of women and mothers, and the 'invasion' of various childhood professionals and the media into the upbringing of children. Children's lives are thought to be more complex than ever before and parents are thought to have lost their grip on the upbringing of their children. These issues have repeatedly been highlighted in the public discourse as well as causes of children's illfare (see Kuronen and Lahtinen in this book; Aitamurto, 2004; Sihvonen, 2005; Jallinoja, 2006, pp 114–115; Alanen et al, 2006). The concern over childhood situated in the late modern may be interpreted as a sign of adults' uncertainty in the face of social change. Late modern society is often characterised as an age of uncertainty, constructing both adulthood and childhood as increasingly ambiguous (for example, Lee, 2001). From this perspective, the debate on childhood can be seen as part of adults' own struggle with their identities in a society fraught with uncertainty.

Second, certain unexpected emotive catastrophes dissolved a collective sense of security. These events include the 2001 terrorist attack on the World Trade Centre in New York, the December 2004 Tsunami in South East Asia, and separate cruel and incomprehensible criminal activities committed by Finnish youngsters described in the media as having been brought up in 'good families' (see Table 4.1 earlier in this chapter). These incidents raised evil as a topic of discussion and initiated a debate on a value conflict within the conventional social order. Aitamurto (2004), who has studied the media debate on the Myyrmanni case, argues that what was shocking was the information given by the media that children from 'ordinary families' were capable of committing crimes. This caused parents to panic: could this happen in our family as well? Childhood researcher Marjatta Bardy (2001, p 4), along with her colleagues, refers to the above-mentioned World Trade Centre attack in the preface of the report called *Mikä lapsiamme uhkaa?* ('What threatens our children?'):

> Horror, fear and grief made other issues as insignificant as a fly. The outpouring of emotions, thoughts, speeches and incidents has been immense. We decided to focus on the original title of the report, being even more confident that it is our duty to take good care of our children – our descendants.

The report in question was demanded by the government "because of the current social and value changes that threaten children's welfare".

In this light it is possible to understand the attraction of the illfare talk and its emotionally captivating aspect: children's illfare means the illfare of the most essential symbol of permanence and intimacy. Hence, the attraction of illfare talk represents adults' collective pain over the disappearance of the familiar social order. From this perspective, one could think that we are dealing with an emotional reaction here, the way to which has been paved by the cumulative effects of several latent factors of social change.

With good reason, the illfare debate may be characterised as 'adultist', for children's experiences of their alleged 'illfare' are not present in public talk. Chris Jenks (1996) writes that the late modern era has readopted the child, who is symbolically placed to represent permanence and social ties for the adults themselves. At the same time, childhood is constructed as nostalgic.

Finally, in the light of this kind of ethos, it is easy to understand the arousal of social concern on the illfare of children. At the same time, illfare discourse has politicised childhood. The function of the debate can be interpreted to argue for both the childhood services of the welfare state and the adults' (parents') responsibility for children. From this point of view the growing illfare of children can be seen as a rhetorical argument for the support of families/parenthood and their associated services.

Child welfare social work and the argument for increasing illfare

Social concern over children's illfare touches child welfare social work in many ways – there is no doubt that child welfare services have received a great deal of public attention lately. The phenomenon is familiar elsewhere as well, although the role and intensity of publicity in defining social problems varies in different societies (see, for example, Calgraft, 2004, pp 32-3). All of those who have followed the British debate on child protection know the way in which British child protection has been reformed in fits and starts, following attacks of public moral panic of precisely this kind. At the same time, we have become familiar with the names of the children – Maria Colwell, Kimberly Carlile, Victoria Climbié and Caleb Ness – and the tragic events leading to public uproar that have created the need to revise the instructions and practices within child protection. The role of the Finnish media in raising and controlling social problems is still much less blatant and less disruptive to personal privacy than in Anglo-American culture. Nevertheless, even in Finland, publicity and the new, more sensationalist-oriented journalistic practices (see Raittila et al, 2008) contribute to the making of a new type of cultural politics of childhood.

As already argued, the illfare discourse has politicised childhood as a social problem. In the illfare debate, the increase in client numbers visible in child welfare statistics has attracted interest from the media. The growing figures have been used to assert that children's illfare is increasing.[7] For some vague and probably manifold reasons, the increasing numbers of child welfare clients seem to be a topical issue in many other rich western countries as well (see Jenks, 1996, p 21; Sullivan et al, 2008; Holland, 2004, p 17).

The growing number of child welfare clients as a social concern

The most important child welfare statistics used in the debate on children's illfare include the numbers of children and young people placed outside their own homes or taken into care,[8] as well as the numbers of 'open care'/community care clients. In the light of both these figures, the client numbers have increased significantly over the past 10 to 15 years. In recent years, the numbers have been growing even faster that earlier. During the decade 1995-2005, the amount of Finnish children or young people who were placed outside their homes has grown by 50%. The proportion of Finnish young people below the age of 18 who were placed outside their homes in 2005 was 1.1% (Sosiaali-ja terveydenhuolto vuonna 2005, 2006; Lastensuojelulaki, 2007). Culturally, taking a child into care is a strong symbol of children in distress, hence it is often used as the most important indicator of children's illfare. The number of children and young people who are clients of municipal open care child welfare social work has increased continuously for over 10 years, and the total growth during the period has been over 100%. In 2005, 5.4% of Finnish children and young people under the age of 18 were involved with the support interventions of child welfare community care (Sosiaali-ja terveydenhuolto vuonna 2005, 2006).

If we compare the Finnish numbers to, for example, the British we can assume that there are differences in the fundamental ideas of the different welfare systems. As Kuronen and Lahtinen also point out in this book: "in 2003 there were 25,700 children on the child protection register in England whereas in Finland the number of children in community-based child welfare services was 56,379 (with the population of children being 11 million and one million respectively) (see also Pösö, 2007, p 22)". In the same vein, according to the statistics, there seem to be almost 100 times more young people in prison in England and Wales than in Finland. Also these numbers tell their own story about the differences between systems. In Finland a greater number of young people are institutionalised within the auspices of the child and youth welfare systems than is the case in the respective authorities in England and Wales (Marttunen, 2008).

Although the growth in client numbers is shockingly rapid in Finland, it has been typical of the illfare debate to take these figures as a given without asking much about their bases, the practices that led to them or the background to such figures. The debate has tended to equate client numbers with children's illfare. It is possible that growing client numbers are a sign that children and their families are facing difficult life situations more often. However, the figures could also be explained in other ways. They cannot be used directly to assert that children are faring ill.

There are many reservations associated with the use of statistics as an indicator of the level of children's illfare. Tarja Heino and Tarja Pösö (2003), who have studied statistical practices in child welfare, list some of the main limitations in the use of statistics. First, the national statistics available on child welfare are very scarce and consist primarily of numerical data. Due to the predominant statistical practice, knowledge about community care clients in child welfare on the national level is constructed by collecting the total number of clients as well as the number of new clients each year. The figures say nothing about such matters as who the client children are, what their families and circumstances are like, how old they are and what their problems are (Heino and Pösö, 2003; Heino, 2006, p 2). The statistics are compiled to serve sociopolitical interests and the information gathered is meant largely to serve the needs of authorities and the drafting of legislation. This means that priority is given to recording interventions instead of the condition, personal experiences or circumstances of the children subject to the interventions. The reliability of statistics is at times conditional, for statistical criteria are interpreted locally (Heino and Pösö, 2003; Heino, 2006, p 2).

Municipalities have gradually been involved in producing the statistical data. Information concerning the number of community care clients of child welfare in each municipality has been collected since 1992. In 1995, this information was provided by 85% of the municipalities and information from all municipalities has been available only since 2004. The progressive inclusion of all municipalities and more detailed statistical practices (adopted in 2000 and 2002) has caused significant jumps in the figures (Heino and Pösö, 2003, p 585; Heino et al, 2005, pp 6-7). Therefore, the growth of client numbers that is directly readable from the statistics does not transparently reveal an increase in the illfare of children; what it does show is the cumulative number of child welfare clients captured in the statistics. Children are also included in municipal child welfare statistics, though there are variable criteria. The statistics are on the clients of the child welfare system, but the interpretations of when the client relationship begins are not uniform throughout municipalities or even among child welfare professionals. As an example, almost half of the municipalities report that their statistics include children who have received counselling or advice once or twice, while one third of municipalities include only children for whom a community care decision based on the 1983 Child Welfare Act has been issued (Heino et al, 2005, pp 11-12). Thus, the nature of the client relationship on which the statistics are based may vary as to its severity and the municipality. Therefore, the picture of children's illfare that can be derived from the statistics is not consistent across the country.

Using the increasing number of child welfare clients as an indicator of illfare should be treated with caution for several reasons, as has been pointed out above. In fact, a study of child welfare statistics is more conducive to new questions rather than providing direct answers about children's illfare. Joel Best (2001), who has studied the construction of social problems touching children from many angles, would probably define the child welfare client figures highlighted in the Finnish illfare debate as 'bad statistics'. By this concept he refers to an uncritical manner of using statistics to prove that the prevailing social concern is justified. Figures that even originally might be of doubtful importance for the phenomenon are thus removed from their context and easily begin to lead a life of their own in (media) publicity. According to Best, "the solution to the problem of 'bad statistics' is not to ignore all statistics, or to assume that every number is false. Some statistics are bad, but others are pretty good, and we need statistics – good statistics – to talk sensibly about social problems. The solution, then, is not to give up on statistics, but to become better judges of the numbers we encounter. We need to think critically about statistics" (Best, 2001, p B7). We should therefore be accurate when interpreting social problems involving children. We should also challenge, call into question and propose alternative perspectives on the strong and prestigious assertions presented in the public arena on 'children's problems'.

If it is thought that simply being a client of child welfare describes illfare, would it not be equally interesting to record the 'elimination of illfare', which could also serve as a desirable indicator of the impact of child welfare? The increase in the number of child welfare clients could also be studied from the following angles. Could it be taken as a sign of an improvement in children's welfare? There are some suggestions of this kind in the results reported by Heino (2007). Each year, a growing number of children and young people have received professional help and support in their problems.

Or do the statistics reveal that the number of workers dealing with children's issues in the social and health care sector is increasing (see Jallinoja, 2006, pp 68-9), which is reflected in the increase of child welfare clients? As an example, Matti Rimpelä with his colleagues (2006) suggests that some of the increase in client numbers can be explained by developments in diagnosing children's problems. Or are the figures perhaps the result of deficiencies in the functioning of basic services – or of an active local culture that guides clients towards child welfare? British researcher Vicki Coppock (1997, p 159) proposes that changes (such as financial cutbacks) in one part of the service system dealing with children's problems may increase the client numbers in some other part. In Finland, the clients of open care child welfare services have been increasing in almost the same numbers as the numbers of clients of municipal home care services for families with children have been decreasing over the last 15 years (SOTKAnet Indicator Bank 2008).

Clients and social problems beyond the statistics and public talk

The lived experience of child welfare social workers offers an alternative perspective and a kind of mirror to the public discourse on illfare. The everyday knowledge social workers have is contextual and looks at the phenomenon from a close distance – it could also be termed particularised knowledge (Smith, 1987; see also Hänninen et al, 2005, p 106). Does this knowledge reflect and justify the public discussion of the growing illfare of children? What kind of children and problematic situations can be found behind the growing amounts of child welfare clients? What kind of explanations can we find for problem situations from this perspective?

Now we turn our focus on the local culture of child welfare, especially child welfare workers' accounts of their empirical knowledge on the problems of their new clients.[9] We discuss how the knowledge child welfare social workers have of their new clients coincides with the illfare presented in public discussion.

On the basis of the pilot results, the causes for the need for child welfare seem to be quite classic. The most typical profiles found based on the factor analysis of child welfare clienthood are:

- young people with multiple difficulties in their lives;
- different situations where violence is present;
- neglect of childcare and incapacity of parents;
- parents' disagreements and quarrelling with children;
- parents' use of drugs and alcohol combined with criminality and mental health problems (Heino, 2007, p 62).

All of these issues are very familiar in child welfare. A closer look at the pilot data shows the complicated nature of child welfare situations.

The problems that the media has raised for discussion as indicators of illfare are only part of the mass of intertwined problems. Illfare as a general and abstract phenomenon and the causes of it seem to be of more interest than the actual cases of child welfare. By turning to the basic background factors among child welfare clients, we try to get beyond the category of an abstract universal child client case.

Instances of public concern over the social problems of children typically move along a continuum stretching from the assumption of children as victims to the assumption of children as dangerous (Best, 1990). The former refers to younger children, the latter to adolescents. The concern over children's illfare seen in the Finnish media has, however, rarely differentiated children according to age. According to the pilot, the age of clients appears to be of considerable significance. New child welfare clients exist in all age groups. However, most common among them are the under three year olds (and among them particularly babies under one year of age), who made up 30%, and the 14-16 year olds, whose share was 24% of new child clients. The issues of illfare are actualised or child welfare is particularly sensitive in capturing them at both ends of childhood. Inevitably, illfare is manifested in different forms at the two ends. It is interesting that the public concern over children's illfare has been touched so little by the child-based discourse that has become very popular among professionals at the same time. This might provide opportunities to overcome the dichotomy of victim/dangerous child by applying a citizenship thinking based on children's rights. Of course, this approach is not enough to remove the differences in the opportunity of involving illfaring babies and young people.

Discussions with social workers also made it evident that the family categories used in official family statistics do not adequately describe the family situation of children in child welfare. The key to this family variation was that in many cases children's families do not fit into one category. Instead there can be many different changes in family relations and the nature of them can be dramatic. In the pilot data over half (56%) of the children have experienced different changes in family structures – although 30% of children are under three years old. Almost half of the children are living with lone parents but the reasons for lone parenthood can be diverse. Besides divorces and widowhood, it is interesting that almost one third of children have been living their entire lives with only one parent (mother). It can also be counted that 42% of children have been living within the same family – although someone may have moved away from the family, no new family members have moved in.

One interest of the pilot was to look more closely at the family structures and relations of the new clients in child welfare. In the media, divorce and lone-parent families are welcome explanations for the illfare of children. Yet, what seems to make a case in the media is if the family background is 'good' or 'ordinary', which is defined as a nuclear family with two parents and a solid economic status.

Traditionally, a low educational level has been ascribed to welfare risks but in the illfare discourse it has been expected that a growing number of 'the better families' are suffering illfare (see Jallinoja, 2006, pp 166-80). In the pilot it was surprising that social workers knew very little about the working history or the nature of the job (permanent or temporary positions) that the parents of the child welfare clients held. The situation of mothers was better known than that of fathers – one reason for this is the number of lone mothers. On the basis of the social workers' answers the situation of parents can be described in two ways. On the one hand, 40% of the children were living in families where at least one parent was at work. On the other hand, 43% of children were living in a family were at least one parent did not have a work history at all. Instead of exact knowledge social workers described the special labour market situation of the parents in many ways. In these descriptions different hardships, health hazards or unexpected life situations were connected to the labour market situation.

Poverty has historically been one of the main reasons for the need of child welfare assistance. In the pilot, child welfare social workers were asked to estimate the economic situation of their new clients. This proved to be a very difficult question for the social workers. They did not self-evidently know the economic situation of their clients. In their answers they estimated that 4% of their new clients were quite affluent. They did know that over half of their clients received extended or occasional income support. If we look at the situation according to family structure, over half of the children whose families had received income support were living in one-parent families.

When comparing the grass-roots knowledge of social workers to the illfare discourse, one can note that the arguments used in the public concern represent unique and exceptional cases that do not correspond to the vast number of child welfare clients and their life realities. Poverty, lone parenthood, narrowing life conditions and their connection to different psychosocial issues, combined with the age of children are the basis of the pilot. These are the client-related questions that should be discussed rather than a general and undefined growing illfare.

Conclusions: towards multiple ways of knowing the problematic life situations of children

After considering the social concern on the quality of childhood in Finland, we argue that the thesis of the growing illfare of children has functioned very well as a rhetorical concept. It has succeeded in politicising childhood as a cause of social concern. As an analytical concept, however, it is too vague and emotionally loaded – it does not enable appropriate knowing.

From the perspective of social welfare work with children it is important to ask about the nature of the context that the illfare debate has created for identifying and solving problems involving children. The following things, at least, appear to be evident. First, children are not involved in defining the problems that touch them and the overall adult image of the child is quite pessimistic. Second, the concept of social problems that is created in the discourse is narrow and simplistic. There is no multidimensional knowledge of the phenomenon, nor is it called for. The causes and solutions of illfare lie in experiences defined by (professional) adults who are media savvy. These causes and solutions often seem to concern either the health or the state of mind of individual children or the level of the child–parent relationship. Information on the children's living environment, peer relationships or material circumstances is not widely discussed in the debate.

It seems to us that there would be room for more precise and complex knowing on social problems concerning children. On the basis of the preliminary results of the pilot, we argue that it might be more useful to speak about problematic life situations related to, for example, poverty, lone parenthood, mental health issues and drinking instead of the illfare of children. These kinds of problematic situations of life are quite typical and well-known causes for the need for child welfare social services (Forssén, 1991; see also Blomberg et al in this book). The examples of 'illfaring children from good families' that are raised as a topic in the media are, however, not evident at least as clients of child welfare services. When we concentrate on dramatic newsworthy incidents, there is the danger of overlooking the more common problematic situations. When it comes to the increasing numbers of child welfare clients as evidence of the growing illfare of children, it seems to us that we could see the growing numbers as a consequence of lowering the service threshold of the Finnish child welfare system (see also Blomberg et al, this book), changes in the totality of the child service system and changes in professionals' modes of action, along with the changing nature of the problems children and their families are facing.

It is likely that the way in which social concerns are framed, presented and discussed in the media can decisively influence officially instituted policy and child welfare professionals and parents' actions. At the moment, Finland is full of examples of different development programmes and projects, started at different levels, justifying themselves as prevention or reaction measures to children's illfare. One concrete example is the *Sosiaalialan kehittämishanke* (National Development Programme on Social Welfare) (2004-07) initiated by the government (see Kallinen-Kräkin, 2008), one part of which was a child welfare development programme. Another example of national projects is the *Lapsi- ja nuorisopolitiikan kehittämisohjelma* (Childhood and Youth Policy Development Programme) (2007-11) governed by the Ministry of Education. There are a lot of examples of different smaller projects as well. Many of these have been based on the increased illfare of children – without the actors ever defining what they really mean by illfare. Simply using the two Finnish words for children's illfare as keywords brings up numerous such projects with the Google search engine. The project descriptions show that they include work with problems with widely divergent contents and degrees of severity.

Media attention creates a strong pressure on politicians and professionals working with children's problems to do something about the illfare observed. Uncertainty and threatening images also bring out expressions of the responsibility felt by adults. Social workers in child welfare may become the subjects of a particular accountability and control. What kind of knowledge do they then resort to? What is the cultural politics of childhood that will then be adopted?

Emotionally loaded public concern easily promotes the adoption of quick solutions and rapid intervention – a kind of reactive knowing. Our times favour rapid action, but this involves the danger of repeating simplistic thinking patterns in solving social problems. To take an example, the idea that parents and professionals simply ought to behave in a certain way and then children's illfare could be prevented is a fairly simplistic method to solve complex social problems. Many British researchers on child protection consider that 'an analysis of learning by mistakes' and most risk evaluation meters developed for child protection work are problematic in the anticipation of problem situations threatening children. For example, Irene Stevens and Peter Hassett (2007) consider the former sensible only in a situation where the problem is repeated in exactly the same form as an earlier 'bungled child protection situation', which is a rather unlikely scenario. Similarly, they consider that most evaluation meters developed for child protection are based on linear cause-and-effect thinking or positivistic knowledge. Such knowledge is not useful in solving the most complex social problems, which are what child protection social workers often encounter, even if we had all existing factual knowledge on children's problems at our disposal. Linear knowledge cannot be used to predict the course of events for individual children, which is something ecological theory, for example, has known for long (see Garbarino, 1992). This is also strengthened by an analysis of successful client relationships in child welfare where success cannot be shown by simple meters (Ritala-Koskinen, 2003). Knowledge of causes and effects and quantitative knowledge have become a stable part of the general cultural understanding of scientific knowledge, and this is likely to be the reason why the media also values knowledge related to the causes and prevalence of phenomena above all other knowledge. Such knowledge is, of course, of great value, but applying this – or any other kind of knowledge – to the solving of social problems should cause one to think about the conditions under which the knowledge was produced and on what phenomena it is therefore applicable.

If we accept the assumption that at least some of the social problems considered as children's illfare are complex in nature and difficult to gain an overview of, then the danger threatening Finnish children is not so much illfare, but the risk of a regression of knowledge and action, which is caused by the panic felt by responsible adults and by attempted solutions that do not work with the particular problems (an adaptation of Venkula, 2005, p 79). Fuzzy and complex social problems require a more extensive and less easily accomplished study, for the solutions are not ready made and repeatable, but must be created during a process. What is essential is the understanding of the combined effect of the various factors and the recognition that change is the norm in human life. Child welfare social workers are likely to possess plenty of experiential knowledge of working like this, at the 'interface of chaos', where the essential issue is actually not gaining complete control over the problems, but alleviating them sufficiently (Stevens and Hassett, 2007, p 131). In this situation, such kinds of knowledge as emotions, tacit intuitive knowledge, everyday knowledge, moral reasoning and experiential knowledge are necessary in addition to evidence-based scientific knowledge (Venkula, 2005, pp 119-20; Forsberg, 2006; Taylor and White, 2006). The ability to combine several of these different ways of knowing is essential in solving fuzzy problems. In contrast, the generation of scientific knowledge needed for particular situations is often a slow process.

In the debate on 'capturing' children's illfare, the multiplicity of the problems has to some extent been recognised and the solution that has evolved in several contexts is multiprofessionality (for example, the national *Varpu* and *Perhe* projects – see Kallinen-Kräkin, 2008) or multidisciplinary research (see, for example, the website of the Ombudsman for Children in Finland, www.lapsiasia.fi/en/frontpage). To function properly, these require that the knowledge bases of all parties are identified and the knowledge required in the solving of complex social problems is diversified. For it is often the case that the more distinguished experts there are in their own field, the more specialised they will be and the less practised they are in looking at phenomena from the viewpoint of another field. This is often a crucial obstacle to the success of multiprofessional support work or multidisciplinary research (Venkula, 2005, pp 118-19).

The illfare discourse in itself is less essential than the question of what other discourses, practices and ways of knowing it is related to; in other words, how the illfare discourse is used in practice. These are the combinations that generate the cultural policy of childhood for each era.

Notes

[1] We are aware that the concept of 'illfare' is not English. The closest English word would be 'psychological ill health', but this term does not totally catch the meaning of the Finnish public discussion. The concept of illfare is used as an umbrella concept to describe a range of problems affecting children and is understood also as an opposite to the concept of 'welfare'.

[2] When we were finalising this chapter, public concern on children's illfare was reactivated as a result of two school shooting tragedies, which are extremely rare in Finland. The first tragedy happened in 2007 at the Jokela High School where an 18-year-old male student killed seven students and the female principal of the school. The other shooting happened in 2008 at the Kauhajoki Polytechnic where a 22-year-old male student killed 10 students and one teacher. Both of these events, where the assailant was not actually a child, have been in the media connected to the children's illfare discourse. The content of the public discussion that arose after these shooting cases is not included in this chapter.

[3] Aino Ritala-Koskinen, one of the authors, was a co-researcher in the pilot. One of the ulterior motives for the pilot research was to take seriously the fact that, on the national level in Finland, the only information concerning clients in child welfare, which is annually tracked, is the number of clients and the growing trend of the client figures. The project was conducted as a joint process of social workers and researchers. The Internet questionnaire that social workers completed regarding 330 new clients of municipal child welfare services in 2006 was formulated collaboratively. So the empirical knowledge of social workers was already present when it was defined what was important to know about their new clients. Social workers were asked to answer the questions on the basis of *what they knew about their clients*. Answers were a combination of factual knowledge and social workers' accounts of the problems their clients had, but the answers also tell us what kinds of issues social workers are well aware of or not aware of in their clients' lives. In the context of this chapter we have used this pilot data from a restricted perspective.

[4] Generally, the reform of the law is seen as successful because it now better suits the spirit of the international agreements on human rights and the rights of the child. The new assessment and decision-making procedures fixed by law aim to safeguard the rights of children and families.

[5] These numbers are only trend setting; they do not cover all of the discussion of the topic in the newspaper. For example, adding the words 'young people' besides children would exponentially add to the items (see Sihvonen, 2005).

[6] The *Helsingin Sanomat* is the only nationwide daily newspaper and has a strong institutional position in Finnish society. The newspaper is independent and non-aligned. The *Helsingin Sanomat* is actually the largest subscription-based newspaper in the Nordic countries. The paper's weekday circulation totalled 430,785 copies in 2005 in a population of some five million people (*Helsingin Sanomat*).

[7] In Finland, Stakes (National Research and Development Centre for Welfare and Health) used to be the body that annually collected the statistical data on child protection. On 1 January 2009, Stakes was merged with the National Institute of Public Health and together they formed the new National Institute of Health and Welfare.

[8] 'Children and young people placed outside their homes' means children and young people who have been placed outside their homes by the decision of the municipal welfare board as a support intervention within community care, as a taking into care or as after care.

[9] See note 2.

FIVE

Supporting families: the role of family work in child welfare

Marjo Kuronen and Pia Lahtinen

Introduction

In Finland, for the last 10 to 15 years, there has been increasing interest and investment in so-called family work in the field of child welfare. In spite of the extensive family policy in Finland and in the other Nordic countries providing universal financial support and social and health services for parents and children (for example, Ellingsæter and Leira, 2006; Eydal and Kröger, this volume), there is a growing concern that universal family policy measures are not enough. It is emphasised that families need more specific and targeted support in parenting and taking care of their children.

Related to the deep economic recession in Finland in the early 1990s, there has been growing concern regarding the increase in and more complex problems of families and children. Most often mentioned concerns are connected to: neglect in care and upbringing of children; increasing numbers of children taken into care; high and long-term unemployment and its consequences for children; increasing rates of poverty among children and families with young children; violence, alcohol, drug and mental health problems in families. Furthermore, there have been discussions concerning the hardening of, and more demanding conditions where parents are taking care of their children in today's society – for example, problems in reconciliation of work and family life, loosening social networks, and cutbacks in financial support and services for families (for example, Salmi et al, 1996; Bardy et al, 2001; Forssén, 2006; also Chapter Four by Forsberg and Ritala-Koskinen).

Along with the increasing concern about coping of families, new forms of services, methods of working with families and even a new professional group called family workers have emerged in the fields of child welfare, health care and education. Under the name of family support, prevention, early intervention and early support (Heinämäki, 2005; Uusimäki, 2005), different forms of family work have become very popular in Finland in the last 10 to 15 years. Family work includes a variety of activities, such as 'family cafes', mutual support groups, family centres and professional help at home, which target either all families or more specific groups of children and parents. Both public organisations and NGOs in the field of child welfare, but also in health care and education, have developed a variety of activities under the title of family work, often in specific short-term projects,[1] but increasingly as an integral part of municipal child welfare services.

In municipal child welfare, family work is firmly related to social work with families and children but it is not practised by social workers. As a recently developed new form of work and because of the changes in the educational system, family workers are professionally a heterogeneous group. Task division between social workers and other professionals in social services is defined in the 2005 Act on Qualification Requirements for Social Welfare Professionals (272/2005) and in the recommendations given by the Ministry of Social Affairs and Health (Sarvimäki and Siltaniemi, 2007), but a specific professional qualification is not yet required in family work.[2] In the early 2000s, a national survey on family workers in municipalities showed that two thirds of family workers had upper secondary vocational education in health and social care, and one third of them had a polytechnic education (equalling to a BA level degree) in social care or in social pedagogy. Many of them had some additional further education in the field of family work (Auta lasta ajoissa, 2004, p 42). Considering the demands of working intensively with families with complex problems, it has been discussed what would be the correct level of education for family workers, and what kind of professional skills and knowledge base family work requires (Reijonen, 2005, pp 13-14).

On account of its different forms and activities, several Finnish researchers have described the field of family work as confusing (Heino et al, 2000), 'cunning' (Reijonen, 2005) and indefinite (Uusimäki, 2005). They have asked what family work actually is, how it should be defined, what are its objectives and methods (Lahtinen, 2008), who should provide it, and are these family interventions effective in supporting families and children (Westman et al, 2005)? Researchers have either tried to analyse and classify the diffuse field of different practices and development projects (Heino et al, 2000; Uusimäki, 2005) or studied one specific form of family work (Kaikko, 2004; Korkiakangas, 2005). However, some of them have taken distance from the current professional practices and discussions by trying to define and analyse family work more theoretically, referring widely to professional interventions in families with young children (Nätkin and Vuori, 2007).

In this chapter, the discussion on family work relates to current practices, but at the same time maintains a critical distance from them. The authors also make a distinction – even if not a very firm one – between family support and family work. Family support is used to refer more generally to ideological discussions and aims concerning the needs and problems of children and families, whereas family work refers to concrete actions taken and specific forms of (professional) intervention to provide 'support' for families. Furthermore, the chapter concentrates on family work provided within child welfare services that is organised by local authorities, and targets families and children who are assessed to be in need of corrective and more intensive intervention in their everyday life. In this context, family work in Finland most often means offering professional help to families in their own homes.

The chapter begins with a brief review of the international discussions on family support, mainly in the other Nordic countries and the UK, followed by an overview of the historical background of the development of family work in Finland. The second part of the chapter analyses the current state of family work in child welfare and its objectives, targets and methods. As the chapter concentrates on public child welfare services, professional roles of social workers and family workers in child welfare need to be discussed. Furthermore, questions will be raised concerning the role of service users, families and family members, in family work, especially with regard to connections and possible contradictions between supporting parents and protecting children, between adult and child perspectives in family work. The authors argue that actual practices of family work should be carefully analysed instead of presenting its ideal descriptions and abstract 'support talk', and that the aims and methods of family work should be clarified.

Family support in the international context

The idea of families needing support is not a new one and not only discussed in Finland. Ever since the 1970s, there has been a wide interest among 'family experts' in family education (Yesilova, 2007). Finnish midwives and public health nurses in maternity and child health services have provided social support and guidance in parenting (Kuronen, 1999). Also in social work, 'family orientation', influenced mainly by systemic family therapy, has been one of the leading professional principles for several decades (Forsberg, 1994, pp 1-5; Juliusdottir in this volume). However, the tone of discussion centred on family support seems to have intensified in recent years and has caused real changes in the service system.

In English-speaking countries, family support is the concept used to refer to both the political and ideological aims and the actual practices and programmes targeting families (Millar, 2005). For example, in the UK and Ireland, there has been an increasing interest in family support, but also discussions concerning the unclear nature of the concept and its contents (Penn and Gough, 2002, p 17; Featherstone, 2004, pp 1-6; Dolan et al, 2006). There are studies that analyse actual family support programmes (for example, Dolan et al, 2006 in Ireland; Artaraz et al, 2007 in England) or evaluate their outcomes and effectiveness (Moran et al, 2004 in England; Tilbury, 2005 in Australia). In addition, there has been a lot of critical discussion in the UK recently among social policy and social work researchers about family support. These researchers have analysed the political origins of family support, its ideological background, and changing relations of families and the state as a consequence of the new policies (Penn and Gough, 2002; Featherstone, 2004, 2006; Gillies, 2005).

According to Brid Featherstone (2006, pp 6-7), family support has replaced the previous term 'prevention' and extended the scope of families targeted in family support programmes. Many researchers in the UK refer to the Labour government's political objectives in family policy and child welfare stated in government papers, such as *Supporting families* (Home Office and Voluntary and Community Unit, 1998) and *Every child matters* (DfES, 2003). The main critique towards family support is related to its ideological basis. It is argued that the aim is to put more pressure and moral responsibility on parents, especially on mothers, but at the same time extending surveillance of parenting and family life instead of targeting the 'real problems', such as poverty of children and families. Val Gillies summarises well the main points of this critique:

> Reflecting an increasing professionalization of childrearing practices, recent policy documents have emphasized the need for all parents to have access to support, advice and guidance. Implicit in this approach is the notion that 'socially excluded' parents in particular are isolated from the information and assistance that enables effective parenting. Meanwhile, the concepts of poverty and inequality are becoming increasingly detached from government definitions of social exclusion. Policies addressing the 'condition' of exclusion commonly emphasize a perceived disconnection from mainstream values and aspirations, as opposed to marginalization from material resources. In the case of family policy, interventions framed within the discourse of 'parenting support' stress the importance of helping parents to do the best they can for their children. However, tacit moral judgements direct the nature and type of support that is promoted, with a particular emphasis placed on advising and 'including' marginalized parents. (Gillies, 2005, p 70)

Most researchers have concentrated on analysing government policy statements, but some of them, like Helen Penn and David Gough (2002), have empirically studied different family support programmes. In their case study of one local authority, they come to the conclusion that: "The emphasis in most of the services was primarily on assisting with psycho-social functioning or child care skills rather than providing resources of economic, health, child care, or leisure and recreation facilities that could improve the general life styles of families" (Penn and Gough, 2002, p 29). They call for actual, financial support for families instead of advice and education.

The critique also points out increasing state control over family life. British researchers are often very critical and sensitive towards state intervention into family life and define family support as controlling intervention rather than positive support. In the UK, child protection has mainly intervened in severe child abuse cases. In this context, family support is probably seen as an extension of child protection and state control over family life. However, there are also opposite arguments. After evaluating outcomes of family support programmes, Patricia Moran and her colleagues (2004, p 127) argue that, in spite of the heavy debate about the appropriate boundaries beyond which the state should or should not intervene in family life, the message from the literature they studied shows that most parents welcome offered support measures.

The strong critique of many British researchers towards the state control differs from most Finnish discussions on family support or child welfare. A reason for this might be different ideologies and models of child welfare/child protection (Hearn et al, 2004; Pösö, 2007; Blomberg et al in this volume), different family policy and welfare state systems (Eydal and Kröger, this volume), and different situations of families with young children. Furthermore, in the Nordic countries, the barrier between family and the state is lower than for example in the UK; 'family goes public' and state intervention into family life is understood more positively and is usually socially accepted (Julkunen, 2006, p 29). In Finland, and in the other Nordic countries, extensive support for families and children is prioritised against more controlling measures, and state intervention is seen more as services and support than control and surveillance. Still, contradictions and tensions between control and support is one of the basic questions in social work and in child welfare also in Finland (Pösö, 2007). However, family support in its practical form as family work fits well into the broad idea of child welfare and the state responsibility for the well-being of children and families. Finnish critique on family work has pointed out that interventions into family life are too weak rather than too heavy and controlling. For example, social work researcher Johanna Hurtig (2003) has strongly criticised family work for being too 'gentle', cooperative and way too understanding towards the parents, which might mean ignoring children's need for protection in and from their families.

In the other Nordic countries, it seems there is no critical debate centred on family support as there is in the UK, or lively professional discussion and development regarding family work as there is in Finland. Margareta Bäck-Wiklund (2000, p 52) argued some years ago that, unlike in the UK, in Sweden universal family policy measures and economic support for families with young children have been discussed and developed, instead of ideological and moralistic political debate around 'support for families'. Also Guðný Björk Eydal and Mirja Satka (2006, p 312), in analysing Nordic welfare policies for children, understand support for parents as being universal services and financial support, such as parental leave schemes, equal access to institutions of early education and schools, health care services, and a system of various schemes of financial support for families with children, including child/family benefits. These are aimed at creating equal living standards and equal opportunities for all children rather than more selective support for certain 'problematic' or 'excluded' families. In the Nordic countries, researchers have been more interested in universal family policies – and more recently childhood policies – and services for families and children (Ellingsæter and Leira, 2006; Eydal and Satka, 2006) than in targeted family support or family work.

What is common, however, in the Nordic countries – at least in Finland and Sweden – is the discussion that all families with young children need support in their everyday life and childrearing, and different activities have been developed to provide it. In Sweden, it is discussed under the title of *föräldrarstöd* (support for parents) introduced by *Statens folkhälsoinstitut* (the National Health Department). It focuses on interventions to avoid psychological problems for children and to improve parent–child attachment (Bremberg, 2004). Also, in Finland, this is one approach known widely as family support, early intervention or early support, but also as family work, and it has been adopted, for example, in the nationwide *Perhe-hanke* (Family Project), which has even taken some influences and examples from Sweden (Paavola, 2004).

In the field of child welfare, however, it seems that, in the other Nordic countries, the term 'family work' is not discussed and used in the same way as it is in Finland. In Sweden and Norway, working with families in child welfare seems to concentrate on developing and utilising different forms and methods of family therapy, and on other specific methods such as family group conference, Marte Meo, Parent Management Training and PRIDE-method (Hansson et al, 2001, p 12; Schjelderup et al, 2005). Some of these are also well known and used in Finland along with family work.

The roots of family work in Finland

At the beginning of the chapter, increasing public, political and professional concern for psychological ill-being or 'illfare' (see Chapter Four by Forsberg and Ritala-Koskinen) of children and families was mentioned as an important background for developing new forms of working with families in child welfare. Furthermore, at least since the early 1980s, family orientation as an ideal – and rhetoric – has been common and 'fashionable' in Finnish social work. Different forms of family therapy and systemic and functionalist understanding of the family have inspired family-oriented social work. The problems and symptoms of one family member are seen as a problem of the family system, and as problems in communication and interaction between family members. Thus, family relations and interaction in the family have been the key targets of professional intervention (Forsberg, 1994, pp 1-5; Forsberg et al, 1994). In this context, family work could be seen as a step towards more concrete family-oriented methods of working with families in child welfare.

Even though the concern about children's psychological ill-being on the one hand and a family-oriented approach to social work on the other have certainly influenced the emergence of family work, the authors have identified two more concrete roots for family work in the Finnish child welfare system. Both of them relate to reformulations of the service system. First, cutbacks in universal social care services for families with young children, especially in home help, have been replaced with more targeted family work for specific groups of families. Second, within child welfare services, there has been a trend towards community-based services, preventive measures and early intervention instead of taking children into care (Pösö, 2007, p 72). In the following, these two roots will be looked at more closely.

Home help changing into family work

Home help for families with young children was developed in Finland in the 1930s, first, by a child welfare organisation called the Mannerheim League for Child Welfare and, later, since the 1950s, as a public social service organised by local authorities. The original aim of the then-called 'visiting homemaker system' was to support and help poor mothers with large families in the agrarian countryside by sending a trained woman into their homes. Practical help in housekeeping, but also enlightenment and advice were the cornerstones of the occupation, understood as 'occupational mothering'. In the early years of the scheme, the main task of the homemakers was to replace mothers' work in times of illness, pregnancy and childbirth, not only in childcare and homemaking but also in farm work – even in milking cows (Simonen, 1990, pp 42-3). Gradually, municipal homemaking became a universal social care service, not only in the countryside, but also in urban society.

Since the 1980s, because of demographic changes and the increasing need for home help for older people, home help for families with young children as a public social service has gradually become more and more limited, and it has now practically become unavailable as a universal service (Leinonen, 2003). At the beginning of the 1990s, almost 60,000 families received public home help services, whereas, in 2003, there were less than 15,000 families getting them (Bardy et al, 2001, pp 65-8; *Lääninhallitusten keskeiset arviot*, 2004).

Home help for families provided by local authorities gradually changed to become more selective and means-tested. First, in the 1980s, a specific part of home help was renamed intensive family work. Satka (1994, pp 323-30) summed up that, in 1980, there were 80 municipalities (out of a total of 464 municipalities at that time) in Finland providing intensive family work. Intensive family work was first invented by the Mannerheim League for Child Welfare, the same large national NGO that had previously established the system of visiting homemaking. Intensive family work provided practical help but the aim was also to influence the parents, especially the mothers, by providing education and advice in childcare and homemaking (Nupponen and Simonen, 1983). By the end of 2003, about 75% of all the municipalities in Finland had replaced their home help services with more selective and child welfare oriented family work (*Lääninhallitusten keskeiset arviot*, 2004, p 112).

Previously, families were able to get temporary practical help for childcare and housework as a public service. Now they have to buy it from the NGOs and increasingly from private companies. In addition, the content of family work has changed from working *for* to working *with* families, especially with mothers, and from practical help with housework and childcare to psychosocial work, advice, education and social support. In the last couple of decades, family work has rapidly replaced home help and has transformed from being a universal social care service to being a selective supportive service for families who are service users of municipal child welfare (Bardy et al, 2001).

From residential care to community-based child welfare

In the mid-1980s, remarkable changes took place in child welfare social work in Finland along with the 1983 Child Welfare Act,[3] giving priority to preventive measures and adopting a broad understanding of child welfare instead of the earlier, more limited and narrow child protection. Orientation and discourse in child welfare started to change from reacting towards preventing problems, and supporting families and children rather than removing children away from their own homes. This aroused a need to find new forms of support for families and children at home instead of placing children into institutional care.

One consequence of this was that residential institutions 'opened their doors' and instead of providing institutional care directed their work towards helping children and parents in their own homes. These new activities of residential institutions were called 'family work', 'family support work', 'family-oriented work' or 'open care'. Many of the institutions also changed their names from being a 'children's home' into being a 'family support centre' (Pösö, 1990, pp 192-5; Forsberg, 1998). This kind of family work has been described as being located in the middle ground between institutional care and family support (Heino et al, 2000, pp 14-18).

Social work researcher Hannele Forsberg (1998) has studied professional culture in the family support centre and compared it with child welfare work done by social workers in municipal social work offices. According to her, this new form of work was established to answer to the critique about the bureaucratic, problem-oriented and expert-dominated child welfare system. It was believed that it could create space for more informal encounters with families and recognise the value and importance of biological parents in child welfare. Its professional framework was based on family orientation and solution-focused brief therapy concentrating on positive aspects and strengths of the families, parents and children instead of on their problems (Forsberg, 1998, pp 128-33).

The trend towards prevention and early intervention meant strengthening family orientation in child welfare (Forsberg et al, 1994; Forsberg, 1998). It could even be argued that supporting families rather than protecting children has been the major ideology in the Finnish child welfare in recent decades (Pösö, 2007, pp 72-6). In recent years, however, there has been ever increasing numbers of critical voices concerning children's right to be cared for, protected and heard as individuals. It has been argued that family orientation might mean 'adult centredness': supporting parents instead of children, orienting to their strengths instead of problems in childcare and protecting parents' right to privacy – at the cost of children's well-being and safety (for example, Hurtig, 2003). The critique has been taken into account in the new 2007 Child Welfare Act, which came into force at the beginning of 2008. It was preceded by the 2004-07 nationwide Development Programme in Child Welfare, which had a strong influence on the contents of the Act.

As discussed earlier, emphasis on prevention and early intervention is related to the Finnish and Nordic broad understanding of child welfare instead of a more narrow understanding of child protection. However, there seems to be a contradiction between the ideology of support, early intervention and helping children and families in their own homes and the numbers of children placed into care. According to the statistics, there was an actual decline in the 1980s in the numbers of children placed outside home but this trend had started already in the 1970s, years before the 1983 Child Welfare Act. In the early 1990s, the numbers of placements started to rise again and have done so ever since (Stakes, 1998, 2006). Even if one has to be careful in interpreting these statistical trends for various reasons (Heino and Pösö, 2003; see also Blomberg et al in this book), it seems that the ideal of supporting families and children in their own homes has not prevented taking children into care, not even into institutional care. In international comparisons, Finland still seems to be a country where the numbers of children, even very young children, and young people in institutional care are higher than in other western European countries. In addition, the number of children registered as clients of municipal child welfare services is very high compared, for example, with England (Pösö, 2007, pp 77-8). Furthermore, it seems that children and families stay as service users longer than before (Forssén, 2006, p 108). This all means that, simultaneously with the high numbers of children taken into care and cared for either in foster families or in institutional care, community-based child welfare has extended and new forms of work, often called family work, have been developed in the space between the two.

Thus, according to the authors' interpretation, family work in child welfare has developed from at least two different and opposite directions. On the one hand, universal and more practical help in daily life for families with young children has changed to more selective and targeted interventions for families and children who become service users of child welfare services. On the other hand, there have been aims to avoid and replace harder interventions into family life with more delicate measures of control and support. The primary answer to both of these needs has been family work.

Current family work in child welfare

Today, family work is among the most popular community-based services in child welfare. Almost every municipality in Finland provides some kind of family work and the rest of them are planning to establish posts for family workers or to set up projects to develop their family work. For the first time, family work is also mentioned and recognised in the new 2007 Child Welfare Act (417/2007, 36§)[4]

73

as one of the supportive measures in community-based child welfare services. It is described in the proposal for the Act as follows:

> Family work is work done at the homes of families, for example, discussion help or support in everyday life provided by family workers. Family work can support parents as educators, assess parenthood or provide support for children. (HE 252/2006, pp 155-6)

Family work is offered mainly for families where parents are assessed as having problems in coping with parenting, problems with alcohol or drugs, or mental health problems, related to neglect of their children (*Auta lasta ajoissa*, 2004). According to the recent report by the Regional Administrative Boards, the biggest obstacle for providing and developing family work is the shortage of resources. Despite massive inputs already invested in family work, new posts for family workers and different forms of activities that have been established, almost half of the municipalities reported that they were not able to arrange services for all families needing them (*Lääninhallitusten keskeiset arviot*, 2004). Furthermore, a large survey of family workers in the municipalities revealed that the number of families for one family worker varied quite dramatically – from one to three, up to 30 families (*Auta lasta ajoissa*, 2004, p 42).

Finland is a Nordic welfare state where the public sector, mainly local authorities, bears the main responsibility for the provision of social services, including family work. However, municipalities may provide the services themselves, in cooperation with other municipalities, or by purchasing them from private service providers. Especially in the urban areas, it is typical to have a mixture of providers of family work including local authorities, NGOs and private service providers (*Auta lasta ajoissa*, 2004, p 37). The fact that some of the rural municipalities are only now planning and establishing their family work models forms a future challenge. If family work is understood as a service that should be offered throughout the country, how can its availability and quality be secured?

Objectives and theoretical frameworks of family work

Ideally, family work is described as being target-oriented and systematic work done with and in families according to a 'family work plan' (Kaikko, 2004, p 8). It should also be based on the needs of the family (Korkiakangas, 2005, p 58). Uusimäki (2005, pp 51-2) highlights an extensive list of tasks that should be carried out in family work – for example, prevention, early intervention and support, caring, correction and control. These high expectations also reflect on the objectives of family work, which are manifold and often expressed at a rather abstract level. Some of them are explicit whereas others could even be called 'hidden' objectives.

The most overtly expressed and frequently mentioned objectives of family work are preventing children from being taken into care and supporting parenthood.

Avoiding taking children into care might also be such a self-evident – or perhaps even hidden – objective of family work that it is not openly expressed to the parents –or even to the children (Hurtig, 2003, p 27). Other expressed objectives of family work are, for example, supporting a child's school attendance, assessment of parenthood (Hurtig, 2003, p 27), securing children's growth environment, helping families to cope with their problems and supporting families to find their own resources (Hyytiäinen and Ouni, 2000).

In the objectives of family work, there are expectations that are not easy to fulfil simultaneously or that are even conflicting: On the one hand, family work is aiming to protect children in families – and even from their families. At the same time, family work should support the parents and parenting. The latter aim is often the one overtly expressed. Family work is part of child welfare but, still, protecting and securing the well-being of the child is a complex matter in family work and in child welfare in general because 'the best interest of the child' is not easy to define. Furthermore, it has been emphasised that the objectives of family work should be agreed together with family members, avoiding professional 'target language' and defining objectives from above. Finding the needs and objectives of the family is perhaps one of the most crucial questions in family work (Heino et al, 2000, p 192). Therefore, it is important to specify the objectives and indicate them more concretely and in everyday language, so that they would be clear also for the parents – and children as well. That would also make evaluation of the progress, results and quality of family work easier.

Family work can be seen as 'both/and' rather than 'either/or' work. First, there is a tension between control and support. Family workers have to balance between working as partners of the adult family members and securing the welfare of the child. Second, family work is done in a professional–client relationship, which consists of loyalty and professional responsibility at the same time. Loyalty is necessary for constructing a confidential relationship and responsibility refers to a duty to intervene when required. Third, in family work there is a tension between voluntarism and obligation to accept help. There might be conflicting views between the expectations of service users and professionals. Finally, family workers have to balance between closeness and professional distance with families and family members they work with. The longer and more intensively they work with the family, the closer and more personal the family becomes for them (for example Heino et al, 2000, p 194; Hurtig, 2003; Reijonen, 2005, p 10).

If the objectives of family work are manifold, somewhat unclear or even contradictory, so are the theoretical frameworks[5] that family work is based on. Family work can be seen as a meeting point for a variety of theories and practices influenced by educational, psychological, social-pedagogical, social work and sociological approaches. The most often mentioned orientations and frames of reference for family work in child welfare are child protection and child oriented family work (Määttä, 1999, pp 96-7), but family systemic or system theoretical orientations, social-pedagogical orientations, and strength and solution focused orientations are also often referred to (Kaikko, 2004, pp 13-18).

In the analysis based on interviews with family workers, Myllärniemi and her study group (2007) found a wide range of terms and concepts that family workers used in describing their work. These included early support, rehabilitation, empowerment, supporting the welfare and development of the child, assistance in upbringing, assessment of parenthood, supporting the everyday life and family relationships, therapeutic orientation, consulting and advising the family, and controlling and following up families' everyday life. According to Myllärniemi (2007), these terms express and organise what family workers "imagine they are doing" rather than describe actual, concrete work with families or open up the more specific meanings of these terms, which refer to different theoretical frameworks. The co-author of this chapter in her piece of empirical research (Lahtinen, 2008) found similar descriptions when analysing texts written by participants in further education for family workers. In addition, there were references to social pedagogy, family orientation, dialogue and partnership. It would be important to clarify and classify theoretical frameworks for family work, but also to study the actual, concrete contents of daily work, to get from the abstract ideals and rhetoric to actual work practices.

Methods in family work: practical help, 'tricks' or supportive discussions?

As mentioned earlier, when comparing family work with home help services, practical help in housework and childcare have transformed to a large extent into psychosocial advice, education and social support. In addition, there are a variety of more specific methods and tools taken into use in family work. Often these methods have been developed originally for other purposes. These include family therapeutic interaction techniques, strength and solution focused methods, methods developed in pedagogy and early childhood education, and child-oriented methods influenced by the sociology of childhood.

Methods of family work in child welfare have been classified into at least four categories: discussion methods, activating methods, consulting and practical support in everyday life, and non-classified other methods. Discussion methods include, for example, discussions with individuals, families and groups; family counselling; negotiations; network meetings; and therapies. Activating methods include art therapy; occupational therapy; adventure education; organising camps for families and children and so on. Supporting everyday life means practical help in parenting, childcare and housekeeping. Other methods include drug rehabilitation for the whole family or community work, which are services offered outside the family home (Heino, 1999; Hurtig, 2003, p 28).

Since the 1990s, there has been a strong tendency in Finland and elsewhere towards developing methods, systematic models and tools for child welfare (for example, Schjelderup et al, 2005). In Finland, more systematic methods and models that have been developed and taken into use include, for example, systematic child-oriented assessment (Möller, 2004), family group conferencing (Heino, 2001) and other network methods (Seikkula and Arnkil, 2005), supportive peer groups for both children (Taitto, 2002) and adults, and life story methods (Bardy and Känkänen, 2005). New tools have been developed especially for working with children, such as 'feelings weather charts', 'strength cards' and 'healing story books' (for example, Välivaara, 2004). But new tools are also used with parents – for example, network and role maps (Helminen and Isoheiniemi, 1999; Airikka, 2003). Development of these new methods and tools has also affected and extended to family work.

The spectrum of methods and tools used in family work has diversified in recent years. Role and network maps, and different games, cards and forms belong to the family worker's 'toolbox'. It is expected and assumed that, by using these concrete tools, family workers can work more effectively in challenging family situations than they can by discussing. Using the new methods and tools could be seen also as a current 'fashion'. Heino et al (2000, p 195) warn about using methods just as a part of routine. Without recognising, reflecting on and evaluating the orientation beyond methods or tools, using them can be detached from the objectives of the work. Therefore, it is important to ask how, why and for whom these tools and methods are used in family work. Are they being used merely as 'tricks' and for the sake of the methods themselves, so that it looks as if something more is being done rather than just discussing around the kitchen table?

The variety of different methods mentioned in relation to family work is widespread. Yet, in child welfare, family work itself is understood as a method used in social work with families and children. Family workers today are more often than before turning into professionals concentrating on social interaction with family members and using more specialised methods and tools, rather than providing practical help in domestic work and childcare. It is important to ask, is this really the kind of support that families need and how is it helping the children?

The role of the 'family' in family work

In the professional language of family work, it is emphasised that the objectives should be set up in partnership with families. However, it might lead to a situation where the targets set up with service users are different from those defined professionally without their knowledge. What might remain unspoken are the controlling and assessing aims of family work. When talking about family work in child welfare, the threat of taking the child into care is always lurking behind positively expressed supportive targets if the family situation does not improve or if the parents refuse to cooperate with child welfare workers, including family workers. Parents and professionals probably both know this but it is not necessarily openly discussed.

Family work has a strong 'whole family orientation'. Accordingly, the objectives are defined from the point of view of 'the whole family', which might hide and ignore the different or even conflicting needs of different family members, women, men, girls and boys. As discussed earlier, there is a possibility of conflict in family work between supporting parents and protecting children (Hurtig, 2003). It is important to ask who is seen and heard, whose problems and needs are recognised, and who are worked with in family work.

When students of family work described their methods in family work, most of them wrote about adult or family oriented methods and less about the methods of working with children. There were a few of them who mentioned face-to-face work with young people. The child was seen in relation to the parents, friends and professionals, or even as an 'instrument' to do something for the parents. For example, mother and child going out together was seen as important, not because that would give the child a good time and some time together with the mother, but because *the mother* needed some fresh air and cheering up (Lahtinen, 2008). There seems to be a strong assumption that children are helped by helping their parents (see Forsberg, 1998, pp 193–4).

Johanna Hurtig (2003) emphasises seeing and hearing children in family work and argues that, if the professional focus is on the child at the very beginning, it will last through the whole process. According to her, in child welfare an understanding of the individuality of a child, seeing children as a part of the family, asking children their experiences and views of their everyday life, and taking the everyday life experiences of the child as an essential part of collecting information and assessing the situation are important (Hurtig, 2003, pp 91–2).

In family work, it is necessary to ascertain the position and individual needs and rights not only of children, but also of women and men. Brid Featherstone (2004, pp 7–14) calls for a feminist analysis of family support. According to her, that would allow the unveiling of gender-neutral language such as 'family' or 'parent' and the analysis of gendered family practices. Furthermore, it would help to see power relations in families and discuss such problems as violence and abuse. Finally, it would give recognition of and support for caring activities in families. In Finland, family work has hardly been analysed or discussed from a feminist or gender perspective.

Several studies show that social workers and family workers most often work with women in the families. Lone mothers and their children largely make up the numbers of service users of family work and child welfare in general (for example, Kaikko, 2004). Nevertheless, they are discussed in gender-neutral terms as families or parents, ignoring the specific problems that lone mothers face in their everyday life. Mothers are probably recognised and discussed in actual encounters between family workers and mothers but not in professional texts concerning family work. For example, students of family work often mentioned women's specific needs and activities (Lahtinen, 2008, p 64):

> There's been a group for the mothers living in the area. Family workers took their children out so that mothers could talk and chat without interruptions. They met each other at the group meetings about once a month.

On the other hand, fathers seem to be invisible and absent in family work practices, in the same way as in all child welfare work (see Featherstone, 2001; Forsberg, 1995). They are not at the centre of the focus of the work as the mothers are and it is the mothers who are connecting fathers and family workers. There were several comments in the empirical data by one of the authors that family workers *should* work more with fathers – but they actually do not do that (Lahtinen, 2008).

Because of the strength and solution focused orientation in family work, strengths rather than problems in parenthood are emphasised. That might mean that, together with gender-neutral and family-systemic orientation, problems between parents in their relationship might be ignored. Positive orientation does not allow for discussion on and work with problems such as male violence in families. What is needed in both research on and practical development of family work is careful analysis of the positions of, and possible specific methods for working with, individual family members (Featherstone, 2004).

Conclusions

In spite of the cutbacks in other social care services and financial support for families with young children in Finland (for example, Forssén 2006), there has been an increase in resources allocated to family work focused on early intervention and support for families in their homes. Preventive, solution focused, strength and family oriented work is offered for families who are seen to be in need for professional assistance in parenthood, in improving interaction and communication between family members, in household tasks and in control of their life in complicated and demanding situations. In addition, family work in child welfare is offered in situations where more corrective measures are assessed to be needed. Family work in child welfare is firmly related to social work and is even seen as one of its methods. However, there are some tensions between them, as family workers do not want to be only the 'handmaidens' of social workers – professionals putting into practice the decisions made by the social workers. On the other hand, family workers do not want to take the responsibility that belongs to the social workers, which often means unpleasant and difficult controlling interventions into family life.

Even if the official aim of family work is to prevent problems and intervene as early as possible, in practice it is often started when families are already having complex and difficult problems, are not motivated and committed, or are already beyond the help that can be offered by family workers. In child welfare, family work should be offered earlier than is often the case today. That is why family work is actively developed also in basic services for families with young children, such as in maternity and child health centres and in day care.

When looking at the historical roots of family work, it is important to see what has disappeared or been ignored along with the expansion of family work. Clearly, home help for families with young children has almost completely disappeared as a universal public social care service in Finland. Needing help in cleaning, cooking or childcare is no longer seen as a reason for getting public services. However, that would make the everyday life of families easier in some crucial situations and might even help to avoid such problems where family work is now offered.

What has not disappeared or diminished is taking children into care. In fact, the number of children placed outside the home, either in foster families or in institutional care, has steadily increased since the early 1990s along with the number of children in community-based child welfare services. It is too simple to draw a clear connection between the need for family work and preventing taking children into care (Heino et al, 2000, p 186). However, the crucial question in family work is the balance between helping the parents and protecting the children. Entering a private home is culturally and professionally sensitive, and sets special requirements for the family worker in working and communicating with adult family members. It is difficult to bring up questions concerning children's psychological ill-being, maltreatment and serious family problems. The place of the child in family work as the one needing protection remains unclear (Hurtig, 2003, p 4). Johanna Hurtig (2003) calls this "the dripping model of helping" where helping parents is understood as the most adequate way to help children. If the parents benefit from the help so do the children – eventually. This is a rather negative and gloomy view of the possibilities of family work to help and protect children. Myllärniemi (2007, pp 85-6) instead already sees the focus in family work to have changed to the child and to the secure and mutual relationship between the child and his or her parents.

There are many challenges for further empirical research and practical development of family work. What should be studied further are the elements of support, control and assessment in family work. Is family work helping children or the parents? It has not been discussed enough who is controlled and/or supported and how. This makes the objectives of family work unclear to the service users – and maybe even to professionals themselves. It is also important to discuss further the division of labour and responsibilities between social workers and family workers in child welfare (Myllärniemi, 2007). Furthermore, different models, methods and tools have been developed for family work, but are they used and how, do they work and do they help? There is too little research currently available to answer these questions.

More should be discovered about the actual practices of family work instead of making simple ideal descriptions. What do family workers actually do in and with families and with family members? A new research approach might even be needed, which Silva Tedre (2004) in connection with the care of older people calls "distaste-materialist research approach to caring". It concentrates on the actual contents of the work, small everyday events, caring as bodily experience for the carer and the care receiver, physical space, and even dirt and smell and other distasteful aspects of the work.

When looking at the future of family work in child welfare there are several possible directions it could go. It might be that the current situation continues where objectives, methods and forms of family work are 'wild' and manifold.

On the other hand, it seems that the current 'spirit' in child welfare – expressed, for example, in the new 2007 Child Welfare Act (417/2007) – is geared towards more systematic, documented and regulated work processes and methods, as well as coordinated structures and guidelines (Heino, 2008). This might also be the future direction in family work.

Notes

[1] A nationwide Family Project (*Perhe-hanke*) took place in Finland in 2005-07, including 17 local projects supported by the Ministry of Health and Social Services, and run jointly by local authorities and NGOs (www.sosiaaliportti.fi/fi-FI/PERHE-hanke/).

[2] The Ministry of Social Affairs and Health has recently given recommendations for the task structure of professional social services, including child welfare. The recommendations are based on the 2005 Act on Qualification Requirements for Social Welfare Professionals. According to the Act, social workers with a master's degree in social work have the main responsibility in municipal child welfare and in its decision making. In these recommendations, family work in child welfare is defined as belonging to "social welfare supervisors" having a polytechnic degree in social care (Sarvimäki and Siltaniemi, 2007, p 7). It remains to be seen whether the recommendations will make family work more professional and increase the qualification requirements of family workers.

[3] In 1983, two significant new Acts were issued concerning children's welfare in Finland: Lastensuojelulaki [Child Welfare Act] (1983/683), and Laki lasten huollosta ja tapaamisoikeudesta [Child Custody and Right of Access Act] (1983/361). The 1983 Child Welfare Act was replaced with a new one at the beginning of 2008.

[4] The new 2007 Lastensuojelulaki [Child Welfare Act] (417/2007) is much more precise and extensive than its predecessor from 1983, including detailed regulations concerning, for example, needs assessment for every new client within three months, the legal right of the service users – both children and adults, the rights of the child to be heard and regulations concerning children taken into care.

[5] We use 'theoretical framework' here in the context used, for example, by Malcolm Payne (1997) and Karen Healy (2005) when identifying different social work theories and defining them as "theories for professional practice to refer to formal theories that are intended to guide and explain social work practices" (Healy, 2005, p 92).

SIX

Family-focused social work: professional challenges of the 21st century

Sigrún Júlíusdóttir

Introduction

This chapter is written from the historical and professional point of view of family social work development. Although based mainly on research on, working with and teaching about families in Iceland, the perspectives are integrated with experiences from the other Nordic countries and the US. The ideological roots of the pioneers working for the benefit of families and children's welfare on different levels are looked at. The relevance of preserving the original spirit of the holistic approach when working for contemporary psychosocial welfare is highlighted. In the perspective of the earlier, conflicting dualism of client-centred practice versus theory development, it is argued that the family therapy movement from the 1950s had a close link to and crucial influence on family-centred social work. Consequently it also played a significant part in the 20th century epistemological development in social work.

Postmodern thinking and values with increased democratisation and revised ideas on the nature and function of power have radically influenced social work and changed the conditions, definition and meaning of its position and role. This is discussed in the context of some prominent social theorists' critical analysis of the social processes, such as Michel Foucault's writings on the concepts of power and autonomy regarding the helping professions. The methodological shift from corrective interventions towards partnership, conferencing and negotiating in family social work is analysed as part of a paradigm shift concomitant with professionalisation in social work.

The *family concept* is discussed in the light of current social changes; globalisation, fragmentation, family values and the Icelandic-Nordic idea of family solidarity are examined with reference to recent family research. It is argued that the reflexive effects of postmodern processes are essential for the emerging reconstructions of families and family relationships, and that people and politicians need help from professionals with theoretical skills and contextual understanding to handle these transformations. The challenges of the family social workers in the 21st century have much in common with the 100-year-old phenomena related to the turbulence and intensive social changes of that period. It is important not to miss the present as well as the future link to the past.

The ambiguous advocacy of social work

As is well known, social work started as a part of the co-evolutionary processes of eco-social change, urbanisation and political movements, and developed in parallel with the social turbulence, inequality and conflicting interests in the modern industrial society of the early 1900s. Social work as a profession evolved through its contextual understanding of individuals and groups in their struggle to adapt to the new social conditions and social phenomena following World War I and II. The initial character of social work was also shaped by forces similar to those that lay behind the early 20th century women's rights struggle for equality regarding personal freedom, social participation and education, as well as that of the trade unions/labour movements. The origin of the category is thus both politically and ideologically related to the moral ideals of philanthropy, volunteering, ethics of human rights and social reform thinking (Rojek et al, 1988; Soydan, 1999; Juliusdottir, 1999, 2004; Pettersson, 2001). Swedner (1993) has analysed the three main motives from the initial phase: charity motive, stabilisation motive and solidarity motive.

Although deeply rooted in the missionary thinking of freedom, justice and equality, seeing every human as a goal in itself, general social work soon acquired a critical position as a prolonged arm and tool for the state and municipalities in "regulating the poor" (Fox Piven and Cloward, 1971) and in their controlling efforts in guiding clients with reference to protection, "law and order" (Richmond, 1899).

In spite of the powerful role models in the area of advocating social reforms and change on the macro level on the basis of theoretical knowledge and research, it seems that the initial basis of philanthropy and intensive involvement in badly situated clients kept appealing strongly to the profession and its leaders. Although claiming advocacy for children, single mothers and other minorities, usually manifest in working explicitly for their short- and long-term interests, the obligation to serve simultaneously in the name of public authority made social workers often suspect in the eyes of clients – and the public. Gradually their activity was identified with bureaucratic functions, "friendly visiting" or control actions. The ostensibly beneficial interventions were met with scepticism creating the dilemma of social work as a profession. Phrases like "the good bureaucrat", "the unloved profession" or "the kind social worker" were also frequently heard but did not convey professional authority or autonomy.

Loyalty to impending tasks and daily obligations to clients and employers appealed strongly and probably prevented emphasising self-interests or giving priority to long-term professional interest. According to Boszormenyi-Nagy's theory of entitlement and invisible loyalties, ambivalence towards self-realisation and insecurity of entitlements may make up a taboo against feeling entitled to growth to a further extent than the obligating loyalty to the past – compare the history of loyalty to pity (Boszormenyi-Nagy and Spark, 1973; Júlíusdóttir, 1993). Reframing this heritage of 'history of pity' into a 'history of heroines' (Davis, 1973) may play a part in dissolving ambivalences. Identification with and loyalty to the pioneers' progressive efforts create conditions for feeling entitled to professional capacity and autonomy. Examples are Jane Addams' social reform work at the client level and her struggle for socioenvironmental improvements through theoretical researching and publications in the US (Addams, 1902, 1910), which was acknowledged, for instance, in her winning the Nobel Prize for peace in 1931.

Following the initial phase the second generation of US social workers improved their skills predominantly at the clinical level where the developing casework method was reinforced in close cooperation with professionals from medicine, psychiatry and psychoanalysis. With reference to the new perspectivism (von Bertalanffy, 1968) and the systemic approach in the 1950s and 1960s, the case was not exclusively the individual – the family and significant others were also included in the treatment process. This was probably an important phase for the development of family therapy as well as professional social work in a broader sense (Pincus and Minahan, 1973; Hårtveit and Jensen, 1999).

In this period academic social work training was not available in the Nordic countries. Instead it was quite common for ambitious Nordic social workers to go to the US, especially during the 1960s, for graduate education and training, both in 'traditional' casework and in family therapy. This provided them with new skills and status in the home country and many of them became advocates of more specialised training in social work, although this was often restricted to clinical practice in treatment settings, schools, probation or therapeutic work in social institutions. Even if casework required graduate training it hardly enhanced theoretical development, but rather played its part in delaying research activity in social work in the US and the Nordic countries. Working on the micro level during this phase was, however, often interpreted as rejecting the importance of the macro level and deceiving political ideology. You were either a (micro) 'saloon social worker' or a (macro) sociopolitical activist.

In the third phase emerging in the 1970s a somewhat similar hampering dualism appeared in the process of academisation of the category, more precisely that of theory and practice. Interest in developing concepts and theories of social work or other research activity was seen as a threat to the loyalty towards clients. The belief was that one was *either* a practitioner (social worker) and loyal to the 'parental/caregiver role' *or* a theoretician/researcher (someone else) – a black and white picture of antagonism. This conflict loomed large both in training and in the service institutions. It culminated in 1970-90 while the educational programmes were being included in academia in Sweden, Finland and Iceland, but remained in colleges in Denmark and Norway. Two models can still be differentiated in Nordic countries but they are developing with a more direct focus towards coherence – for example, because of the Bologna declaration on comparability and compatibility in higher professional education (Juliusdottir and Peterson, 2004).

For social work as a modern academic discipline and profession, the (often conflicting) loyalties to these roots have brought and probably will continue to bring (however, in a different way) the profession a quite special position among other helping professions – for instance, through the holistic approach and its emphasis on humanism and professional ethics. Recognising these roots as the foundation of the profession implies a holistic understanding of the connection between influential macro–micro forces in people's lives. Besides the concept of *change* the concept of *family* or rather *family relations* is still the very core and common denominator in social work in whatever context or methodological approach.

Developmental forces: paradigm shift towards knowledge, power and autonomy

With reference to the earlier discussion, it is hypothesised that *two* main factors have been influential in the process of release from the first phase position that was dominating into the middle of the 20th century. *One* factor is the methodological development in family therapy, the clinical family research and its relation to social work. It was initiated by the Palo Alto group and their scientific work at the Mental Research Institute (MRI) on human communication (Watzlawick et al, 1967; Bateson, 1972) where social worker Virginia Satir was one of the prominent people (Satir, 1964). She contributed with the professional ethics and approaches from the holistic ideology of social work and with creative linking of theory to practice and vice versa. This was, however, not acknowledged at that time (personal communication from Paul Watzlawick and John Fish at MRI, Palo Alto, October 1994; Peggy Penn at a conference, Germany, summer 2001; and Lynn Hoffman at KCC Family Therapy Summer School 2005). The theoretical as well as the clinical contribution of Lynn Hoffman (1981) and other family social workers was also of considerable importance in enhancing theoretical thinking and conceptual development in family social work.

The other factor is the slowly evolving research-based practice in general social work (which started to flourish in the US in the 1970s and in the Nordic countries in the 1980s). It was influenced by the critical discourse on the role of professionals sustaining the manipulative state control of public institutions like mental hospitals, schools, prisons, social and health services (Szasz, 1970; Illich, 1972; Foucault, 1973). The theory of Jürgen Habermas (1963/73) on subject-object positions in human interaction had a crucial impact on a new understanding and development of a revised client–worker relationship, which was also reflected in a new conceptual framework. The critical debate on the family as a closed repressive system (Cooper, 1971; Laing, 1972) was, interestingly enough, concomitant with the most fruitful methodological development in pragmatic human communication, the concept of change and the freeing effect of family therapy for individuals (Watzlawick et al, 1967, 1974).

In family therapy the idea of individual dysfunctions was rejected and replaced by emphasis on system phenomena. The goal was not to cure or adapt the individual (to family, society) but rather focus on his/her personal maturity and strengths through differentiation from dysfunctional relationships (Bowen, 1978). This approach appealed to social workers and may even be seen as a basis for the breakthrough of the concept of *empowering* in client work. Simultaneously the acknowledgement of phenomena of strengths such as *resilience* is increasing (Walsh, 2006; Ungar, 2008).

According to Thomas Kuhn's (1962/80) definition of paradigm, different research subjects and disciplines require different methods and tools to suit different tasks making up the set of practices that define a scientific discipline at a particular point in time. Thus any academic subject and discipline has to develop a basic understanding of its own meaning and its common concepts. Jerome Bruner discusses in his book *Acts of meaning* how meaning is "a culturally mediated phenomenon that depends upon the prior existence of a shared symbol system" (Bruner, 1990, pp 69, 73). The process of constructing meaning in any context is a response to sociohistorical circumstances. A profession's shared symbol system and co-created meaning shape its culture and common understanding (Bruner, 1990; Gergen, 2001). This relates to both the profession itself and its common understanding of meaning of client work creating professional competence and advocacy.

On the path towards integrity in social work certain phenomena have acted as stumbling blocks (Juliusdottir, 2004). As mentioned earlier, invisible loyalties, dichotomous thinking, heterogeneity and imbalances regarding attitudes and factual concern with theory and research are such examples (Juliusdottir and Karlsson, 2007). According to a social constructivist view, educational reforms and identity development can be processed through a narrative reconstruction on individual and group levels linked to interactive co-creational processes in the professional discourse (McNamee and Gergen, 1993/2004; Shotter, 2002).

In the 1970s Frankfurter School critical analysis of the concepts of authority, power and patriarchy was pervasive in Europe, including Scandinavia, creating new grounds for the development of family social work (Adorno et al, 1964/50; Habermas, 1963/73). The influence of these works might be said not to have become manifest and acknowledged in social work until the critical writings of Michel Foucault had been studied, digested and given the appropriate and acceptable *meaning* for social work – a process that took several decades (Chambon et al, 1999). His analysis, definition and exemplification of the concept of power and its application to (helping) professions – for instance, social workers – have contributed to the development of a new professional paradigm. Two key concepts in that developmental process are *autonomy* and *democratisation*, both highly actual in work with human interaction in family relationships. Autonomy is developing through empowerment of the professional role with strengthened theoretical basis and independent research on the one hand, and the subsequent democratisation rejecting paternalism but encouraging client involvement and participation on the other.

Today, family social work based on knowledge research reflects the professional autonomy of social work and the new methodological approach reflects democratisation and sociopolitical advocacy (Munro, 2001; Seim and Slettebö, 2007). Feeling yourself entitled to autonomy and power opens the way to work for the benefit of others. We will now look at the revised social landscape of functions and phenomena confronting the contemporary family social worker.

Changed family concept: from social obligation to individualisation

The concept of family is changing. In the 21st century *structures*, forms and order of things are on the retreat, while *content,* relations and continuous transformations within and around families are gaining importance. The original meaning of the term for family in Icelandic, *fjölskylda,* comes from the root *fjöl* (as *fler* in Nordic languages) = diverse, multi or many, and *skylda* = obligation. Thus the composite word *fjölskylda* can be read as referring to *multiple obligations.* The family institution was supposed to consist of a team, a group of individuals, who had reciprocal obligations towards each other. This relates closely to the idea of *solidarity* and *altruism* rather than *egoism* or *individualism* (Juliusdottir, 1993). People interfered and did not leave the other alone when in need or trouble. The family system was more than the sum of the individual parts. This is still quite applicable in Iceland as families have considerable palpable obligations in a way somewhat different from the other Nordic countries, as discussed elsewhere in this book.

Generally, the idea of family is changing from its function as a structure of (legal, economical and moral) common interests and legal obligations towards a framework of a loosely coupled love-based membership. Therefore it is questionable how realistic a *unit for change* it is today (McKie and Cunningham-Burley, 2005). We see people's globalised life and the whole world in fragmented parts. From an ethnomethodological point of view, the family construct is seen as the social body that has the means to create the conditions of its own verification and therefore its own reinforcement, which imposes itself permanently on reality.

The French social theorist Pierre Bourdieu has discussed the family critically, referring to it as "a fiction" or "realized category" and even as "a well founded illusion", as it is produced and reproduced by the state and its prolonged arms – for example, the professional categories, including family workers, which guarantee it the means to exist and persist as a unit of consumption. We have to cease regarding family as an immediate datum of social reality and rather see it as an instrument for construction of that reality, thus moving even beyond the ethnomethodological challenge and asking *who constructed the instruments of construction that fit so well for the market* (Bourdieu, 1996)?

In the middle of the last century *the family* was defined, in Nathan Ackerman's (1937) terms, as *a psychosocial unit* in a dynamic interaction with the social forces. *The* family flourished as an acknowledged unit for treatment for some decades. Instead of *the family* professionals we might now talk about various dynamic shapes of family forms or lifestyles but, above all, *relationships and intimacy* (Jamieson, 1988). In their book *Parent therapy* Jacobs and Wachs (2002) present a modern treatment paradigm, a relational model, claiming that there is no identified patient, only a parent–child relationship to which both parent and child are continuously contributing. The relationship itself becomes the focus of the treatment and the deconstruction of its multiple meanings the primary goal.

The increasing individualism in postmodern society is strongly affecting human relationships, lifestyles and personal interactions, implying that the question of *solidarity* in family relations needs more concern in our practice. However, the basic assumption in family work is the ethical and ideological belief in the value of helping people to *join each other and relate* through their emotional ties and reciprocal solidarity. I will come back to that.

A changed meaning of change and interventions

The concept of change is changing. In the 20th century family workers looked at themselves as *change agents* (Pincus and Minahan, 1973). There was no question that this change was supposed to bring about some corrections within *the psychosocial unit* towards adaptation and thereby *to* enhance stability in society. In that sense the change was aimed at *a* certain solution. It was oriented towards helping people to better handle their family obligations and roles, reach stability in work and personal life, and be part of the social environment in order to be *included* in society.

As a result of the transformation of social processes and of mentality, the role of family workers is no longer that of promoting change for adaptation. This creates a new understanding both for ordinary people and for social workers (Beck et al, 1994; Sennett, 1998, 2004). This general observation includes, for example, the changed attitude towards the concepts of *responsibility* and *involvement* in other people's lives, as well as the idea of human rights. The idea that the individual is responsible for himself and his destiny is related to what Rose (1996) discusses as the increasing effects of the *centrifugal forces* in society – a concept also well known from Helm Stierlin (1981) when theorising about family dynamics – meaning that people have a tendency not to worry about other people's eccentricities, distress or even criminality, as long as it does not involve any trespassing of their own terrain. This centrifugal force is a phenomenon opposite to the *centripetal force*, which refers to the urge to interfere, wanting people to adjust, belong to the community and be included in society.

The changed attitude – and sometimes rejection – towards the maxim of being 'your brother's keeper' actually comes close to the tendency of ignorance and exclusion of individuals and groups, which might in some way be threatening to self-interests. People are considered to be responsible for themselves and even to have the right to destroy their lives if they 'choose' to do so. The idea of public intervention, paternalism, is retreating.

Theorising about social modernity in a similar vein is found in Young's (1999) writings about the acceptance of disorganisation, or what he calls *entropy*. This concept originates in physics, but is also applied by the Italian Milan therapy team when theorising about family interaction (Selvini-Palazzoli et al, 1978). In the social context it implies that people neglect the unusual, bizarre or deviant behaviour and accept variances and anomalies in society. This acknowledgement of deviance is simultaneously an *exclusion* and rejection of it as a natural object of concern in human society.

In this connection, Young talks about *bulimistic* (throwing out) society as opposed to the earlier *cannibalistic* (taking in) society. It is thought provoking how young people's increasing eating disorders might be seen as a parallel process to the transformation of these social processes. The cannibalistic kind of a society was characterised by formal rules and social legislation about people's lives, which was intended to control and guide them often far beyond their human right to self-determination, as, for instance, when the poor and the criminals were objects of control and corrections. Today, exclusion and neglect are instead of more concern (Young, 1999).

This changed attitude to social responsibility is certainly making the role of general social workers and other family workers debatable and the idea of interventions quite controversial. But changed conditions enhance development and shape new solutions. Instead of seeing the situation in this impossible either-or/then-and-now context it can be defined as being in the wake of a ship (Phillipson, 1989), where the conflicting forces and heavy groundswell are full of new provocative and urgent issues to handle. In his discussion about the crisis of the rapid progress from modernity to post-modernity, Zygmunt Bauman (1991/95) also points out in theorising about *liquid modernity* that people are not bound to be crushed or drowned by these waves and streams. On the contrary, family social workers are confronted by challenging tasks, as people need help and guidance to handle their anxiety and the disorganisation that accompanies the turbulence of the wake.

The new approaches built on the more democratic subject-subject ideology have been efficient, as well as the revolutionary influence of constructivism developed from philosophy. It is in accordance with the systemic approach in family work, now increasingly reaching out to the broader environment, the working places, organisations and cultural work (McNamee and Gergen, 1993/2004).

The discussion of social change in this section will now be coupled to some crucial aspects of post-modernity concomitant with globalisation.

Individualisation, family values and solidarity

Individualisation

The changed idea of *social responsibility* relates to increasing *globalisation*, bringing us to further deliberations on the concept of individualisation. The general definition of the term refers to a two-sided coin (Beck and Beck-Gernsheim, 2002, pp 13-19; Beck-Gernsheim, 2002). On the one side is the dissolution of the earlier given social lifestyles. This weakens the traditional values and concepts such as class, gender roles, family and neighbourhood. The new processes produce inevitably new, alternative lifestyles, which make up the other side of the coin created by the global, however not always visible, institutionalised demands, controls and (regulating) obstacles – just working at another level.

Individuals are taking on the emotional cost arising from the benefit of the global transformations as they are confronted by the contrasts of being stable or mobile. Sometimes it requires individual strength to move to another city, country or even continent to get the best career or educational opportunity. Sometimes it demands a strong conviction to prefer the security and stability of staying at home. Emigration to another country with foreign culture and alien religion, with consequential mixing and social adaptation, might often be complicated. Family social workers know much about the problems met by the families in these cases (Gómez and Guzmán, 2006).

Social exclusion, increased acting out of hatred and prejudices cannot be isolated or written off because the youngest generation and teenagers are mixing with each other – in different public settings, schools and sports – without regard to colour, race or ethnicity (Weingarten, 2006; Tochluk, 2007). We are also to a still greater extent having cross-national companies as well as cross-cultural and cross-religion marriages –now even in Iceland where immigration is also increasing rapidly.

Thus, through the labour market with its 'invisible' principles, the individual is integrated in a global network of restrictions. They are aimed at the individual and do not take family interests or human relations into account. The fragmentation and shortcuts of our time have been an object for research by several social critics trying to understand the modern social (dis)order (Beck et al, 1994; Beck and Beck-Gernsheim, 2002). Richard Sennett (1998, 2004) argues that 'flexible capitalism' refers to the *flexibility* of the human being as the essential feature for the new economy. People are increasingly willing to move and adjust to different new places and so on, believing that 'being flex' will bring them a more happy life in the *new* place and *new* conditions. Family ties and obligation to another person may in this context make life more complicated and cause frustrations. The idea of making a traditional commitment such as a marital contract 'until death do them part' may then be seen as an anachronism (Bauman, 2003/04, 2004; Sennett, 1998).

The commitment to work rather than home, work now embracing the global market for both sexes and the implications of this commitment for human relations, are interestingly revealed in Hochschild's (2003) research. The part this commitment to working life plays in divorces and dispersive effects for marriages and other human relations is also critical in the Nordic countries (Juliusdottir, 1997, 2007; Åberg, 2002). Even divorces and reconstructed families suit the new economy quite well – for example, when parents are buying double sets of things, children are travelling between places, the individuals of the ex-family become more mobile as a labour force and so on. In this perspective, it is understandable that more and more people decide not to have children at all, as seen in European statistics.

Values and family relationships

In the Nordic countries rapid change is not always so evident and it seems that family values related to personal relationships are not on the retreat. A discourse analysis of Icelandic newspapers on family issues reveals traditional family values and worries about the 'future of the family'. Lack of time, too much work, early marriages and births, many children and frequent divorces of young parents were the main expressed concerns (Jonsdottir and Snaebjornsdottir, 2005). A nation-wide Icelandic research project, 'Family change: young people's views and values' (FVV) – that is, position and feeling in the family, values and future views (Juliusdottir, 2007) – showed similar signs. Among interesting findings was the 18-year-old young people's demand for more family time and parental concern. Some of the issues were comparable with the recent UNICEF (2007) report of six comprehensive factors for assessment of adolescents' (15 years old) well-being in 21 rich countries of the world. In the case of Iceland, insufficient data on family relationships and children's subjective sense of well-being is striking in this report when you bear in mind that we have complete data on factors like material well-being, physical health and safety, infant mortality, birth rate and weight where we, like the other Nordic countries, score among the highest in the world.

According to the UNICEF report, information on well-being and interaction in the family, 10% of the Icelandic adolescents feel lonely, as outsiders in the family, left out of things or awkward or out of place (UNICEF, 2007, p 45). The FVV findings show that 70% of the adolescents talk daily with parents (less with fathers). The frequency is somewhat lower in the divorced-parent group and much lower with divorced fathers. The overall picture from a number of items concerning well-being in the family shows that those with divorced parents are generally less content, more often feel lonely or depressed and have negative feelings about themselves. This information suggests less personal harmony and less life quality among the young people in the divorce group than the others. The results from both the UR and the FVV project indicate that Icelandic policy makers still support the interest to have children (bring them into the world) and emphasise the development of high-tech health services to keep them physically alive. Recent reforms in Icelandic family law – for example, regarding parental leave and custody issues – imply progressive change towards parental equality, benefitting the welfare of children (Eydal and Gislason, 2008). Young people in the Nordic welfare states are, however, still requesting more concern from their families, a hopegiving sign of braveness to claim their rights to socioemotional well-being.

Family social workers have substantial knowledge about human relationships and also about demographics, legislation, social structures and processes. When also building on their own research they can be influential, both in the public debate and through programmes of family life education, seminars on interpersonal issues such as dilemmas of ethical decision making, as well as constructive counselling and entering into dialogues with families without losing sight of their own cost-benefit interests. I will develop this further later in this chapter.

Solidarity

As described above globalisation is making people confused and insecure about their existence. In times of short-term relations and fragmented lifestyles an urgent and valid task for family workers – and the only way for politicians – in post-modernity is to minimise the effect of these phenomena, for instance through the concept of *human solidarity*. In this context it is thought provoking that recent Nordic research on family solidarity and intergenerational concern shows that family members do assist each other according to their different needs and that this help even increases when the public health service is lacking, for example in Finland (Salmi, 2002). A Norwegian study shows that people are still making savings for their children (Gulbrandsen and Langsether, 2002) and a Swedish study shows the remarkable contribution of relatives when someone in the family needs long-term health care, in spite of relatively strong public resources (Sand, 2002). A recent Swedish study (Björnberg and Latta, 2007) on intergenerational contact and support revealed an apparent although relative family solidarity. In Denmark people are willing to give a helping hand to their neighbours and friends, and 87% are willing to take their parents into their home if necessary (Juul, 2002).

The relatively strong family relations and extensive informal family support in Iceland are well known from both earlier and recent studies (Juliusdottir, 1993; Ólafsson, 1999). The research already referred to on values among Icelandic young people shows signs of sincere interest and concern for grandparents (Juliusdottir, 2007 and 2008).

According to research on divorce in the western world the general trend seems to be that divorce is developing from being a conflict issue towards an issue of reconciliation and parental cooperation with increased gender equality (Ahrons, 1994; Juliusdottir, 2007). We find positive results on solidarity not only in family research but also in studies on volunteering. The general belief that economic and social welfare as in Scandinavia would make people more egoistic and less prone to good deeds or organised charity is *not* confirmed. Nordic and international studies on volunteering show that the better-off societies and people are contributing most generously to such activities. (Juliusdottir and Sigurðardóttir, 1997; SOU

1993, p 82; Gaskin and Smith, 1995; Salamon et al, 2003; Kristmundsson and Hrafnsdottir, 2008).

Interpersonal ethics and solidarity emerging from the capability of developing personal concerns through intimate relationships are of crucial importance for the family worker's compass as a travel guide in the contemporary global landscape of liquidity, risk and choices (Bauman, 2000). With reference to solidarity it is an ethical task to help an individual to build up an inner strength and create his/her own keel and ballast in order to meet the constantly new waves of the *wake* of changes and transformations in life. This is actualised when working in the private sphere with the ethics of love relationships, parental tasks or intergenerational ties, and in working places as well as with larger systems in a broader context.

The discussion of some crucial dimensions of postmodern social change – that is, individualisation, family values and solidarity – implies rethinking the role of the contemporary family social worker.

Challenges of postmodern family social workers

The reader may be reminded of the fact that the basis for family work, just like social work in general, is not and has never been value free. The meaning of the professional title family social worker carries associations in people's minds with caring and responsibility with an ethical connotation. Family workers are, however, acting in a very fragile framework when activating inherent creative forces to promote health and well-being in family systems, and they often work in the field of tension between help and (guiding) control. The contextual understanding coming from the systemic approach creates 'farsightedness', reaching out from the family core to the broader, social environment.

Family social workers are now as ever supposed to monitor how people can increase acceptance and respect for each other in times of global conflicts and fissures. There is an ethically and politically responsible component in that role, on the micro as well as the macro level. Family social workers are not marionettes as Foucault indicates in his previously mentioned keen critique of professionals. They are not co-dependants in manipulating people as objects; instead the role aims at empowering people to resist and reflect before moving in the global economic field (Chambon et al, 1999).

We sometimes hear the appealing message that 'we' live in a world without boundaries, 'we are all in the same boat' in a world that is getting smaller and smaller through the adventurous development of technology and communication. We can agree with Sluzki:

> It *is* a paradox that the notion of a 'global village' coexists with increased regional fragmentation and growing distance between the rich and the poor. The nostalgia for the (illusion of) simplicity of the past – and that social construct, 'normality' – clashes with the challenges of complexity. Change, rather than an exception, seems an ever-present

reality in our lives, and families need help coping with this process. (Sluzki, 2001/02, pp 50-1)

The industrial society, the modern society of new communication and the postmodern times of high-tech revolution and risky lifestyles have all required suitable balancing social efforts. The revised ideas of social welfare interventions and control have now obtained a new reference, which actualises critical reflections on family social work practice.

Family social work at different levels, linking the micro, clinical knowledge to the macro, social-policy level, gives family workers a special position to *mend a broken world* (Kliman, 2001/02) with the creation of a more holistic existence in the midst of general social fragmentations, as discussed earlier. This may, for instance, refer to the split lives of the children of divorce as well as the fragmented lifestyle of young people (Gergen, 1991). It includes making relatives visible as important and valuable collaborators as well as activating other system workers, for example in school, health and social services (Piltz and Gustavsdottir, 1992). It may also refer to the segregated existence of people of different origin or the broken world of people from war or famine, as well as the disorganised lifestyle of families in conflict marriages in the more affluent parts of the world.

Globalisation and increasing mobility urges family social workers to have an inner dialogue asking questions that create deeper understanding of privilege and oppression, how we value and judge difference (Sutton, 2000). It also provides a wake-up call "in what ways we can make further commitments to diversity, identifying ways to reach out to Arab and Muslim colleagues" (Roberto-Forman, 2001/02). They can be backed up by conveying our understanding of the universal importance of meeting children's basic needs for security and reliable relationships.

Working with larger systems includes work on behalf of individual clients through intervening with specific larger systems (for instance, social services, agencies, schools, health clinics) by training, empowering activities and consultation services to organisations, corporations and communities. In this work there is more focus on issues of class, race and cultural context, thus recognising the powerful impact of larger systems on the lives of social work clients. Often our clients may be rather well off economically, have education, work and a home, but simultaneously they may feel underpowered, depressed, tired and sometimes burnt out or they may feel intolerant, irritated and generally decomposed without being able to link it to their life conditions in a broader meaning or to see it in a social context, as a contingency to be avoided.

Empowering other people, bringing them the hope and belief that they can influence and control their circumstances requires a 'politics of optimism' based on a sustainable sense of hopefulness in the workers themselves as well as acting with 'benevolent opportunism', a perspective that emphasises taking advantage of opportunities to use one's knowledge and skill in real situations (Weiss, 2001;

Shotter, 2002). Conveying such understanding is the most fruitful prevention against prejudices and social exclusion (Miller and Garran, 2007).

Summary and concluding remarks

In this chapter an attempt has been made to link the historical roots of social work to the new epistemology, emphasising theory and research making up a paradigm shift of the profession – that is, from a serving, submissive role to that of a change agent with professional autonomy and advocacy for empowerment and benefit of clients in the global context. With reference to recent Icelandic family research, international surveys on family issues and the effects of globalisation, the changed role of the family social worker has been scrutinised. With broad theoretical knowledge closely linked to insight into people's lifestyles and human problems of contemporary life, postmodern family social workers are in a crucial position. By processing professional experience through research and participation in the social debate, it is possible to contribute to deeper insights among politicians and policy makers concerning family relationships and welfare in a broader perspective.

SEVEN

In the best interest of the child? Contradictions and tensions in social work

Reidun Follesø and Kate Mevik

Introduction

> One of the main objectives of the Child Welfare Services is to give children and families help and support that results in lasting positive changes in their lives. To achieve this, we need continually to develop the knowledge-base of children's services. This means we need research informed methods and practice tools that provide evidence of good outcomes ... [In Norway] the family is used as a resource through family counselling and we have achieved new methods in the Child Welfare Services. We participate in creating an equable and knowledge-based child service across the whole country. We are going to accomplish the development of a highly competent service that centres on the child! We are going to listen to the children! (Karita Bekkemellem, Chief of the Ministry of Children and equality)[1]

The introductory quotation is taken from the opening speech at the Norwegian Child Welfare Services Congress, 19 September 2007, made by the recently resigned Norwegian Children's Minister. Under the headline "We want an equal and knowledge-based Child Welfare Services", she refers to some of the commitments made by the Norwegian government to help the nation's most vulnerable children. First, the Minister underlines that "children have their own independent rights". Second, she points out that "the family and the local community are to be involved in decisions and choice of measures taken". Third, Norway aims for "a knowledge-based child welfare service".

The Minister's review of the Norwegian government's commitments highlights the questions that are the focus of this chapter. Her statement provides a glimpse of the contours of three different movements within the Norwegian Child Welfare Services: the movement towards knowledge-based services; the focus on family in the services; and the commitment to ensuring children's and young people's right to participation.

These three objectives will often have parallel intentions and functions; however, this is not necessarily the case. For example, if a request for help by a child and/or family results in the child remaining safe and at home, the outcome of intervention is undoubtedly a good one. If, in addition, this outcome is the result of appropriate, knowledge-based and inclusive methods, this is even better. However, the question we want to address is what happens if the three movements mentioned do not follow each other. Or, to rephrase the question, what, if any, mutual incompatibilities might exist between the three movements? In particular, we ask what space is allowed the child if he/she does not accept the validity or appropriateness of 'accepted' interventions such as family preservation? Our focus is on children and young people who receive child welfare/protection measures from child welfare services.

It is neither possible nor desirable to reach final conclusions in these discussions. Instead, our goal is to initiate debate about the child's place and power in the family, and to consider the dilemmas faced by practitioners if children and parents deeply disagree with each other's understanding of what it means to belong to and be safe in a family. We ask what official constraints are applied when disagreements occur, and whether such constraints provide directions and alternative measures with a view to possible solutions.

The text is written with a Norwegian context in mind, but the questions raised have relevance for all the Nordic countries and more broadly within the western culture. The idea of the family as an institution is strong in the Nordic region, and the same goes for the will to include children and young people in decisions concerning their own lives. The dilemmas that might be found in incorporating the, sometimes conflicting, principles evident at the intersecting point between family preservation and children's full participation will not in this way be limited to a Norwegian context.

The child in the family

The family plays an important role in the constitution of our society – both by virtue of emotional and social ties and as a 'building block' of the daily operations of society. The belief that children and parents belong together is a deeply anchored value in the Nordic societies. Ann-Magritt Jensen (1999) refers to children as the last remaining non-exchangeable primary relation between human beings – while marriage and cohabitation might dissolve the child's relation to its parent's remains. In this way children symbolise stability, integration and lasting social ties between adults in modern society. Our picture of children has changed from being 'the useful labour' to being 'the loved care burden' claims Kjersti Ericsson (1996). The child is important to the family, in the same way as the family is to the child.

The idea of the family evokes positive associations, as indicated in the UN Convention on the Rights of the Child (1989), which states:

> ... the child, for the full and harmonious development of his or her personality, should grow up in a family environment, in an atmosphere of happiness, love and understanding. (Preamble to the UN Convention on the Rights of the Child, 1989)

It is commonly accepted that happiness, love and understanding (all notions open to interpretation) give the best frame around a child's life. In most families these benefits exist, and children and parents grow together in well-functioning communities. In other families love as well as care is in short supply. It is a fact that some children grow up with parents who neglect, ignore or abuse them (Killén, 1991; Bunkholdt and Sandbæk, 1993). The contrasts between the safe and the unsafe family are clear, as Leif's story indicates:

> Christmas was approaching, and for us this was the worst time of the year. I remember waking in the middle of the night on Christmas Eve, mummy was locked up in the bedroom and my sister was trying to get out of her room. Our stepfather had nailed the door shut from the outside. I ran crying and frightened into the living room, he got angry and took the fire extinguisher and held it up towards my face ... I can still remember how painful it was. He threw me out in the snow and locked me out. (Leif in Follesø, 2006, p 42)

There are many children with stories similar to the one Leif tells us. How many children live under such troubling conditions no one knows for sure. What is known, however, is how many children receive one or more support measures from the Child Welfare Services. At the end of 2006 this concerned 40,400 children in Norway. Of these, 33,200 families received relief measures while 7,200 children had moved into either foster homes or institutions according to custody decisions (numbers from the Central Bureau of Statistics in Norway). Behind every number there is a hidden story concerning a child and a family. The stories range from those who temporarily receive relief measures to remedy an acute life situation to those who, over time, suffer the crudest failure of care.

Since 1896, the Norwegian state has had legislation to ensure adequate care for those children who live in homes where they are neglected. However, through the years, faith in the family as the best arena of care has varied strongly. Norway's first law concerning child welfare (Law about neglected children's treatment of 1896/ Lov om forsømte børns behandling fra 1896) reflected a concern for inadequate parents' bad influence on their children, and went far in its recommendations about removing children from their homes to remote places where they were to be raised in institutions suitable for this purpose. Tove Stang Dahl (1992) claims, with reference to Foucault, that the Europe of the 19th century was characterised by a strong faith in the significance of institutions. The 'difficult children' of the Child Welfare Services were to be reformed through the discipline of the institutions, at a safe distance from their contaminating environment, that is, their biological parents.

Subsequent legislation, passed in 1953, was based on an alternative view of how child welfare work should be performed, reflecting a change in emphasis from condemnation, warnings and removals from family towards preventive measures, counselling, guidance and treatment in the home (Hagen, 2001). Current legislation, enacted in 1992, goes even further in underlining children and parents belonging to each other. In the government report (*Stortingsmelding*) No 40 2001–02 concerning protection of children and young people, one can among other things read:

> The starting point for the Child Welfare Services Law and the government is that it is best for children to grow up with their biological parents. This is seen as an intrinsic value for the child, even though there are shortcomings in the circumstances the parents are able to offer the child, and even though there are others that are better qualified than the parents to take care for him/her. Even though deficit of parental care is shown, and even though the deficit may be partly of severe character, the main rule is that one should primarily try to improve the situation by relief measures in the family.

'The principle of biology' is strong in the Norwegian Child Welfare Services. In the directive that follows the government report it states that:

> All measures according to the Child Welfare Services Law must have the Best Interest of the Child in focus (cs Child Welfare Services Law §4-1/jfr Bvl §4-1). The starting point of the Child Welfare Services Law is that to grow up with their biological parents is best for children. (Circular Q-0982, 1998)

One of the consequences of this emphasis is that relief measures in the home must be tried before a possible decision to take over custody. These measures are supposed to be primarily worked out and carried out in cooperation with the parents. However, a survey carried out some years ago shows that the Child Welfare Services in some cases withdraw if cooperation does not occur, even though they are still worried about the children's situation (Havnen et al, 1998). The study indicates that the most important reason why parents are not followed up is the caseworkers' obvious reluctance to do something against the will of the parents. Other surveys also referred to the same dramatic conclusion – when parents resist investigation, cases with potentially serious contents have a tendency to be dismissed.

There is an ongoing discussion in Norway about the weight it is appropriate to ascribe to the biological tie between children and parents as a value *in itself*. The psychologist Vigdis Bunkholdt is among those who have addressed this question, pointing out that there are several documents that underline the significance of family, among them the UN Convention on the Rights of the Child (1989), article 9, the UN's declaration on protection of foster children and adopted children, and the European Convention on Human Rights. These documents assert that nations are supposed to secure human beings' right to privacy and family life, and also that children are not separated from their parents against their will, intentions followed up by the Norwegian government. Bunkoldt claims that the distinctive thing about Norway is the special significance that we ascribe to biological belonging:

> What is special here is that the Norwegian Child Welfare Services have placed the word biology in front of the words family and parents, and by this restricted the concepts of family and parents to refer only to the biological parents and the biological family. In international circumstances on the other hand, one operates more often with an extended concept of family. (Bunkholdt, 2006, p 104)

Bunkholdt underlines the significance of listening to what children and young people themselves say about their relationship to biological origins. She highlights the reliance on opinion and points to the paucity of research-based evidence on this topic. In such a situation, she claims, it is easy to become ideological and insist that what one believes to be right is the appropriate solution. If the Child Welfare Services cannot be open to the fact that different opinions exist about various solutions to the question concerning finding one's biological origin, they may risk making decisions that are not in the child's best interest (Bunkholdt, 2006).

Knowledge-based child welfare services

If we return for a moment to the Minister's speech, we remember her highlighting the necessity for knowledge-based child welfare services: "This means we need research informed methods and practice tools that provide evidence of good outcomes". In the following text, she refers to examples like PMTO (parent management training – the Oregon model) for children and MST (multi systemic therapy) for young people. Furthermore, she underlines that Norway has implemented five MultifunC-programmes for young people with serious behavioural problems, and also that family counselling is a method that is adopted continually by more local authorities.

The Minister asserts that the Child Welfare Services are to be built on methods and measures anchored solidly in research pointing to positive outcomes. A concept often used in this context is 'evidence-based knowledge', founded on the research of evidence-based practice (EBP) and evidence-based research (EBR) (Marthinsen and Tjelflaat, 2003). Traditionally located within a 'medical model', the somewhat ambiguous concept *evidence* has now become widely accepted in other disciplines – including social work and child welfare. Evidence is often translated – if somewhat vaguely – to mean *proof*, and is often attached to scientific research where facts appear as irrefutable. Evidence-based social work has had, and has, a large number of critics, one of whom is the Swedish professor Sven-Axel Månsson from the University of Göteborg, who claims that the assumptions underpinning a concept imported from medical thinking cannot adequately capture the complexity of the processes, relations and conditions that characterise social work (Månsson, 2000).

Corresponding objections are identified by Bjørn Øystein Angel (2003), who argues that the knowledge view of evidence-based programmes is founded on the possibility of relocating knowledge gained from studies on the group level to define and address problems on an individual level. Angel points out that the research approved to be used in evidence-based programmes is faced with rather special demands. It is built on randomised studies, which are put into a database making it possible to carry out meta-studies. From here, generalised knowledge can, in principle independent of context and person, be collected. Angel discusses further how this theoretical and generalised knowledge gives a model monopoly that works as a knowledge norm in our society. The evidence rhetoric is unconditionally powerful: "because the gospel of evidence promises much: a quality secured practice that builds on knowledge" (Ekeland, 2007, p 19).

Evidence-based knowledge and practice could have been made a large and comprehensive topic. Rather than going into the many possible debates, we want to focus on a specific example that presents the views of a girl who has lived large parts of her life under the custody of the child welfare services. Janka was 21 years old when she participated in a project in which young people told about their own experiences with the Child Welfare Services – both good and bad. She says:

> I have the impression that it often becomes 'either/or' thinking. For example when something new from the USA appears that has given good results, it is introduced in Norway with an expectation that this is a new wonder method. It may work, but problems arise if and when this becomes a replacement rather than a supplement to earlier measures. If one looks on children of the Child Welfare Services as a homogeneous group one type of measures may work for all. But this is not the way it works! Many of the measures existing today are about trying to give relief to families. However, one must not forget that some families just do not work, even though relief measures are applied. Sometimes the young person obviously needs to move, but MST is still the chosen measure. This means that the young person stays in the family even though everyone knows that this is a bad solution. I think that I still haven't met a young person who says that he was moved too early. They are removed from the home too late. There may be many reasons for this, partly in relation to the young people themselves. Many have experienced being so strongly attached

to their parents that someone else has needed to intervene and take responsibility for something to happen. No matter how awful the circumstances of a young person are, it might be totally impossible to say that "I want to move!". From the Child Welfare Services' point of view, everything is to be tried first. If your mummy hits you, it is possible to arrange it so that you are not that much at home during the weekends. Or first one has to find out how much she hits. This takes time. A lot of time! And all this time, the child stays in the home, also when the social worker leaves – it does not help that the child who is in an acute emergency situation that the caseworker promises to start on her case the first thing in the morning. Or over the weekend – for a child or a young person these hours or days may become extremely long, and give extensive consequences. (Janka in Folleso, 2006, p 67)

Participation of children and young people

The Child Welfare Services' primary task is to secure a safe childhood for vulnerable children and for families where children and parents' interests are in conflict. To risk talking and listening to children, and including them in genuine participation processes is both important and challenging. However, the requirement that children are to be listened to is constituted both in the UN's Convention on the Rights of the Child and in Norwegian legislation. In the law, it is stated that children from the age of seven, and even younger if they are capable of forming their own views, are to be informed and given the opportunity to express themselves before decisions are made in cases concerning them. It is emphasised in the UN Convention that the child's opinions are to be weighted according to the child's age and maturity (Lov om barneverntjenester, 1992, § 6-3).

This emphasis on participation shows a change in our understanding of children, an increasing recognition of children and young people as citizens with independent rights in our society. Looking back in time, the virtues of obedience and submissiveness were something that both parents and society wanted from their children. Children were to be seen, not heard. Right up to 1950 there are readings about the importance of raising one's children to submissiveness in literature on raising children (Rudberg, 1982; Hagen, 2001). This literature alters in line with new knowledge and the changed structure of society, and can be read as a concretisation of what society demands of its citizens in different social positions (Rudberg, 1982). Hence, one can imagine that qualities like independence and social competence, regarded highly today, are qualities that make it possible for the child to manoeuvre an increasingly complex society. New requirements of employees, such as flexibility and creativity, are qualities that correspond poorly to earlier times' claims for obedient submissiveness. In school, the student who acquires knowledge independently is rewarded, something that demands both social and intellectual competence in children and young people.

In both sociology and psychology there are presentations of new perceptions of children. Sociological researchers have in recent years developed approaches and methods that make it possible to investigate children as active social participants and childhood as a phase in life with its own social dynamics (Satka and Eydal, 2004). Within developmental psychology, increasing attention is paid to children's interaction with their peers, where children both affect and are affected by their horizontal relations. Previously, the vertical relations – between parents and children – were weighted unilaterally.

The Danish development psychologist Dion Sommer (2003a) is one of many important contributors to new research and documentation concerning children's competence in interacting with others. This capacity, he argues, develops in the child's social network, in kindergarten, in school, among peers, in the family – in short where children and young people live their lives. Sommer contributes to an understanding of the child living *here and now*, and with that he challenges the understanding of the child as one that *is becoming* (human beings – not human becoming). The understanding of the child as someone who is to become something else, an adult, implies "a gesture of reducing the child as a person, a gesture towards an objectifying attitude towards the child" (Botnen Eide, 2001, p 205).

New words and expressed wishes to include children as active participants are, however, not necessarily followed up by action. Old practice may continue dressed in a new language costume. Some of the challenges of including children more actively have been discussed by the previous Nordic Ombudsmen for Children, who in 1999 published the debate contribution *The best interests of the child in our time* (Børnerådet i Danmark et al, 1999). This document argues strongly that the implementation of the UN's Convention on the Rights of the Child is both a long and a tiresome process, reflecting the continued privileging of adults' interests and the associated paucity of structures that give children and young people genuine possibilities of exercising any influence. It remains an unfamiliar thought for many adults that children and young people might have something important to teach the adult population. The Ombudsmen claims that, if implementing the Convention is to be made possible, a change in adults' attitude must occur. First and foremost adults must acknowledge the fact that children and young people have a competency that society needs.

Research also reveals that it takes time before new ideas are followed by new understanding. Clare and Mevik (2008) performed a study of Australian and Norwegian social worker education to find out what students in the two countries are taught about children and childhood in the late modern western culture. The study was carried out by examining curricula of the social work courses, followed by elaborative interviews with the teachers in the schools. The topic of the study was a consideration of how well students were taught about children and modern childhood, children's rights, and children's participation and involvement in decision making. In addition to exploring teachers' awareness of new understandings about children and childhood, the researchers asked the teachers to show how they equip students with skills and attitudes that enable them to work with and for children. The study shows that children and children's relationships are given little attention as topics in the social work education in either country. A significant difference between Australia and Norway, however, was the Norwegian will and wish to change this practice.

A conclusion that can be drawn on the basis of this study is that children's rights, constituted in both the UN's Convention and in the respective countries' legislation, are made invisible by the absence of a clear focus on children as citizens with competence and qualities to participate and engage in relations concerning their lives and development. In students' examination papers the "pathologised-appendage-child" (Clare and Mevik, 2008) is depicted, dependent on adults knowing best what children need and want. Even in Norwegian social work courses, where curricula and teaching were changed for the very reason of exhibiting the competent child, students resorted to psychological explanations that have not adapted to a changed knowledge of children's development and growing up in the late modern society. Rather than directly including children, in both countries, the path to the child and to understand children and children's needs goes through parents and other adult authority figures, with an implicit understanding that these adults act in accordance with what is best for children. Similarly, in both countries, the educational focus on communication skills and development of trusting relations is directed mostly towards adults, with the consequence that social workers after finishing education have insufficient knowledge about, and skills in, talking to children with their needs, wishes and competence as a starting point (Clare and Mevik, 2008).

Contradictions and tensions

Let us return to the three arguments outlined in the opening statements made by the former Norwegian Minister. She underlined children's own independent rights; she argued for the involvement of the family in measures taken to support and protect children; and she emphasised the need for a knowledge-based child welfare service. Through our discussions we have pointed to some possible tensions that can occur in fulfilling these intentions. By moving a step further into the reflections, some contradictions can be traced between these three movements in Norwegian child protection.

As in many other countries, an underpinning principle in the Norwegian child welfare legislation is the principle of the best interest of the child. This principle is based on the UN Convention on the Rights of the Child (1989), where we can read in article 3.1:

> In all actions concerning children, whether undertaken by public or private social welfare institutions, courts of law, administrative authorities or legislative bodies, the best interests of the child shall be a primary consideration.

Emphasis on the best interest of the child, however, has to be negotiated along with other interests. In such negotiations, the voice of the child might be weak and some times hard to hear. Research indicates clearly that professionals often avoid asking children about their opinions. One example is to be found in a publication made by the Norwegian legal practitioner Marianne Aasland Gisholt (2007), who has examined whether children are heard in a number of cases in which petitions for transfer of child custody have been filed. Gisholt argues that there are few decisions that impact so dramatically in a child's life as when her/his residence is to be changed and determined. This is well known from breakdown of relationships where children are largely attached to both their parents, and it is most likely that the decision is far more dramatic when it concerns moving to people who are unknown to the child. According to conventional as well as legal texts, the children involved in such circumstances should get a possibility of pleading their case if they are able, and their wishes should be taken into proper consideration in decisions made.

Gisholt has reviewed 70 decisions made by the Norwegian Family Court during a period of two years,[2] and in 56 of these cases a decision was made to transfer child custody from the parents to official authorities. From the total material she shows that, in 34 of the decisions (including 48 children in total), the children's viewpoints were neither referred to nor commented on by the court:

> In the 34 decisions, there are neither statements from the child concerning the actual circumstances, 'witness statements', nor statements concerning the decision to transfer custody for the child. (Gisholt, 2007, p 117)

Of the children referred to here, 26 were under seven years old, 13 were in the age group from seven to 11, while nine children were between 12 and 16 years old.

The main point in this connection is not to document how many times children and young people are not heard, but rather to underline the point that the absence of children's voices is an existing challenge. The examples presented in this chapter give opportunities to raise questions concerning how professionals might explain the frequent failure to include children in such important life decisions. It might be a resistance among both professionals and laymen to see the child as a credible person with opinions and wishes that have to be considered with the same respect and seriousness as the views of adults, which Clare and Mevik's (2008) study indicates. It might also be possible that the child's story, to the degree it is made an object for consideration, is explained and reinterpreted from the assumption that children are immature and lack the ability to understand their own best interest.

There is a possible tension inherent in focusing on both the family and the child in decisions and choices of measures in the Child Welfare Services. The task of the Child Welfare Services starts where parents – according to their own or others' opinions – cannot meet the demands of daily care in the family. The Ministry of Children and Equality states explicitly that the best help children can get will be help given within their families. Child Welfare Service professionals are expected to focus on all aspects of the situation under which families live and to stimulate the latent resources of families. This focus represents a preventive emphasis, expected to result in more well functioning families and fewer cases of neglect, abuse and behavioural problems. The Child Welfare Service is assumed to be in harmony with the declaration, which constitutes the basis of the present Norwegian government.

The conflicts within some families, however, will sometimes be strong and pervasive. Some children and young people clearly state that they *do not* want to stay with their parents; others show great ambivalence. One example, provided by a 20-year-old girl named Helen, illustrates the difficult situation a child can be captured in:

> It wasn't easy for Helen either to make up her mind, or to make good decisions in all the choices she was facing at this time. She really wanted to leave her family home. At the same time she really wanted to stay. Her dream was that her parents would stop arguing, that her mother should recover from her mental illness, and that her family situation should start to normalize. At the same time, she knew this would probably never happen. The child protection agencies started, in cooperation with Helen, to prepare a court case with the intention to place her into another family. Due to Helen's age, a central point in the preparatory proceedings was to take her wishes into consideration. Helen stayed home during the preparatory proceedings. Her parents, especially her father, blamed her heavily for the 'gossip' she had spread about their family. During this period, gradually, the atmosphere in the family changed. Her father's anger turned into sadness and sorrow, and his violent behaviour decreased. Helen didn't know what to believe. Her feeling of having disappointed her parents became an increasing burden, and her hope of a quiet and normal family situation grew. As a result of this confusing ambivalence, Helen finally decided to withdraw her report to the Child Welfare Services. As a result of this, Helen remained in her home, with lack of care and support as a consequence. (Helen in Follesø, 2006, p 55)

In quite a few cases, the Child Welfare Services file a petition for child custody. If the child is under 15 years of age, they are without independent legal rights, but they are appointed a spokesperson who will plead their case during the legal proceedings. The spokesperson meets with the child before the trial with an aim of revealing the child's thoughts and wishes, which are then passed on to the members of the court. Through the spokesperson, the children may, among other things, express a wish to move from their parents and indicate that they want to live with someone more capable of taking care of them. They may, as in Helen's case, tell about their parents' drinking, about violence, fear and loneliness. Even in these cases, and even if the child clearly asks for another home, the child's wishes will not necessarily lead to any changes regarding place of residence. An important question to address, therefore, is how the child's opinions are entered into these decision-making foundations. A tentative conclusion is that the principle of children's individual rights can conflict with the principle of involvement by the family. Given the current dominance of biological arguments, which strongly emphasise the strength of 'blood links' between a child and his/her parents, this question seems to be highly relevant.

Another contradiction can be traced in the co-location of the interest of the child and a knowledge-based child service. It is not possible to enter a comprehensive discussion regarding knowledge in social work within the framework of this chapter, but some specific issues need highlighting. Like many other subjects, social work as a profession strives to define its own knowledge base. According to the Australian researcher Karen Healy, social work faces a number of challenges in this struggle. The legitimacy of any profession, Healy claims, is linked to practitioners' capacity to articulate their own knowledge foundations. One possible answer to this challenge is to build a scientific, evidence-based foundation of the profession. Such an approach, Healy warns, has several limitations:

> ... scientific methodologies based in positivism are often inappropriate for knowledge building about social work practice. One reason is that these methodologies, such as mainstream inferential statistical techniques, seek to establish a linear relationship between one variable (the independent variable) and another variable (the dependent variable). In human relationships, such variables are difficult to isolate. (Healy, undated, p 22)

Similar reflections are to be found in texts written by Pedro Morago, Lecturer at the Robert Gordon University in Scotland. The paradigm of evidence-based practice has, he states, generated:

> ... not only great enthusiasm in many areas of the social work profession but also an intense debate about the transferability of the principles of evidence-based practice from medicine to a discipline that operates amidst particularly complex and multifaceted societal factors. (Morago, 2006, p 461)

In spite of his warning, Morago points at several reasons for embracing the evidence-based approach in the field of social work. The promoters of evidence-based practice claim that, because policy makers and professionals may cause more harm than good when intervening in the lives of service users, their decisions should always be informed by empirical evidence:

> Certainly, the medical literature provides a few examples of how interventions – some of them very popular – the efficacy of which has not been rigorously evaluated, may have harmful consequences for the health of individuals. One of them is the practice of accustoming babies to sleeping on their stomach, which is believed to have caused sudden death to thousands of infants over the last three decades. (Morago, 2006, p 465)

Also in the area of social interventions we can find examples of how good intentions do not always lead to good results. In such a context, evidence-based practice seems to appear as an optimal tool in order to adapt well-informed decisions and to avoid or reduce risk.

It is not at all hard to agree that social work ought to be both helping and supporting, and should not lead to anyone getting hurt. The question, however, is whether evidence-based practice is the right way to prevent people from getting hurt and harmed. There is probably no great disagreement concerning the need for a knowledge-based child welfare services, or that considerations must be made on a professional basis. It is, however, a paradox if a particular viewpoint is given prime status as evidence. Evidence-based practice is being challenged for giving excessive prominence to quantitative methods of evaluation. This might exclude other methods that provide more specific information about people's values, preferences and needs. Such an approach might narrow the understanding of knowledge and prevent the experiences that children and young people have themselves from being given their rightful place in the manifold knowledge base that the Child Welfare Services need. Under these circumstances it is helpful and necessary to remember that all kinds of social work must be understood contextually and communicatively (Ekeland, 2007).

If children and young people are to have the possibility of participating with their experiences in a fair way, there must be arenas in which they feel safe to do so. Such arenas must be created in fellowship – and in this process it is not only necessary to teach children, but also to learn from them. This process might be both difficult and challenging, but still necessary if professionals really are to listen to the children. Such an approach will also influence the way research is carried out and the contributions made through evidence-based research alone are not sufficient. As Healy states, the expertise of service professionals lies less in the command of a specific knowledge base than in the understanding of processes to promote participation in knowledge building within diverse contexts of social work practices (Healy undated, p 24). A participatory approach associated with greater involvement by service users might led to changes in what are trusted as 'truths' in social work.

One possibility of embracing and practising these aspects exists in the *dialogue*. For the case here Freire's definition of dialogue is helpful:

> And since dialogue is the encounter in which the united reflection and action of the dialoguers are addressed to the world which is to be transformed and humanized, this dialogue cannot be reduced to the act of one person 'depositing' ideas in another, nor can it become a simple exchange of ideas to be 'consumed' by the discussants ... It is an act of creation; it must not serve as a crafty instrument for the domination of one person by another. (Freire, 2003, p 88)

Freire's thoughts break with the traditional hierarchical idea that conversations between children and adults are about passing on knowledge from the learned to the ignorant. This includes relations between teacher and student, professional and child under the Child Welfare Services and so on. According to Freire, human beings' opportunities lie in the ability to reflect on and consider their own lives within equal communities where people meet each other with interest, trust and expectation. This requires, however, that children and adults must be valued equally, and that they must be included with the same respect regardless of age, status and position. Furthermore, in an equal relationship, the parties' thoughts, feelings and understandings of themselves will be weighted in the same way, without being corrected or met with a moralising attitude. How can the adult, who is in a powerful position in relation to the child, manage to create a reciprocal dialogue?

Several researchers bring forth the *appreciative attitude* as an ideal to strive for in interaction with other human beings, children included (Bae, 1988; Løvlie Schibbye, 1988; Aamodt, 1996). This requires taking the child's experiences and opinions seriously, and relating to these in respectful and interested ways.

In this chapter we have referred to three different movements within the Norwegian Child Welfare Services and posed questions concerning the role the voice of children and young people might have in this picture. If family preservation is the dominant intervention, what does it take for a child to be given the possibility of breaking out of her/his family? And if the Child Welfare Services are to be based on methods that have a documented effect, what does it take for a child or a young person to get the help they need if the range of methods available does not include methods appropriate to them? One critical objection of these methods is the lack of emphasis put on the child's own wishes and opinions. We have wanted to force the issue well aware of the fact that the field of child welfare comprises nuances and variations that are not included in our text.

There is probably no great disagreement concerning either the need for a knowledge–based Child Welfare Service or that considerations must be made on a professional basis. It is, however, a paradox, as pointed to earlier, if *current knowledge* is equated to *evidence*. This may narrow the understanding of knowledge, and exclude children and young people's experiences. Children's voices are needed in order to accomplish the development of a highly competent Child Welfare Service.

Along with other sources of knowledge, children must have their rightful role in building the manifold knowledge base needed in this area of social work.

Notes
[1] www.regjeringen.no/nb/tidligere_statsraader/minister/taler_artikler/2007/vi-tar-et-loft-for-a-skape-et-likeverdig.html?id=481319
All quotations from the Norwegian texts are translated by the authors.

[2] The period referred to here is 16 April 2004 to 11 May 2006 (Gisholt, 2007, p 48).

EIGHT

Children in families receiving financial welfare assistance: visible or invisible?

Inger Marii Tronvoll

Introduction

This chapter discusses how social workers from social welfare and child protection services can contribute more actively to helping children in poor families. A Norwegian study of living conditions for families with low income concluded that social welfare and child protection services should be able to identify the needs of children in these families, and to provide help in a flexible and non-stigmatising manner (Sandbæk, 2004). There is an increasing recognition that children are active subjects in their own lives, and that understanding of their experiences and coping strategies is important for understanding their existence (James et al, 1998; Sommer, 2003b). Has this understanding become a part of social workers' attitudes about children in families who are dependent on long-term financial welfare assistance?

Child poverty is a global problem, but conditions for children in low-income families has also received increased attention from politicians and researchers in Europe and North America, including the Nordic countries (Backe-Hansen, 2004).[1] Though countries like the US and Great Britain have more serious poverty problems than the Nordic countries, which have more comprehensive welfare systems and greater income redistribution to families with children, the prevalence of child poverty is dependent on the same general causes in all these countries. According to Backe-Hansen's review, there is widespread agreement among researchers that "growing up in poverty, with the multiple risk factors with which this is associated, *increases the risk that children and young people will exhibit more symptoms of social and psychological problems*" (Backe-Hansen, 2004, p 18; emphasis in original).

The family's poor financial situation can be said to have consequences for children and young people's daily life on two levels. The first level concerns the direct consequences of financial scarcity; one has less and can do less than others. The second level concerns consequences in the form of reduced social freedom of action. When children and young people are unable to participate in the same activities as their peers, they have less opportunity to develop relationships and position themselves as equals in relation to friends. This increases the risk of becoming socially isolated and excluded, and it is at this level that children and young people suffer the most (Backe-Hansen, 2004).

In the Nordic countries, it is mainly social workers who receive and process applications for financial assistance from low-income families. These cases involve families who have no income from other sources such as employment or social security, or who have such low income that they must apply for supplementary assistance from social welfare services in order to manage. This professional group, therefore, has the opportunity to gain insight into the children's situation and to consider this in evaluating the family's need for assistance. We have found few contributions in Nordic research studies, with the exception of Hjelmtveit (2004), which provide insight into how social workers relate to children in low-income families. Hjelmtveit's study has an interesting sample, even though it is of limited size, and he combines interview data from children, parents and caseworkers from their welfare office.

There are some qualitative studies that deal with children and young people's experiences of poverty and choice of coping strategies (Tvetene, 2001; Ridge, 2002; Sandbæk, 2004), and surveys have been conducted of children's understanding of poverty and assessment of their family's and their own financial situation in several Nordic countries (Hussain, 2003; Salonen, 2003; Marthinsen and Røe, 2004; Eydal and Jeans, 2006). This suggests that the view of the child as active subject in his or her own daily life has gained increased support in the research community (Eydal and Jeans, 2006).

A review of the literature (Backe-Hansen, 2004) confirms that children and young people are participants in relation to their own financial circumstances and their understanding of this. They choose various problem-solving strategies to manage with little resources, or they get more using means that are considered socially acceptable in their context, as the Icelandic study also argues (Eydal and Jeans, 2006). Children and young people also choose strategies for living with their situation, intellectually and emotionally. Another point that may be special for this group is that they function as financial participants in relation to people in different social contexts. Relations to parents and to peers are especially important.

Sandbæk's (2004) study has a broader perspective, combining data from parents on the family's financial situation with information from the children. The study includes a comparison group, in addition to the main sample of low-income families. Sandbæk finds the study's most striking result to be the differing views of parents and children. The difference between the low-income families and the comparison group is much smaller with respect to children's views of their daily life. This may mean that the difficult living conditions described by parents are less troubling to the children in the age group interviewed, but an equally likely explanation is that the parents do what they can to protect the children. Despite having more limited financial resources than most people, they are able to manage this to some degree. Based on these findings, the researchers advocate measures that can increase the parents' ability to create a good environment for their children. The authors conclude that the Norwegian welfare system should be examined from the perspective of children. Because social welfare and child welfare services are in the best position to assist children in families with special needs, they should be strengthened so that they can do this job more effectively:

> From our perspective, social welfare and child protection services must be better equipped in order to identify children's needs and to be able to meet these in a flexible and non-stigmatizing manner. (Sandbæk, 2004, p 168)

How this strengthening is to be achieved is not explicitly addressed. Many factors can play a role and it is natural to think of structural conditions as being important. In this chapter, however, the focus will be on another approach – how social workers perceive children or, in other words, which discourses about children can be identified in social workers' descriptions of their own practice.

Child perspective as discourse-based practice

Our review of the literature shows that the question of social workers' child perspective has not been studied in particular. There is more literature to be found on how child welfare workers should relate to children than on how they actually do so, and very little on how social workers who administer financial welfare assistance relate to children in the families receiving this help. Another challenge is to find a method or technique to consider how social workers' view of children can be understood, and which possible connection this can have to their way of relating to children, in other words, their practice. Juul (2004) focuses on child welfare workers' perspective on children, which she points out is a complicated concept, and discusses on the basis of a literature review how different practices can suggest different understandings. Another possible approach, which we choose to use here, is to treat how the child is 'seen' as discourses, which enables us to identify and find examples of how children are formed and reproduced within the framework of contextually functioning discourses. The concept of discourse can be understood and applied in different ways (Burr, 2004). It will be most useful here to use discourse understood as practices that systematically create the objects or phenomena we are talking about.

Burr cites Foucault (1972), who is best known for his analyses on the macro-discourse level, where language generates 'forms of thought' or 'regimes of truth', which are often taken for granted until one uncovers how these reflect special historical, political or moral positions. The term discourse can also be used to analyse language used in interaction between people, where the focus is on which word is used and how sentences are created and questions are posed. These two forms of discourse can be seen in relation to each other, in the sense that discourses on the macro level are maintained through discourse-oriented practice on the micro level (White et al, 2006, p 10).

If this chapter had been based on either accessible raw data or the author's empirical work, then it would have been possible to carry out a micro-discourse analysis. This has not been possible for various reasons, so the author has chosen instead to base the chapter on published literature from other researchers. This means that the author must use the empirical material and analyses presented by these researchers, which has resulted in an analysis that is more on the macro-discourse level, while recognising that conceptions and ways of thinking are reproduced through discourse-oriented practice on the micro level.

We will look at social workers' reflections and descriptions of what they do as practices that contain special views of or ideas about children. Hjelmtveit's (2004) report is chosen for closer analysis, because it is the only study that is found about children and poverty that focuses clearly on how social workers think about children in their work. The report gives a thorough presentation of the empirical study, including many quotes from different groups of informants. It is mainly the quotes that are used in this analysis. The author was not in control of the research process that, using this type of approach, led to these quotes and must therefore rely on the original report in this regard. The material used is, however, accessible to the public and can be reviewed by the reader.

The author has also chosen to include a second research study, which specifically examines how social workers reflect on their relationship to children in child welfare cases, so as to avoid having to rely on just a single study (Husby, 2000).[2] The focus in this study is not on children and poverty, although many of the families investigated by child protection do have low income, but rather on how and to what extent social workers in child welfare work together with 10 to 14 year olds in the investigation process. This chapter has also used empirical material from the study, which is presented in a theoretical frame of reference.

By interpreting the texts of these two research reports about how social workers relate to children in their work, it is possible to exemplify how the practices work. It is interesting to see which understandings of children are taken for granted or naturalised in these texts, what makes them possible and, finally, what consequences they might have in the specific context, which in this case is consequences in the form of how social workers might relate to children in their work.

Hjelmtveit (2004) has done a qualitative study for Save the Children Norway of the situation for children and young people in families receiving financial welfare assistance. Interviews were conducted with 17 children and young people aged from 10 to 17 years, 20 parents and 22 social workers from 12 offices in the central Østland area. The sample was relatively limited because access to informants proved to be difficult. Few of the social welfare offices were willing to prioritise the extra work that participation would require and few of the approached families were willing to participate. The 12 participating welfare offices approached 90 families, of which only 17 agreed to be part of the study. There can be many complex reasons for such low participation rates, but, according to Skevik (2005), it is difficult to get people in this kind of life situation to participate in research.

Most of the children in Hjelmtveit's study live with a single mother; only two of 17 live with both parents. About half of the parents have poor health, with noticeable physical or mental symptoms, but it is more striking that over half of the children and young people have their own history of illness and problems. This is a much higher proportion than in Sandbæk's study. With regard to material standards and activities, most of the children have consumer goods such as stereos, video games, computers and cell phones, but they have less opportunity to use these than most children. Parents ration cash cards for cell phones; they do not have Internet access at home and buy few CDs (Hjelmtveit, 2004).

One of the social workers Hjelmtveit interviewed summed up the families' situation in this way: "Poor finances are always part of daily life" (caseworker in Hjelmtveit, 2004, p 3).

The children experience deprivation with regard to material goods like food and clothes, and experiences like vacations and recreation activities, but particularly the teenaged informants said that poor finances limited their social mobility and their friendships (Hjelmtveit, 2004).

Husby's (2000) master's thesis can be seen as a contrast to Hjelmveit's study, because she interviews child welfare workers who can be expected to have children as a focus for their work. The informants in both Husby's and Hjelmtveit's studies work in municipalities where the work is divided between social workers in separate units, where some work with social welfare and others with child protection. This is common in larger towns in Norway. The child protection/welfare workers are mandated by law and regulation to protect children's rights if their parents do not do this adequately. Husby interviewed eight child welfare workers about how and how much they work together with 10 to 14 year olds during child protection investigations. Husby analyses her data with reference to literature on children's rights under case processing and on methods for interacting with children. She found that all the informants said they met the child at least once, but methods varied in other respects.

Three discourses have been identified or constructed in our analysis of these two studies. It is the researcher who identifies the discourses based on an analysis where one looks for underlying ways of thinking about children that can be related to theory, politics or moral judgements. These discourses represent trends in thinking or ideas in society, or parts of society, which are often taken for granted, but which influence social practice – in this case, practice related to how the activity of social workers as a vocational group is organised. This practice then contributes to the reproduction of the discourses, which provides the opportunity to contribute to changes or towards maintaining the status quo.

The first of the three discourses asserts that children's rights are parents' responsibility, the second lets relevant case processing rules guide practice in relation to children and the third focuses on children as subjects in their own life. The discourses appear in different forms and connections, some of which are more influential than others. We will examine what this means and what consequences it can have for social workers as they develop their practice.

Child poverty is parents' responsibility

Several social elements are combined in this discourse, with the political activity related to national legislation and the international convention on the rights of the child seeming to be the most important and the most visible. But together with these is a moral aspect, which exposes parents with long-term low income to risk of moral condemnation. The main feature in this discourse is that parents have responsibility for ensuring that their children are not harmed, also when it comes to how they allocate the family's income. Children's rights have been more clearly in focus since the 1980s through work with the UN Convention on the Rights of the Child of 1989, particularly article 3, and the Norwegian laws on parents and children of 1981, and on child welfare services of 1992 (Ofstad and Skar, 1995; Lurie, 2001). The government has an overriding responsibility to create a framework for children's rights through laws and public services, but the moral power in the discourse is visible when the parents' primary responsibility for protecting the rights of their children is emphasised.

What is taken for granted in this discourse is that it is 'natural' for parents to want to protect the rights of their children. This makes it unnecessary to question whether children's rights can contradict or come into conflict with parents' own interests. Among caseworkers from the welfare office we can see the parental responsibility discourse expressed in statements like these:

> It is somewhat difficult [to protect the children]; it's the parents who have responsibility for their children and for managing finances so that the children have as good a situation as possible. (Caseworker in Hjelmtveit, 2004, p 11)

Sandbæk's study confirms that parents with low income try to shield the children, but the situation is difficult for families living with very scarce financial resources for a longer period. Many of these parents have their own problems, particularly health problems, which reduce their ability to function in different areas. A caseworker in Hjelmtveit's study put it this way:

> These are complicated problems and most try very, very hard to cope. They have very little to go on and no matter how they try, they are unable to live within the allowed budget. (Caseworker in Hjelmtveit, 2004, p 11)

When children's rights are taken for granted as a parental responsibility, the need for others to become engaged in this area and take responsibility for realising this social goal is removed. As long as rights exist only in conventions and laws, they can easily become intentions rather than realities in the child's life.

Parents are also given responsibility for contacting child protection to get help for their child's special needs, but some caseworkers consider it their duty to provide information about what child welfare has to offer:

> It varies whether people want to accept help from child protection when we give them information. If they are a bit overwhelmed they actually appreciate it.

> Many parents voluntarily contact child protection to get help under §4-4 [law on child welfare services]. (Caseworkers in Hjelmtveit, 2004, pp 12-13)

Caseworkers in charge of financial welfare assistance in this study took little responsibility for children's rights. Some of the informants had reflections about this, but these did not seem to have consequences for their practice:

> We have a very big responsibility for seeing these children, and it is very costly if we don't give them help now and are not extra supportive of these families. (Caseworker in Hjelmtveit, 2004, p 11)

The welfare workers do refer cases to child protection services and some also have coordinating meetings with them. Child protection is the agency in our society that has the legal mandate to protect children's rights if their parents are unable to do so, which suggests that a discourse on rights would characterise their descriptions of practice. This discourse is, in fact, not so apparent in the informants' reasons for interacting with the children, but may be seen implicitly in their narratives. It can be interpreted that they take responsibility for protecting children's rights in their descriptions of the information they give the children about the role of child protection, why they have contacted the child's family, what they will do and about the results of decisions that are made. It is rarely stated explicitly, however, as Husby (2000, p 65) points out:

> Only one informant mentioned briefly that children have some rights from the time they are 12 years of age.

Husby adds that the child protection workers who did not take responsibility themselves for informing the child left this more or less up to the parents. The informants justified this alternative mainly by the importance of having a positive, cooperative relationship with the parents in order to make their work less difficult. To risk conflict with the parents by protecting the child's rights can, in their view, be a burden for the child. Negative attitudes and lack of confidence in child protection from the parents seemed to be conveyed to the child, causing them to withdraw and be unwilling to participate in discussion. Some informants chose, therefore, to have little active contact with the child, leaving it to the parents to inform them about why child protection was in contact with the family and what they planned to do.

We see it as a problem that social workers in child welfare leave it to parents to protect children's rights instead of clarifying their own mandate to do this, as required by law if parents for various reasons are unable to do so. But precisely the fact that child protection will intervene when parents are unable to perform adequately gives child welfare social work a double role (see Kuronen and Lahtinen in this volume). This agency has both helping and control functions, which can make it difficult to find a useful balance in cooperating with children and parents. When the reason the child needs help is that parents have good enough child-raising ability but inadequate financial resources, it is to the child's advantage that help can be given by caseworkers with responsibility for financial aid. Referrals to child protection in such cases should be unnecessary, because it means an extra burden for the clients and the risk of experiencing uncertainty and stigmatisation, which the child should be shielded against.

View of children in the rules for case processing

The clearest discourse, which is most easily identified in the narratives provided by informants in both Hjelmtveit and Husby's studies, is focused on case processing. The most important elements are principles about equal and fair treatment of the members of society, which are important values in our society. Rules and procedures are based mainly on public regulations and municipal standards, but also can have developed as professional norms for individual workplaces. Social workers, as public employees, have a strong obligation to their employers to follow the case processing rules and procedures. There is nonetheless a certain flexibility that can be utilised and variations in local practice often develop among different units. Social workers also have the opportunity to inform their employers if local regulations have consequences for service users that can be seen as unfair or unintentional.

Here, practice is presented where the view of children is dominated by how children can and should be taken care of in accordance with the prevailing case procedure (due process) rules for the particular agency. Focus is on routines and procedures for the work, and not much on the underlying rights. Caseworkers in Hjemtveit's study put it like this:

> I believe that we see the child, but it is child protection which, in a way, has the formal responsibility for the child, it's the adults who are our clients, and it is finances which are, in a way, the main point of the contact.

> We don't see the children very much, I would say, we're not good at bringing in the whole family to see how they function, so we don't get information until things have gone very badly. But children are

not originally our main focus. We are not good at seeing the family as a unit.

The total situation was better handled before social welfare and child protection services became separated from each other. (Caseworkers in Hjelmtveit, 2004, p 12)

Caseworkers handling financial welfare assistance acknowledge that children's situation should be taken care of, but they rarely do this themselves because they are guided by rules mandated by law and official guidelines, and by municipal standards for welfare assistance. From a rule-oriented approach, it is child protection services' responsibility to focus on the child's situation, to the extent that the parents are unable to safeguard the child's needs. This is rarely questioned; it is taken for granted in the sense that it is accepted that rules must be followed, even if this means that the child's need is made less visible. Many caseworkers express understanding and empathy for the parents' situation, and it is, therefore, not difficult to imagine that this must have consequences for the child's situation:

The most characteristic trait for long-term welfare recipients is their lack of energy. This restricts them, things they have not been able to do or collect, and it becomes a vicious circle where it becomes more and more difficult to manage the demands of daily life. (Caseworker in Hjelmtveit, 2004, p 11)

The consequences of the case processing discourse's dominant position are that the children's needs become invisible or non-existent for social workers who are in a position to do something to help the child. Leaving it up to parents who have as difficult a situation as these quotes would indicate to safeguard the child would appear to be an abdication of responsibility. This is not intended as one-sided criticism of social workers' actions. It must be emphasised that it is the dominant position of this discourse that contributes to a practice that makes children invisible in families in need of financial welfare relief. This reflects the priorities and preferences of many actors and groups in society in positions of influence and responsibility. Social workers in Norway are largely public employees who have the duty to follow the rules that apply to their occupation, as these are articulated in laws and regulations. Most experience also considerable job pressure and maybe limited space to reflect over issues related to their work practice, such as to 'see' the child. These are only articulated in special situations, as when a researcher asks these questions.

Strong rule orientation and much job pressure pertain at least as much in child protection services as in financial welfare assistance. Emphasis on case processing rules is apparent in the arguments that child protection workers give for why they must meet the child, at least once. Husby puts it this way:

> Their experience is that professional reasoning and recommended decisions are first considered to be good enough, professionally, if they have at least had one personal contact with the child. (Husby, 2000, p 92)

Contact with the child is tied to decision making. Work in a child protection investigation is expected to lead to a decision by a given deadline, and it is considered important to work in a goal-oriented manner and to consider what is needed to reach a decision in the case.

Oppedal (1997) points out, meanwhile, that case processing will also be inadequate when children are not heard, in the sense that their viewpoint is not clearly expressed in the case documents. The authorities that will make the decision lack, therefore, the basis for emphasising the views of the child. It is a special kind of invisibility, when children in the case processing discourse become a part of the procedure and not a human subject who the whole child protection process is intended to help. This would require another discourse, which reflects another understanding of children.

The child as subject and participant

The subject discourse is found where emphasis is placed on seeing the child as an individual being and as an active subject in his or her own life, who exercises influence and is in turn influenced by others. Children can be said to have their own reality with feelings, thoughts and experiences.

This 'child perspective' has been introduced to the social debate by researchers on children and childhood, including sociologists (Frønes, 1995; Näsman, 1995; Corsaro, 1997; James et al, 1998; Alanen, 2000) and social psychologists (Tiller, 1990; Sommer, 2003b). The roots can be traced back to phenomenological philosophy, but also to the increasing emphasis on individual freedom and responsibility in western society during the last decades with neoliberal ideology and political influence (Frønes, 1995).

It is debatable to what extent it is possible to gain access to another person's reality. In the case of children, access can be complicated by the fact that children have an important part of their existence in arenas together with other children where it is not easy for adults to gain admission. Children are experts on their own situation as children based on their own experience and encounters. It follows from this that children should be heard in matters that concern them, because they have a special competence about their own situation, which others cannot be expected to provide. It can be a challenge for adults to gain insight into the child's thoughts and experiences. This is partly dependent on the child's ability to communicate, but to a large extent dependent on the adult's ability to stimulate the child to dialogue by preparation of opportunities for communication and giving sufficient response to the child's message.

A practice that is grounded in this view of the child seems to be almost entirely absent for informants with responsibility for financial welfare assistance. The only meaningful expression that can perhaps be interpreted in this direction is when the caseworker discusses his experience with second-generation social clients:

> There are many children who come to see us when they are 18 years old. They want an apartment and money and everything, and their parents have provided for them for so many years, so now the municipality can take over. (Caseworker in Hjelmtveit, 2004, p 13)

Some of the informants from child protection tell, however, about a more active way of relating to children, where the child as subject is prominent (Husby, 2000). These child protection workers consider it their task to be a supporter of the child, both giving and receiving information throughout the process, including informing the child of the results of the investigation. When they succeeded with this, they were able to provide space for the child's influence. The child's statements influenced decisions and actions along the way and the result of the investigation. The children's influence was most apparent in the cases where the child showed trust and openness in relation to the child protection worker. The child's trust seemed, however, to be connected to whether or not the worker had established a positive and cooperative relationship with the parents. The subject discourse brought with it in this case an opportunity that benefited both the child and the parents.

Consequences for practice of discourses

There would be little reason to investigate social workers' view of children if it were not possible to assume that these implicit conceptions affect their actions and decisions and therefore have consequences for their practice. We will follow this line of thought a little further and consider how different discourses with differing positions and possibilities for action can lead to different types of practice. Let us first consider this for caseworkers in the social welfare office. They do not 'see' children very much and abdicate responsibility for them until the child becomes 18 years old and can apply for financial welfare assistance themselves. Hjelmtveit says that the question of 'social inheritance' is addressed by parents, young people and caseworkers. Both children and parents expressed concern about the child becoming a second-generation welfare recipient. If caseworkers see children as being forced to follow in their parents' footsteps through some form of social inheritance, will this mean that they are relating to the children more as victims of a process of socialisation than as active participants in their own lives? An alternative interpretation is that this is about social learning rather than social inheritance. The children learn within which discourses the caseworkers operate and which positions it is possible for them as service users to take within the framework this establishes.

In order to see this alternative interpretation, it may be a necessary precondition that one sees people as active subjects who are actively learning and participating in their own lives. This kind of viewpoint has the potential to see possibilities for development and learning of positive behaviour as well as unwanted behaviour. Such an understanding reflects a subject discourse where service users, both children and parents, are seen as active subjects in their own lives. This way of thinking gives both helpers and service users positions as active participants with the possibility of exercising influence, creating and changing. Seeing such possibilities can provide hope, which can provide motivation. Motivation can help to release energy and strength. Both children and parents want a better future for the child than dependence on welfare assistance. This desire is an important resource that caseworkers could make use of if they emphasised cooperation with children and parents and developed a good working relationship. The following quotes from Hjelmtveit's report show that children and young people have strong desires for the future:

> I don't want to have it like that! I will really get an education and earn a salary and not live on social assistance ... but I'm afraid that if I go there I will become dependent upon social assistance, and I'll give up. (17-year-old girl)

> From when I was small, I have not been able to afford things like the others, so I have decided that I'm going to be rich when I grow up. (16-year-old boy) (Children in Hjelmtveit, 2004, p 7)

Sandbæk's study suggests that parents try to protect their children from the consequences of the family's poverty, and that they will probably be positive and cooperative partners for social workers if they are given the opportunity (Sandbæk 2004). Parents' concerns are also expressed in Hjelmtveit's study. One mother says:

> It bothers me that, for financial reasons, I am not able to give him support for activities where he could have done well and strengthened his self-confidence. The opposite happens when you don't have money, then I can undermine his self-confidence instead of improving it. (Mother in Hjelmtveit, 2004, p 9)

Instead of cooperation, many parents felt that they were opposed and forced to use much time and effort on a battle with employees of the social welfare services (Hjelmtveit, 2004). This suggests that a too one-sided focus on rights and the case processing discourse might act to limit social workers' freedom of choice, placing them in a control and conflict position in relation to the service users, rather than a cooperative position. There is a danger that Sandbæk's recommendation for strengthening social welfare and child protection services, so that they can better meet the needs of children, will not have the desired effect without expanding the conceptual basis for social workers' practice. This should include a view of service users as active subjects in their own lives. Such a view allows greater potential for developing cooperative relations with families with children, where social workers' efforts can supplement and strengthen those of the child and the parents to improve their own situation. Such cooperative relationships often demand much work, but will lead to a better result for the children because the helpers are part of the same team.

Based on Husby's study, it can be argued that this is also relevant for child protection workers. The informants who related to the child as a subject and active participant throughout the investigative process gave the child space for influence and helped to assure that their rights were protected. If necessary, the child protection workers negotiated with parents and children about ways of doing things that they could accept. This might mean that parents were allowed to be present during their conversations with the child, or that parents were informed ahead of time what issues would be taken up with the child, or that the child and sometimes the parents could influence where the conversation would take place. There is also a clear example in Husby's study of the absence of subject discourse and how this limited freedom of action in the case. A child protection worker initiated a case after receiving a risk report about a stepfather's violence towards a 12-year-old boy. She chose to relate to the family as a whole and to study interaction in the family using Marte-Meo observation techniques without talking to the child. She had contact with the adults and had several conversations with the mother, before deciding to meet the child. Husby interpreted the child protection worker's view of the child in this way:

> She didn't relate to the child as an autonomous individual, a person with their own right to participation, to receive information, and to have the opportunity to express himself ... The problems experienced by the child are not articulated in the case. The caseworker defined the child's situation in a certain way: interaction problems in the family. This understanding of the problem may not be wrong, but it's not certain that it was sufficiently nuanced with respect to the child's own view of the problem. (Husby, 2000, p 83)

Juul (2004) also wants to find a way to relate to the child that is more consistent with emphasis on children as subjects. She asks whether child protection workers have sufficient competence in talking to children. This conforms to findings by Husby (2000) who points out how striking it is that child protection workers use so little of their knowledge about children and about activities for facilitating good communication with children. They use basically the same approach that they use for conversations with adults, without questioning this. It is taken for granted until the researcher questions this. There should be much room for improvement here. Juul expresses how important it is to enable the child to communicate:

> When child protection workers don't talk to the child, they don't find out what they are struggling with and what competence they have, and it becomes difficult to give the child adequate help. (Juul, 2004, p 20)

Conclusion

We are back to the starting point for this chapter: how social workers think about children in families that are dependent on financial welfare assistance for longer periods.

The review of the literature shows that interesting research on children and poverty is being done in many countries, but few researchers have focused so far on how social workers relate to children in low-income families.

The analysis has found and discussed discourses that reflect different ways of relating to children. Through this analysis, the individual expressions have been given a broader meaning because they have been placed in a larger context and have been considered in relation to discourses at the social level. The discourses describe trends in ideas that influence the formation of opinions and ways of thinking among people. They can operate simultaneously and are not mutually exclusive. The possible connections that are presented here can contribute to the ongoing debate about child poverty and hopefully lead to new understanding. Adult responsibility for children's rights and the necessity of rules to guarantee citizens equal and fair case processing are important principles for public employees. The author has argued for supplementing these ways of thinking with the idea of 'seeing' the child as an active subject, as a means of providing more effective help to families with children. Because ways of thinking influence the practice of workers, but also are reproduced or maintained through practice, there is a potential here for change. This can happen through ideas that help to raise consciousness about which ways of thinking form the foundation for practice.

This chapter is, however, based on limited material and there is clearly a need for more research on this important topic. Backe-Hansen's (2004) review of the literature suggests that poverty is often one of several risk factors in the child's development. It is important to see the various factors in relation to each other in order to reach a balanced picture of the child's situation. A recommendation from Sandbæk (2004) and her Norwegian research group to strengthen the resources of social welfare and child protection services to better meet the needs of children would seem to be a logical solution. Social workers who relate to individual families will have access to information about various risk factors and the professional competence to place this information in a broader context. The question remains whether they will use this information to assess the child's situation in the family. As discussed in this chapter, there is reason to believe that such a strengthening of services will not have the desired effect without a change in the basic thinking about social work practice in the direction of more thinking about and relating to children as subjects and participants in the families receiving long-term financial social assistance. This aspect should, therefore, be brought into the continuing debate about how this strengthening of services can best be achieved.

Sandbæk also contends that the children's needs must not only be acknowledged but also met in a non-stigmatising manner. This makes it less relevant for social workers with responsibility for financial social welfare assistance to pass this task to child protection services if there are not reasonable grounds for doubting the parents' ability to care for their children. Some children and parents in low-income families could avoid having to relate to child protection as an additional agency if the discourse about children as subjects and participants in their own lives became more widely accepted among social workers.

Notes

[1] Through a grant from the Norwegian Research Council, researcher Elisabeth Backe-Hansen from the Norwegian Institute for Child Development and Ageing (NOVA) has completed a literature survey of how children and young people manage to grow up under difficult living conditions, and how this affects the child's development both short and long term. The review is based on Norwegian, Nordic and international (English-language) research literature.

[2] Others have also examined this theme from somewhat different angles (for example, Killén, 1991; Claussen and Tiller, 1997; Oppedal, 1997; Sandbæk, 2002; Juul, 2004).

NINE

Listening to children's experiences of being participant witnesses to domestic violence

Margareta Hydén

Introduction

The notion that it is harmful for children to be exposed to violence growing up in a family in which mum is beaten has received increased attention during the past decade. Studies from the US estimate the numbers of children exposed to some form of physical violence between their parents during their childhood ranges from 20% (Henning et al, 1996) to 37% (Holden et al, 1998).

In a review article, Edleson (1999) presents 84 studies describing psychological and developmental difficulties among children witnessing violence in the home. The children show significantly more signs of uneasiness, anxiety, depression, post-traumatic stress and aggression than other children do. Being exposed to one's father beating one's mother might also lead to other long-term effects, such as distrusting others and a pessimistic outlook in terms of influencing one's own life situation. Because witnessing domestic violence can terrorise children and significantly disrupt child socialisation, many researchers have begun to consider exposure to domestic violence to be a form of psychological maltreatment (Peled and Davis, 1995; Somer and Braunstein, 1999). Some even argue that it is the most toxic violence children can be exposed to (McAlister Groves, 2001), and that its consequences have only recently begun to be understood (Adams, 2006). This is why the study of children who have experienced intimate partner violence in their homes is of great concern to research in social work. It is one of the most urgent and comprehensive challenges for researchers in social work to provide knowledge that may contribute to the development of services to these children, I will argue.

Nordic countries are generally regarded as global welfare role models in terms of their image of being gender equal, child friendly and culturally tolerant. Research from the Nordic countries that has critically examined how men's violence in families is perceived and responded to in the Nordic context has found that this is an over-simplistic image (Eriksson et al, 2005). How many children, then, are exposed to this toxic violence in the Nordic countries? As in all research concerning sensitive topics, it is difficult to get a reliable estimate of prevalence. In a Swedish study of child abuse involving 1,764 children of middle school age, 10% of the children stated that they had been exposed to domestic violence at least once and 5% that they had been exposed often (SOU 200, p 72). Save the Children Sweden interviewed 1,761 18 year olds and 12% stated that they had seen their father/stepfather abuse their mother at least once (Rädda Barnen, 2006). A Norwegian study of violence concludes that every third child of a battered woman has witnessed the abuse of his/her mother (Haaland et al, 2005).

The study 'Children experiencing domestic violence' that forms the basis of this chapter,[1] is part of a series of studies that aims to understand how women, men and children make sense of acts of marital woman battering. This work has led to comprehensive reflections on methodological issues (see Hydén 1994, 2000, 2005, 2008). Taking a child's perspective is much more than simply 'listening to the voices of children'. It also involves acknowledging the kinds of spaces that must be offered to make it possible for the children to relate their experiences and the analytical steps that must be taken in order to understand them. The basic concerns can be worded as follows: What does it take for the informant to narrate, and researcher to listen to, accounts concerning painful life experiences including intimate partner violence? What kinds of physical and social spaces (that is, social practices and relationships) must be created to make it possible to tell and listen to these accounts? And what kinds of analytical steps must be taken in the search for answers to questions about how women and men make sense of (that is. how they define, interpret and explain) acts of marital woman battering? In the previous studies, these concerns have been related to encounters with adult men and women as perpetrators and victims of intimate partner violence. In studies of children's experiences of their mothers being beaten, methodology (that is. the ways to mount the inquiry and conduct the analysis) is even more critical. In such studies, listening to the children's experiences is essential.

In the first part of the chapter, attention will be directed to some of the methodological steps that need to be taken to meet such methodological concerns. In the second part of the chapter, some of the narrative accounts of children's experiences of their mothers being beaten will be explored. The chapter ends with a discussion of how the results can be used for further research, as well as for the development of social work practice.

Conceptualising children's experiences of violence towards their mothers

The first of the methodological steps is aimed at finding a useful way of conceptualising the child's experience. Useful concepts are those that are designed to shape thinking and bring with them ideas concerning methodological issues. They present analytical possibilities as well as boundaries and indicate what questions need to be addressed.

Researchers in early studies used the term 'witnesses to violence' (see Wolfe et al, 1984; Peled, 1993) in their efforts to conceptualise children's experiences. The term 'witness' was to some extent later replaced by 'exposure (to violence)'. The basic argument for this replacement was that 'exposure' is more inclusive, as it includes watching, hearing and direct involvement, as well as experiences of the aftermath (see Holden et al, 1998; Fantuzzo and Mohr, 1999). The term 'experiencing violence' has also been used, with the argument that it captures the children's perspective (see Peled, 1993; McGee, 2000). The concepts 'witness to violence' as well as 'exposure' or 'experiencing violence' have been well suited to a research paradigm focusing on the various forms of symptoms or other noticeable signs of the negative effects of living in the midst of violence. These concepts are also conducive to differentiating between being a direct and an indirect victim of child abuse and neglect.

In spite of their usefulness, however, the concepts 'witness to violence' and 'exposure to violence' are not very well suited to the exploration of incidents in which mum is being beaten from a child's perspective. In all essential matters, the concepts reflect the adult's perspective. They position the adults as the acting subject and the children outside the action. The concepts address the fact that the violence takes place between people of considerable significance for the children and that they are affected objects of the adults' action. This may be unintentional, but is nonetheless harmful and the cause of suffering. Further, being positioned as 'witness' indicates powerlessness, guiltlessness and subordination to the acting subjects.

At this point, someone may object: "Why are these concepts not well suited for understanding what it means to experience that mum is being beaten? Don't concepts such as 'witness to violence' or 'exposed to violence' in fact provide a solid ground for studies from a child's perspective? Aren't 'witness' and 'exposed' in fact words that cover children's experience very well?" I can agree – and object. They still present an indirect way of learning about children's experience, as a reflection in the eyes of the adult observer.

This indirect way of learning about human experiences is not uncommon. As concerns children, this indirect way of gaining information is in fact regularly used, since children are not generally viewed as important sources of knowledge about their own experiences. "It is historically a novel idea to ask the child how he or she felt and let him/her tell what happened when one suspects or observes that a child has been exposed to violence at home", states Hannele Forsberg (2002, p 307) in her pioneer work on children's feedback on helping practices of shelters. Of course, as long as parental authority has existed, fathers and mothers have questioned their children regarding their whereabouts – and have expected prompt answers. But being invited to give their individual perspective and being allowed to finish their own thoughts without interruption, rather than rely solely on adult interpretations of their lives, are more rare experiences in children's lives. In spite of all the efforts made to gain sufficiently solid knowledge about men's violence towards women to be able to act against it, we have failed thus far. To date, we have not utilised children's experiences and taken them seriously as valid information. We need to know much more about their unique contributions to this field of knowledge.

In my previous work, the concept 'participant witness' (Hydén, 1994) was introduced for conceptualising children's experiences. The concept 'participant witness' situates the child's experience in context – that is, in the child's own life and social circumstances. Even if children are not directly involved in the violence, they can never be totally passive bystanders, observing what is going on in their lives from a distance. Further, 'participant witness' constructs the child's position as multi-layered and ambiguous. Every one of the stories a child can tell about the violent event makes a contribution to a deeper understanding of this complex experience. 'Participant' indicates a subject position, agency, power and being an insider. 'Witness' indicates the opposite: an objects' position, lack of agency, powerlessness, vulnerability and being an outsider.

I am aware of the fact that I am taking a risk by conceptualising children's experience of violence towards their mothers in a way that emphasises not only their vulnerability but also their agency. There is a risk that I will be understood to be suggesting that the children's vulnerability is not to be taken too seriously or that the parents' responsibility could be conditional and shared by the children. I am not suggesting anything of that kind. My overall ambition is to contribute to the knowledge of the distinctive features of the act of violence towards women in close relationships, as it appears in the views of their children. What I want to emphasise is that, even if children have limited or no influence over what is going on when they experience violence in their lives, it is the children's lives in which the children inhabit the subjects' position.

Research strategies

The second methodological step concerns the development of useful research strategies that will serve the purpose of taking part of the children's perspectives. Useful research strategies are those that are designed for meeting children in, or creating, safe spaces where they can talk without being at risk of being victimised again. The two research strategies that most frequently have been used so far fall into the categories observations and interviews.

Observations

Previous studies have mainly based their understanding of children's situations on their mothers' statements or observations made by other adults. Children's conduct has been observed or measured using standardised tests and measurement scales. To sum up, most research about children who have experienced violence towards their mothers has been carried out on them rather than with them. This research strategy has been successful when it comes to direct attention to the existence of the children and their suffering, as well as the forms of violence they are subjected to. It falls short, however, if we want to know the children's view on what constitutes the violent act and the children's reaction to it.

The problem with relying only on maternal reports has been discussed (for example, Jaffe et al, 1990; Kilpatrick and Williams, 1998; Litrownik et al, 2003). One example of the character of the problems was revealed in a study of 692 children (Litrownik et al, 2003), based on the mothers' as well as the children's reports. The mothers reported that 14% of their children had witnessed a family member being hit. When the children themselves were asked, one in three reported that they had seen adults hit each other in their homes. Most mothers do not want to believe that their child has witnessed and been affected by the violence (Jaffe et al, 1990).

Interviews

Interviewing is one of the strongest methods for exploring children's own interpretations of their lives. Using interviews, researchers can study topics in children's lives that are highly salient yet are rarely discussed, such as violence or other sensitive issues (Corsaro, 1997), but it is a method that must be handled with care. Child studies of sensitive issues such as violence bring power issues to the fore in more than one way. The researcher must be aware that the power imbalance is heightened compared to studies including adults, because of the age and status differences. Ways of dealing with this power difference include group interviewing, creating a natural context, using multiple methods and engaging in reciprocity (Eder and Fingerson, 2002).

In all research devoted to the study of social problems and difficult life circumstances, there is a risk of overemphasising and encouraging storylines concerned with powerlessness and suffering, and underemphasising alternative storylines. This may lead to an unintentional further disempowerment of the vulnerable and powerless. For methodological as well as ethical reasons, it is of great importance to develop methods that do not add to the powerlessness of vulnerable children. What I like to emphasise is that there are often opportunities for people to be positioned simultaneously in more than one field of existence, in more than one territory of identity. These opportunities are more limited for children than for adults, which makes it particularly important to provide them with enough space and to listen carefully to their own expressions of their sense of personal agency. In studies on being a participant witness to domestic violence, personal agency is associated with the perception that, as a vulnerable child, one is able to have some effect on the shape of one's own intentions and that the world is a least minimally responsive to the fact of one's existence.

Connecting to social work practice – new possibilities

In my studies of children's experiences of being participant witnesses to domestic violence, the most important part of my empirical network has been an outreach programme for abusive men and abused women, with group therapy as its main offering. A children's programme has now been added to the adult programmes. During the past decade, programmes for children witnessing domestic violence have been established in Sweden. The vast majority of these programmes are run by specially trained social workers and psychologists, and are based on group psychotherapy. The following wording of the aim of one of the programmes is valid for most of them:

> To set aside obstacles for the children to allow for a positive development, through working with experiences, thoughts and questions about the violence. By giving the children a possibility to get to know others with similar experiences and through telling each other about these experiences, the unimaginable can be made imaginable. This will allow the children to express different feelings, in regard to the violence and perpetrator, as well as the victim. (Socialstyrelsen/National Board of Health and Welfare, 2005, author's translation)

All researchers dealing with sensitive and painful issues in direct contact with the sufferers have to face the ethical dilemma that follows the request to vulnerable individuals to speak about their suffering and pain without being sure of their ability to offer a safe space or be in the position to bring substantial relief in exchange. Under the right circumstances, social work practice has the potential to offer a safe space as well as relief. In addition, it has the potential to be an arena for the study of sensitive issues that need to be addressed. Successful social work research is dependent, not only on a solid network of colleagues, but also on a solid empirical network. Having a close cooperation with research could be very rewarding for social work practice and offer possibilities for the reflection on and implementation of results. It is important to emphasise, however, that social work practice and social work research are separate activities, meaning among other things that research participants have to give separate informed consent for participating in research.

Research on social work practice and psychotherapy are generally concerned with issues of outcome measures and effect sizes, and not with therapy as a speech event with the capacity to offer space for children to communicate difficult experiences. My basic argument for considering these speech events as rich sources of knowledge concerns the fact that social work practice and psychotherapy provide us with an institutionally established practice in which problems in the individual life do not have to be separated from society and culture. Within the frame of psychotherapy, for example, stories can be understood as, and also analysed as, strategies for organising personal experiences into culturally intelligible scripts.

But these arguments pose new problems concerning the question of how well narratives in general, and those produced in a therapeutic setting especially, can clearly portray a child's personal experience. If we ask children to talk about their personal experiences of violence by encouraging storytelling in a group therapy setting involving other children and therapists, how near the 'real' experiences are we? A story, after all, is a rhetorical structure, which is meant to provide – sometimes try to launch – a perspective on what happened.

This question is an issue under debate between 'realists' and 'postmodernists' and is too far reaching to be dealt with in this chapter. What is important to emphasise, however, is that even an answer to an apparently simple and straightforward question such as "Can you tell me about what happened?" represents only one possible version of the event and that the story is always shaped to fit the audience in one way or another. What is also important to emphasise is that, when a child tells about what happened when dad beat mum, he first and foremost talks about his experience of that event, not about the event itself. Following Patterson (2002), from these perspectives we can envisage the activity of narration and the activity of listening to a narrative as the creation of a particular space, or a place in which 'to be'.

Conducting the analysis

The third methodological step I would suggest is aimed at developing a useful way of conducting the analysis. A useful analysis does justice to the children's accounts. Narrative analysis is proposed as well suited for this purpose for a number of reasons, I will argue. First, narrative analysis takes as its point of departure the fact that storytelling is one of the most important and powerful forms of creating and communicating the meaning of life experiences (Mishler, 1999). Early in life, children take part in stories and learn to use the story and its form to explore the world and share experiences (Nelson, 1989). Second, narrative analysis preserves particular histories of individuals, resulting in an accumulation of detail that is assembled into a 'fuller' picture of the individual or group (Riessman, 2008, p 11). Third, attention to sequences of action distinguishes narrative analysis – the investigator focuses on particular actors, in particular social places, at particular social times (Riesmann, 2008, p 11). For all these reasons, narrative analysis is well suited to the investigation of sensitive topics (Hydén, 2008).

Despite the story's basic form for communicating meaning, stories are often difficult to tell. American linguist Patricia O'Connor (2000) argues that there are three kinds of stories: stories one likes to tell, such as those about graduating from college; stories that must be told, such as those about practical issues; and stories that cannot be told, such as those about sexual abuse. I would like to add one more category, characterised by ambiguity, containing stories that no one likes to tell, but need to be shared. These are stories about experiences of strange, painful and perhaps confusing events – such as being witness to violence. The need to narrate painful and strange experiences is part of the very human need to be understood by others, to be in communication even from the margin. Therefore, attention to human suffering means attention to stories.

Narrative analysis

Although there is a growing interest in narrative analysis within the social sciences, there is as yet no single analytic approach that can provide the definition for narrative analysis. The term 'narrative' carries many meanings and is used in a variety of ways, often synonymously with 'story'.

Elliot Mishler, one of the major figures in introducing narrative methodology in the medical and social sciences, has developed a framework for understanding the different approaches to narrative analysis. This framework is based on what are commonly understood as the three different functions of language: namely, meaning, structure and interactional context. If the researcher is primarily interested in the actual events being talked about, he/she focuses on the content of the narrative. The researcher might be more interested in the form of the narrative, that is, the way the story is put together. The interest may also lie in the performance of narratives and the interactional contexts in which they are produced. All narratives have a narrator and an audience, real or imagined, and the potential of narrative to be powerful or to be used strategically can only be realised from within this dialogic relationship. The 'I' who narrates does so in dialogue with diverse others. These others include actual or imagined people and other versions of the self that are composed and recomposed in stories by the self and stories about the self. The narrating 'I' strives to manage this multiplicity; stories are always told to an 'other' self, another 'me' and another 'you' in actual and imaginary social worlds (Mishler, 1995).

Catherine Riessman (2008), another of the major figures in narrative methodology, gives the following definition:

> Briefly, in everyday oral storytelling a speaker connects events into a sequence that is consequential for later action and for the story. Events perceived by the speaker as important are selected, organized, connected and evaluated as meaningful for a particular audience. (Riessman, 2008, p 3)

It is quite a demanding task for a young storyteller to live up to the standards of a fully developed narrative. Selecting and organising a narrative, and connecting it and evaluating it as meaningful for a particular audience, in accordance with Riessman's ideal, calls for competence more along the lines of what an adult can accomplish than what a child can. Even if children early in life take part in stories and learn to use the story and its form to explore the world and share experiences (Nelson, 1989), they will be limited by lack of experience and training in telling stories. Nevertheless, I have found Mishler's and Riessman's definitions to be useful starting points for the analysis of children's stories of witnessing violence. I have also found the frequently cited structural model developed by American sociolinguists Labov and Waletzky (1967) helpful (Table 9.1). This model is particularly useful for gaining an overview of narrative material and for comparing full stories or parts of stories.

Table 9.1: Labov and Waletzky's structural model of narrative form

Narrative element and composition	Description of the narrative element
Abstract (A)	Summary of the subject matter
Orientation (O)	Information about the setting: time, place, situation, participants
Complicating action (CA)	What actually happened, what happened next
Evaluation (E)	What the events mean to the narrator
Resolution (R)	How it all ended
Coda (C)	Returns the perspective to the present

Source: Elliot (2005, p 42)

Gaining access to children's stories

In the study of children's experiences of witnessing violence towards their mothers, I combined interviewing with 'connecting to social work practice'. The social work practice I connected to was the group therapy programme for children who were or had been participant witnesses to domestic violence. It consisted of 20 meetings, each lasting one and a half hours. Each session evolved around a theme, such as what violence means, what feelings the children had in relation to the violence and what they did when violent episodes occurred. Different kinds of stimulus material were used, such as drawings of violent situations, drawings of the contours of a body (used for connecting feelings with bodily experiences), films, paper, crayons and pencils. Each session started with looking back at the previous weeks' theme, and the children were asked if something had happened since the last session or if there was anything special they had thought about. The basic message the therapists conveyed was that the children were not alone, even if one might feel completely alone at times. Free speech about what had happened was encouraged.

The data used for the study consisted of tape-recorded and transcribed group therapy sessions. In addition, individual interviews were conducted with most of the children. The basic aims of the study were to gain an understanding of the children's own conceptions of domestic violence – that is, the words they used to describe it and the meanings they ascribed to it. One point of particular interest consisted of the children's narratives of how they acted in relation to the violence and how they positioned themselves in relation to mum, dad and siblings.

When I analysed the recordings over time, it was evident that the therapists gradually established a more safe and trustworthy space. Some of the children expressed how pleased they were at having access to such a space, in phrases such as 'the best thing about these group meetings is the group' or 'the best thing about the group meetings is that the group exists. I never want to leave.' During the first sessions, the group leaders were very active and the children very quiet. This changed in the later sessions.

The data used for this chapter is from the third session with seven children (12 to 14 years old) and one male and one female therapist. The children had all been participant witnesses in severe cases of violence and many had been physically abused themselves (Table 9.2).

Analysing children's stories

Table 9.2: Children appearing in the excerpts[2]

Dina	15 years old. Lives with her biological father, mother and four siblings. Is extremely afraid of her father. Dina has been physically abused by her father.
Eva	13 years of age. Eva's stepfather subjected her mother to violence for five years. Eva and her sister Elsa have been exposed to severe violence, and have been physically abused themselves. Their mother and stepfather are divorced.
Christine	13 years old. Has lived at a women's shelter for seven months with her mother and brother, Magnus. Christine was exposed to her biological father's violence. Her father has been reported to the police.
Nadja	14 years old. Nadja has lived with her biological father, mother and twin brother. She has been exposed to her father's violence all her life. Her father has been arrested as a result of his violence towards the mother and has now left the family. Nadja is afraid that he will return.
Simon	12 years of age. Simon and his sister have been exposed to their father's violence towards his mother all their lives. The father has been arrested as a result of his violence towards the mother.
Max	14 years old and the twin brother of Nadja. Max has been severely physically abused by his father.
Pontus	12 years of age. Pontus has witnessed his father beating his mother and his father's girlfriend. His father has also physically abused him. Pontus's father was in jail during the time of the group sessions.

The analysis was conducted on the original Swedish transcripts and has been translated into English. First on my analytical agenda was to get an overall picture of the conversations I had on the tapes: what are they talking about? The second question was to identify the narrative: does this talk have a storied form or is it something else? The third question concerned the overall meaning: what is the narrative about; what kind of situation is reflected in the narrative; who are the protagonists; how are they related? The fourth question concerned the form of the narrative: how is the narrative structured; what elements is it composed of; what are the functions of these elements? Finally, I was interested in the interactional feature of the narrative: for what kind of audience is the narrative told; what are the contributions from the listeners – do they support or prohibit certain versions of the story; do they contribute as active co-constructers or are they passive listeners?

Trying to escape – forced to listen

In the tape-recorded sessions, there were conversations about small and large topics, like 'What happened in school today', 'I was late because my bike was broken', or 'I'm afraid to go home because my mother's abusive boyfriend might be there'. When talk about the experience of violence was identified two topics frequently emerged, namely fear and avoidance. Sometimes these were presented as related topics, in which case avoidance was a consequence of fear. Sometimes, they were presented as occurring in parallel. The children told of different actions, all aiming at avoidance, with fear as an omnipresent companion. Three different storylines, all concerning memories of violence, made up sub-themes of the overall themes of fear and avoidance: audio memories, visual memories and relational memories. These are all memories of efforts to escape the violence and of how these efforts failed to a certain extent. Some of the children were successful in their efforts to avoid seeing the violence – but less successful when it came to avoiding hearing it. Some children were able to find some comfort in being bodily close to a sibling, and could hide with him/her and avoid seeing the violence – but could not avoid hearing it and were continuously fearful.

Audio memories

At the third meeting, three boys and three girls are present. They are shown a drawing of a little boy and a girl who is a bit older. The children in the drawing are standing alone in a room. In the doorway of the next room, one can see a man and a woman. Their body language indicates disagreement and an upcoming fight. The therapists make the request "Well, now it's up to you to decide what's going on here and to tell the story; tell us something about what happens and what is about to happen". The children discuss this in two separate groups, the girls in one and the boys in another. They then report their conclusion back to the therapists. They are in agreement that the children are very scared and that they are hiding together while they can hear the adults shouting at each other. But what are they shouting about? "Money" is one suggestion. "About who is going to get the children" is another. The therapists ask them if they have heard their parents screaming and fighting, and they all answer that they have. "Can any of you remember hearing your parents fight?" the therapist asks. "Yes I can", one of the boys answers:

Excerpt 9.1: Simon and Pontus's story "Disgusting, smashing sounds"

Therapist I:	How does it sound?
Simon:	Smash.
Therapist I:	Is it loud or …
Simon:	Maybe like someone crashes into the door or something.
Therapist II:	Is there someone else who has this kind of smashing sound in your head?
Pontus:	I do. Disgusting. It's the kind of thing that makes it impossible for me to sleep.

This conversation, directly following the comments on the drawing, is quite fumbling. It includes no complete story. It results in an evaluation, however ("Disgusting. It's the kind of thing that makes it impossible for me to sleep") and, interactionally, has the function of a door opener to a series of short narratives about audio memories of violence.

The following story is characterised by its dialogical form, which is a distinctive feature of most of the narratives; or, if not directly reflected in the narrative, the dialogue between the narrating child, the other children and the therapists is the interactional context of all narration in the sessions:

Excerpt 9.2: Pontus's story "If I had only known how to use the remote control I would have turned the volume up"

Pontus:	But once I put myself and the dog in the big room, once when mum and dad were fighting.
Therapist II:	So you wouldn't hear, or?
Pontus:	Or see.
Therapist II:	Or see, to protect yourself then?
Pontus:	Uh huh.
Therapist II:	What did you think then when you were there in the room?
Pontus:	I turned on the TV and I watched the TV and shivered like crazy.
Therapist II:	Do you remember what was on TV?
Pontus:	No.
Therapist II:	I don't think you do, right, I don't think you think about what's on TV.
Pontus:	I mostly heard Dad screaming. I heard it in spite of the TV. If I had only known how to use the remote control I would have turned the volume up.

Pontus's story is full of action. At the same time, he gives his audience little orientation concerning the circumstances of the fight. He gives a suggestion for resolution ("If I had only known how to use the remote control"). By not being present in the room where the violent act takes place, the children, like Simon and Pontus, may succeed in positioning themselves outside the situation, in that they don't see what is going on – but they are not as successful in positioning themselves out of earshot.

Visual memories

The following conversation, directly following Simon and Pontus's reports of the disgusting smacking sounds they have heard, concerns visual memories – that is, those who the children are participant witnesses to if they do not escape from the scene of violence. This short story marks the transition to a phase in the session characterised by more intensity from the children:

> **Excerpt 9.3: Dina's story "He hit her right in front of us"**
> Dina: But he beat her right in front of me and my
>   younger sister and he beat us too. And that wasn't
>   all that fun.
> Pontus; Nadja; Simon (all together): DID YOU HIT HIM THEN?
> Dina: I dunno, but if I had been able to I would've killed
>   him.
> Therapist I: But this, that one seeks comfort with one's siblings,
>   has that happened to you?
> Dina: But Eric actually hit mum in front of me and my
>   little sister and he even hit us too, so it wasn't all
>   that fun.
> Many voices: DID YOU HIT HIM THEN?
> Dina: I dunno, but if I could've, I would've killed him.

What I think is worth acknowledging here is that the majority of the children are active in asking – or are they suggesting – that Dina should have hit the perpetrator. Therapist I tries to intervene, but is not successful. The last complicated action that is presented ("I dunno, but if I could've, I would've , killed him") could be read as a suggestion for resolution. Dina never hit him, but she might think that it could have solved her problems?

Relational memories and fear

The next story is Nadja's story. Nadja and her twin brother, Max, are very close. They attend the therapy group together.

Excerpt 9.4: Nadja's story "When I called the police I couldn't even talk"

Nadja:
Umm like my parents started fighting like
and he [the father] always screamed like.
I got scared and went and hid and like
he always hit us.
My little brother would walk across the bed he was
so scared and like
when he hit her when I called the police like.
He hit her out there then my mum was going to
go to the laundry room and my other brother who
was there with my little brother at home didn't
dare come out then like.
When I called the police like
I couldn't even talk and then like
I was going to throw a rock at him but he was too
far away.

Nadja's story is like many of the stories in that it is very action-oriented and gives almost no orientation. The last paragraph could be read as the end of her story – or as the beginning of a new one, or as a complicated action in an infinite line of complicated actions.

Excerpt 9.5: Eva's story "I hide in the shadows pretending I'm not there"

Eva:
But like I heard mum and David fight
and when I heard him hitting her
I went into Elsa's room
cos we had like a door without a door
then I went to her and lay down on her bed.
She was also terrified she was actually shaking.
I remember that we fell asleep then.
We had a billiard table they were in there
hitting each other and we had a bar in there
and I remember mummy hiding behind it
cos I went out to look when I heard a door slam
and like I went out to look.
I didn't know if David was still there but I thought
so.
I always have the door open and like listening to
what they say.

> I hide in the shadows pretending I'm not there and
> then I stand there and watch.

Eva's story is more complex compared to the other stories. It is action-oriented like the others, but a bit more oriented towards the listener. It starts with an abstract ("[this is what I did when] I heard mum and David fight") and throughout the narration provides the listener with some orientation. Eva and her sister, Elsa, are very scared. They are hiding together in Elsa's bed and they fall asleep. When they wake up, Eva has to get up and see if the violence has stopped. She has done this many times before – leaving when a violent situation starts and hiding, but still wanting to have some control over what happens. Because of her need for control she forces herself to both listen and watch the violence.

Advice for social workers and teachers

There is one story that remains to be told before this chapter is put to a close. It is a story that is composed as an 'instruction' to teachers and social workers about how to act when they meet children who are participant witnesses to domestic violence. It arose in an interview with a 15-year-old girl, Helen. Helen was participating in a therapy group for teenagers and agreed to be interviewed, because she had so much to tell.

Helen's life has been permeated by violence, neglect and constant breached trust from adults. This interview is difficult, for both narrator and listener. Helen's stories are filled with so much pain and sorrow that they challenge my position as listener. I ask her if she really wants to continue and she says she does. I become more and more uncomfortable at the thought that the interview will soon be over and we will go our separate ways. I do not want her to leave with a pitch-black story as the conclusion. Therefore, near the end, I take control over the interview and steer it away from what we had agreed to talk about – Helen's experiences of domestic violence – which has made us both feel melancholy and disempowered. I steer the interview towards the active and powerful:

Excerpt 9.6: Instruction book for helping children who are participant witnesses to violence

Margareta:	I know there are people out there wanting to help. I thought we can finish with you and me making a little instruction book on what people can do to help children. Helen's instruction book – to whom then, to the counsellor, to the teacher?
Helen:	To school personnel.
Margareta:	To school personnel. And what should be in it?
Helen:	Get to know your students.

Margareta:	Get to know your students, that's the first paragraph?
Helen:	Yeah.
Margareta:	Okay, then we have paragraph two.
Helen:	If you see that they feel bad ask them what's going on.
Margareta:	Ask what's going on?
Helen:	Uh huh.
Margareta:	And then as paragraph three, maybe what to ask them in a little more detail?
Helen:	Yeah first ask how it's going with them.
Margareta:	"Helen, how's it going with you?"
Helen:	Uh huh, I say, "It's all right I guess, sort of".
Margareta:	Okay … that wasn't such an easy answer, what should they ask next? Question two I mean.
Helen:	"How's it going for you at home?"
Margareta:	Okay.
Helen:	And then I answer, "It's not good".
Margareta:	Okay.
Helen:	And then they ask, "What's happened?" … I say, "There's fighting going on at home and mum's being hit". "Do you think we should contact the police or social services and help you with this?" Then I say "yes".
Margareta:	Then let's say that the police come to your house and protect you and social services … is it the same thing with them or what do you think they should do?
Helen:	They should go there.
Margareta:	Right away or?
Helen:	Right away immediately.
Margareta:	Okay so social services come and they say, "Hello there, we're with social services".
Helen:	Yeah and then they should check the environment in the house. If there's food in the fridge. What condition the parents are in, if they see any liquor bottles, any drugs, if they think the environment is okay, if the room's filled with smoke or something.
Margareta:	So I see in front of me a list. Go to the refrigerator. Open the refrigerator: no food. Or open the refrigerator: food
Helen:	If there's food there it's okay because then the kids will have food at any rate. And if there's no food there or old sour milk then "what's this?" Because

	the parents should have money to give the kids food.
Margareta:	And if there's no food there?
Helen:	Then they ask, "How long have you gone without food and why isn't there any food?" and then they should ask the kids because the parents might be lying, then they should ask a kid "How long have you gone without food and is it like this often?" My brother and I usually got to eat at grandma and grandpa's so we had to walk there. We left at 11.00 and got there at 12.00 and got some food. Then we went home to mum, sitting there with her beer bottle watching TV. But I think the most important thing for the social workers to is to get some food for the children. Before they try to talk to them. You cannot talk if you are starving.
Margareta:	So in the instruction book for social services it would say, "If the kids haven't had any food in two days start with going to eat".
Helen:	Yeah because otherwise you can't think about anything other than that you want food. And you may keep talking while you eat.

This interview could serve as an example of co-construction of a story of the life circumstances of a girl who is a participant witness to violence. The interviewer chose the 'instruction book' narrative genre; through the suggestion that the continued narrative be subjected to this form, Helen was placed in a powerful position as the imagined author of such a book – competent people who explain to others how they should behave. As the imagined author, Helen continued to tell about her life from an active change perspective. The interview was infused with energy and quite a bit of giggling, at the same time as it was gravely serious.

Conclusions

It is tempting to develop the writing of the instruction book as the conclusion part of the chapter. I will not do this specifically, but I will highlight certain points that I think can contribute to the discussion on social work with children and families in general, and social work with children exposed to violence in their families in particular.

In the children's narratives, the police often appear as someone you call or who you want someone else – for example, your school – to contact. I believe this reflects the children's understanding of the situation as well as their understanding of the police. What is happening is acute and dangerous, and must be stopped.

The police are always on duty and put a stop to dangerous things. Helen brought up the school's significance. All children go to school – if teachers know their pupils they can tell if they are faring poorly and can act on it. The police, school and social services are all mentioned, and the children's narratives point in the direction of the importance of cooperation.

Common to all the children's narratives is that their siblings are spoken of as important, as those with whom they share their living conditions. This is something social workers should take note of, and allow siblings to stay together in efforts of help and support.

What Helen brings up in her instruction book is the importance of social services reacting concretely to children's social situations. She says nothing about wanting the social workers to talk about the children's social situations – that is, to exaggerate the children's need to reflect on their situations, when they themselves are more action oriented. She points more in the direction of encouraging children to be retrospective and at the same time be oriented towards the future in order to identify concrete situations to act on and raise questions such as, "what should be done if it happens again".

The theme of aggression surfaces in all conversations with the children. When Dina tells her story, the other children repeatedly ask: "Did you hit him then?" Dina answers: "I dunno, but if I had been able to I would have killed him". Nadja's brother throws a rock at their father, but misses him. I think this aggression needs to be addressed. The children first and foremost need to receive credit for their efforts to react, support themselves and perhaps try to stop the violence. If the anger is not addressed, however, the children are left to relate to it completely on their own.

Notes

[1] The research project 'Children experiencing domestic violence' is supported by grants from the Swedish Council for Working Life and Social Research and from the Swedish Crime Victim Compensation and Support Authority.

[2] All names have been changed to assure anonymity.

TEN

Now you see them – now you don't: institutions in child protection policy

Tuija Eronen, Riitta Laakso and Tarja Pösö

Long history notwithstanding

In Finland, residential institutions for children began to be separated from those for adults at the end of the 19th century and their number began to grow. Gradually they acquired a strong, though by no means uncontested, position in Finnish society and child protection. Institutions began to dominate social welfare in general. From the 1960s onwards, however, it was increasingly criticised for being too focused on institutions and, since then, the ideal forms of care and nursing have been considered to be situated primarily outside residential facilities (Eriksson, 1967; Savio, 1989). At the moment, however, a fairly high number of children and young people are placed in residential child protection facilities. In spite of this, these facilities receive only occasional attention in the context of social policy, the professional development of the social welfare or research. This ambivalence – that, on the one hand, these facilities are strongly present in society, but, on the other, they are outside the central contents of child protection policy – is what interests us in this chapter.

The words, "Now you see them" in the heading refer to the fact that, at the moment, over 8,000 children and young people are placed in residential care on child protection grounds (*Lastensuojelu*, 2008). This figure makes up about half of the children placed outside their homes. We will return later to a discussion of whether the figure is large or small, but undoubtedly the number of children and young people in residential care equals the population of a small Finnish town. Since placement in residential care is a strong social intervention in childhood and family relationships, the number reflects society's opinion on what constitutes a suitable childhood and family life. Residential placement covers many individual life stories in the facility and the events before it.

The words, "now you don't" in the heading refer to the fact that the monitoring, evaluation, development and research of residential child protection facilities in Finland are anything but regular or intense. The situation is markedly different from Sweden, for example, where a state organisation provides funding to direct the activity of child protection facilities, as well as research and development concerning them. Research on residential facilities is scarce in Finland (Eronen,

2007). Another significant issue is that work in residential child protection facilities has not been properly included in the social sector educational policy.

Child protection tends to acquire public visibility because of and through its shortcomings (Kendrick, 2008). In the United Kingdom, widespread attention has been attracted by official negligence or procrastination contributing to the deaths of children in their homes because of parental violence. In Ireland, in May 1999, the Irish government issued an apology, on behalf of the state, to the tens of thousands of children who grew up in Ireland's industrial schools, because the children had been subjected to physical and sexual violence during their stay in these institutions (Rafferty and O'Sullivan, 1999). Humiliating experiences of residential care have caused a public outcry in Sweden and Norway; while, in Finland, shortcomings linked to similar facilities seem to be bypassed with silence. A few years ago, an employee of a private facility died when a young resident knifed him. The news was discussed for a few days and then forgotten – in spite of the fact that such things as the number of young people placed in this facility above and beyond its capacity could very well have sparked off a critical debate on the activity of the municipalities that are responsible for placements, or on the monitoring authorities, or on the general morals of residential care.

The ambivalence, "Now you see them – now you don't", thus continues to exist in a cultural silence. In recent times, however, it has been somewhat shaken, as the structures of residential service provision – as well as those of all other welfare services – have changed. When the number of private facilities has become higher than that of public facilities, and when residential placements are commercialised and bought and sold as products, residential facilities are acquiring a new visibility. Therefore, the conflict we have located is topical.

Our chapter presents an actual description of residential child protection in Finland. The materials we have used consist of reports, statistics and studies on the facilities, and we interpret them on the basis of culture and child protection policy. Although our subject is Finnish residential child protection in particular, we also use data from the other Nordic countries whenever possible, in order to be able to contextualise the Finnish debate on residential facilities and on the activity of those facilities, both of which are contradictory, silent and recently also market oriented.

How much is much?

When Turid Vogt Grinde (1989, pp 183-7) described the Nordic child protection practices at the end of the 1980s, she considered the essential trends to be the decrease of residential placements and of places in residential child protection facilities, the blurring of the boundaries of residential care, and an emphasis on the various support measures provided by community care and the parental responsibility for upbringing and care, instead of increasing the scope of residential care. In her opinion, the trends were similar in all Nordic countries. A couple of decades after this analysis it is obvious that residential care is still with us, but the focus has changed in line with Grinde's predictions: judging by Nordic statistics, the share of residential care in substitute care has gone down. It would seem that foster care is the most frequent form of child protection in the Nordic countries, judging by the numbers of children placed. Only in Iceland is the situation different: there the predominant form is residential care. (NOSOSCO, 2005, pp 270-6) It is also clear that current child protection policy strives continuously towards more and more preventive child protection, to the extent that, according to some opinions, the Nordic child protection policy committed to the universal welfare state is in danger of neglecting its task of protection (Pringle, 1998).

Children are placed outside the home on somewhat varying principles. In Denmark, for example, the figure also includes placements of children with disabilities. However, it has been estimated that, even if those children were excluded, the figure of Danish children placed outside the home would still be higher than in the other Nordic countries (see Table 10.1). The figures for Finland include children placed outside the home for reasons of child protection. Similarly, the upper age limit of children placed varies from 16 years (Iceland) to 20 years (Denmark, Finland and Sweden). Between the years 1993 and 2001, the number of children placed increased in all these countries, but the increase was strongest in Finland. It is interesting that Denmark and Finland not only have the highest numbers of children placed outside the home, but also the highest numbers of voluntary placements. In Denmark and Finland the share of non-voluntary placements in 2003 was 13% and 16% of all placements, respectively. The number of non-voluntary placements was the highest in Norway: in 2003, they made up 62% of all placements (NOSOSCO, 2005, pp 66-7, 264-7). The question as to whether or not a placement is voluntary is always complicated. The figure does, however, create the image that child protection facilities are not labelled simply as places of involuntary detention.

In a study of Nordic statistics, Sweden and Norway emerge as strong proponents of foster care. Inside each country, different trends may be discerned. As an example, the use of residential care in Iceland has increased between 1993 and 2003, while, in Sweden and Norway, it has decreased during the same period. In Finland, the proportions of foster and residential care remained more or less

Table 10.1: Number of children placed outside the home in 2003, proportionate to the size of the age group (under 18 years old)

Country	Children placed outside the home (per 1,000 children, according to the age classification of each country)
Denmark	14.3
Finland	11.4
Iceland	7.1
Norway	9.7
Sweden	8.9

Source: NOSOSCO (2005, p 67)

the same during this period. What is essential and important in looking at the time series is the obvious difficulty of finding a shared content to what is meant by foster or residential care. The compilers of the statistical publication referred to earlier state that, among other things, in Finland and Iceland even foster care implemented as a business enterprise is recorded as "foster care", while in other countries the classification is different. It is evident that the forms of foster care are not defined uniformly and a comparison of data from different countries highlights the difficulty concerning definitions.

Even when we look at data on one country alone, definitions prove difficult. It is almost impossible to gain an overview of units providing substitute care, for the names used to describe them do not necessarily describe the nature of their activity. During the past decade, the substitute care units in child protection have acquired multiple forms and the number of private (professional) group homes located in the terrain between residential and foster care has clearly increased. In Finland, the National Research and Development Centre for Welfare and Health (Stakes), which is responsible for child protection statistics, decided in 2005 to categorise (professional) family group homes as a separate form of substitute care. As they had earlier been classified under foster care, the profile of substitute care changed somewhat.

Since then, family group homes have been set up adjacent to residential units and, in practice, some of the units calling themselves 'family group homes' are private residential facilities where the person in charge does not live with the children, but the work is organised in shifts, as is typical of residential facilities. For this reason, demands have been voiced that the concept of family group home should be clarified so that a unit would be classified as a family group home only if the family parents live round the clock with the fostered children (*Lastensuojelulain kokonaisuudistustyöryhmän muistio 2006*, pp 132-3). It is not, however, necessarily possible to distinguish residential child protection facilities, family group homes or foster homes on the basis of how many children are placed in each, for the maximum number of children allowed in one department of an institution (section 59 of the new Child Welfare Act, 317/2007, valid from 1 January 2008), a family group home or, with certain reservations, a foster home is seven children. In a residential child protection facility, a maximum of 24 children can be housed in one building.

The issues related to definitions of substitute care and placements outside the home not only challenge the statisticians, but also reveal something of substitute care and child protection itself. It is rare to find unambiguous contents. When speaking of residential care, one speaks of many ways and practices of 'making a residential facility'. Research literature often refers to the concept of 'the diversity of residential care', stressing the multiple ways of how one enters residential care, how it operates, and what its goals, ideologies and even its facilities are (Milligan and Stevens, 2006). Marie Sallnäs (2000) describes the residential facilities as hybrids, thus stressing the difficulty of defining them. As an example, residential facilities can include many aspects characteristic to foster homes and the homes of 'ordinary' families. Residential facilities are no longer identifiable by means of unambiguous spatial arrangements, staff structures or operational practices, which would distinguish them once and for all from practices termed foster care.

If the concepts are not clear-cut, it is difficult to say whether the number of children and young people placed in residential facilities in Finland is high or low. In 2007, according to the Stakes statistical bulletin (*Lastensuojelu*, 2008), 5,526 children and young people were placed in foster families and 8,095 children in residential care, out of which 2,676 children and young people were placed in family group homes. Altogether, 1.2% of the children under the age of 18 were in substitute care. The estimates of the prevalence of residential placements are always relative. On the basis of the above information it would, however, seem that the number of children in residential care is probably higher than in Sweden and Norway. The comparisons we have made also seem to show that there are clearly more Finnish children and young people in residential facilities than, for example, in Scotland (Francis et al, 2007) and there are considerably more residential placements of children under three years of age than in many European countries (*Mapping the number* …, 2005, p 36).

Comparing the figures on children and young people in residential care with statistics from Europe (Petrie et al, 2006, pp 37-9), Finland would not seem to be particularly oriented towards residential care, but neither does it seem to be a country that avoids residential placements as forms of substitute care. Finland is not included in the comparison in Table 10.2, but we can draw some conclusions by comparing the previous information on Finland with the information on Denmark. In a European comparison of child protection facilities, countries that often resort to residential placements include Germany, Denmark and Belgium. In contrast to this, in the United Kingdom, attitudes towards residential placements are critical, and few placements are made in proportion to the child population and the number of people within child protection. However, Petrie and her team (2006) stress that the figures are difficult to compare, because statistics are compiled differently in different countries and there are also different views in society concerning the responsibilities of the individual, the parents and society. As a concrete example they mention that, in Germany, residential statistics include

Table 10.2: Number of young people in residential care

Country	Young people in residential childcare	% of all looked-after children
UK	10,371	14
Flanders	3,086	53
Denmark	5,907	54
France	52,400	38
Germany	82,051	59
Netherlands	9,000	47

Source: Petrie et al (2006, p 37)

young people who use the supported accommodation services provided by a residential facility, until their 20th birthday.

What is essential for this article is that, in any case, there are so many children and young people in residential care in Finland that the lack of debate and research on such facilities cannot be explained by the infrequency of the phenomenon. In fact, different comparative data, despite its many problems, would seem to suggest that we would actually be well advised to discuss this matter, which even in quantitative terms is an important phenomenon in Finnish society.

Residential facilities as arenas of child protection work

Debate on the professionalism, theoretical base and place in society of residential child protection work in Finland has changed. During the 1960s and 1970s, the professionalism and place in society of residential work was made more visible by critical opinions that brought the concepts of humanism, education and the relationships between community and the individual into the debate on residential care (Goffman, 1961; Eriksson, 1967; Basaglia, 1972; Kaipio, 1977). This was followed in the 1980s by an almost complete silence concerning research or theories on work in children's homes. After this, the discussion focused on how the care units themselves could select their frame of reference and how they looked after the children in their care and what gender-based care practices this produced (Kyrönseppä and Rautiainen, 1993; Pösö, 1993). The debate again became more heated in the early 2000s; interest then focused on issues arising from children's need for special care and the development of certain work methods. Within clinical psychology and child psychiatry, studies have focused on the need for care related to the mental health of children placed in institutions and partly also that of their parents, on how to evaluate this need and on various risk or protective factors (Pasanen, 2001; Hukkanen, 2002). Several projects have developed methods of special care for residential work (Tervonen-Arnkil, 1999), methods to improve the independence skills of children in residential care and methods to support long-term educational work (Tuovila, 2001). These challenges, which have become topical for child protection work in the 2000s, appear to focus mainly on methods. Similarly, the report on foster care presented by a national task force (Känkänen and Laaksonen, 2006) emphasises the development of residential work as an issue concerning methods and the need for special care.

The European debate on residential child protection work has asked how it should be understood primarily as work and which disciplines form its theoretical basis (Crimmens and Milligan, 2005; Smith, 2005; Petrie et al, 2006; Andersson, 2007; Johansson, 2007). Residential child protection work has been seen to have links to social work, social pedagogy and the care and upbringing of children and young people. In Scotland, for example, residential child protection work is understood as a practice that shares the theoretical basis of social work and is thus part of it. In certain countries of northern continental Europe and central

Europe, residential child protection work is understood from the viewpoint of social pedagogy or the upbringing of children and young people. Understanding residential child protection work as something connected to social pedagogy and its research tradition is typical of child protection work, especially in Germany. This debate is quite unfamiliar to Finnish child protection debate. The question of whether residential child protection work should be linked primarily to social work, the upbringing of children and young people or social pedagogy does not evoke passionate responses in either researchers or practitioners.

In Finland, practitioners of different fields are involved in residential child protection work: health care professionals, youth workers and social work professionals. Competence for residential work may be gained after a basic education in several fields (education, social work and health care). What is interesting is that, whatever the educational background, no studies focusing on residential work are required as part of qualifications for the jobs in residential care. Nor are such studies offered by the current Finnish educational system, for the social work educational reforms in the 1980s and 1990s eliminated residential work as a specialisation area. Before this it was possible to specialise in residential work within both secondary and tertiary social work studies. In contrast, certain special needs of children and young people – among which alcohol and drug addictions are expressly mentioned – are considered to require specialised education and experience after the basic education. The eligibility criteria for residential work are loosely defined in legislation. The new Child Welfare Act, which came into effect in 2008, states that the eligibility criteria of the personnel must take into account the special needs of the clients and the nature of the activity of each unit (section 60, Child Welfare Act, 417/2007).

In units offering 'home-like' services to children and young people of various ages, residential work has a different face from, say, units providing services for boys with an alcohol addiction (Kemppainen, 2006). Residential child protection work also differs considerably from individual- or family-oriented social work because of its collective nature (Smith, 2003, pp 234-44). In a study by Marie Sallnäs (2000), the ways in which workers defined their work emphasised a 'home-like' atmosphere and sharing of ordinary daily life with the children and young people placed in foster care. Work in children's homes is characterised by a repetition of daily patterns, the sensitiveness of the work, the infinite variation in the relationships between the professionals and the children, and long duration.

In residential facilities, daily life is shared with children and young people of widely varying ages, varying characters and often with varying backgrounds and families. The work requires that the professionals are flexible and sensitive in encounters with children of different ages, and equally are capable of responding to their basic needs, which at their simplest relate to the repetition of sleeping and waking, eating, washing, getting dressed and undressed, or to the privacy or communality of the facilities, or the upholding of residential or non-residential practices in daily routines. Such issues as how the child is escorted safely to sleep, how his or her wishes are noted in deciding about the events of the coming week or how his or her questions and problems are listened to in the middle of the unit's daily routines might sound small and negligible. However, when repeated, they form moments of experience during which the quality of residential child protection work is also being defined. The long duration of residential work includes both the time that is spent daily with the children and the duration of the child's client status; at its longest, this may begin in babyhood and continue until the child attains majority. The relationship may also continue as an intergenerational relationship between the professional and the child even after the child has left the children's home. (Törrönen, 1999; Laakso, 2008).

This day-to-day work, its possible variations from one facility to the next and making the daily work visible is gradually attracting interest in Finland (Eronen and Laakso, 2006) as well as elsewhere (Anglin, 2002; Ward, 2004; Smith, 2005). An emphasis on the daily work strengthens the importance of residential work; what is essential is not only the various interventions or special programmes, but also the ordinary life lived with the children. This emphasis forms a challenging relationship to the societal policy surrounding the residential facilities. When the facilities operate on commercial principles and their services are priced as part of the market orientation of welfare services, it is precisely the daily work, being close to the children and the repetitiousness of daily life that are difficult to commercialise. If they cannot be sold, they will not be bought either. A second challenge to the work in substitute care is children's rights and how they are realised in residential care. In international debate, the rights of children in residential care have arisen only in recent years, when people have started to think and provide instructions about how children's rights should be implemented in residential facilities (Guðbrandsson 2006; Draft UN Guidelines, 2007). It seems that in Finland this debate has yet to be started.

Children and young people in residential care

Residential child protection facilities in Finland receive children of all ages. At the level of legislation, residential facilities are not designed for particular age groups (as is the case in many countries), but the facilities accept both babies and teenagers. Child protection practices may stress the importance of foster care for the smallest children. Nevertheless, infants may be repeatedly placed in residential facilities (Bardy, 2001, p 52). Consequently one can claim that there is a strong reliance in Finland on residential child protection as a milieu in which children and young people may grow up and as support in difficult situations.

Through the UN Declaration of the Rights of the Child and the national legislation, Finland is committed to respect and safeguard the rights of children. The child has the right to resources, participation and protection. However, residential facilities in Finland have not been evaluated from the viewpoint of children's rights. It is only very irregularly that one hears the question of what sort of resources, participation and protection the children's homes, family homes or substance abuse care units are providing for children and young people. Little attention is also paid to who the children are who spend their childhoods in residential child protection facilities.

No comprehensive description exists in Finland of children taken into custody and placed in residential care. The information on national child protection does not cover issues of that type (Heino and Pösö, 2003). However, reports exist on children taken into custody in individual cities and municipalities. According to a report on the capital region, the factors recorded as constituting the need for a custodial intervention undergo an obvious change when the child becomes 13 years old. When children under 13 years are taken into custody, the grounds are linked to the addiction and mental health problems of the parents and to shortcomings in the basic care of the child, while, when the child is over 13, the grounds listed include the indiscriminate behaviour of the young person, manifestation of mental symptoms, substance abuse and conflicts at home, as well as difficulties at school. As a category, the difficulties and inabilities related to parenting do not distinguish the different age groups. However, in the over-13s group, for more than every second person, a parent has requested that the child be taken into custody (Myllärniemi, 2006, pp 38-40).

Concerning the causes of custodial decisions and their links to the choice of placement, the most extensive information is available from the municipalities that make placements. Research on the subject is scarce. There is cause to assume that the links are complex. As an example, a placement in a reform school – which represents a residential facility for 12 to 17 year olds who are 'difficult to care for' – has been found to be based equally on an accumulation of long-term problems or several attempts to support the child and the family and on situations that have taken an acute turn for the worse (Kitinoja, 2005, pp 265-7).

Looking at Finnish research on child protection facilities – which, as was noted above, is scarce – it is possible to find some descriptions of children living in residential facilities. In fact, the research constructs two different images of children in residential care. One of them directs an analysing gaze to the child through risks, problems and diagnosis. It defines the grounds of custodial decisions and the children's service needs. In this case, the data sources often rely on client documents. We call the children thus described 'children in need of services'. The other image is constructed of the children's own narratives and the researcher's face-to-face conversations with the children, confused and often also wordless because of an experience that is difficult to describe verbally. We call these children 'children in residential care'.

In the light of texts by several experts, the 'child in need of services' is seen as a bundle of problems, an accumulation of risks and difficulties before, during and after residential care. Research interest has been directed to the life situation, risk processes and protective processes of fetal alcohol syndrome (FAS) children in care (Viittala, 2001); the developmental risk factors and protective factors, symptoms and need of psychiatric care of children in residential care (Pasanen, 2001); and the psychosocial problems of fostered children (Hukkanen, 2002). A study of the documents concerning young people in reform schools shows that psychiatric diagnoses occupy an important role, as do placements in substance abuse and detoxification units before placement in the reform school (Kitinoja, 2005). The young people may have experienced several care relationships that have been interrupted for several reasons and also several concurrent ones. Seen from this angle, the service needs of children in care and particularly of those in residential care are special as regards both the therapeutic support required for learning and the development of boundary-setting practices.

In contrast, the 'child in residential care' is encountered eye to eye. The studies, often qualitative in approach, document the fact that the experiences of the children and young people have stopped the researcher in his or her tracks. In research of this type the children are described through experiences and emotions. Childhood in child protection facilities is associated with many experiences of being hurt and neglected, but also of belonging and participation (Eronen, 2004). Pösö (2004, p 66) has emphasised 'the solemn eyes' as a strong observation made during a research relationship. The solemn eyes belong to young people who report difficult experiences and are looking for someone to listen to their descriptions of what they have gone through. The solemnity is mixed with sadness and sometimes a faint rebellion because of the hurts that the young people have encountered in their lives. Elina Virokannas (2004, pp 32-3) has interviewed young people in substance abuse treatment and she highlights the contrast between the stories recounted within youth and substance abuse research and the narratives of her young interviewees. In substance abuse and youth research, narratives about belonging to a group or a culture are emphasised, while, in her research, the features emphasised in the young people's narratives were loneliness, lack of belonging and the fluctuation of identity on both sides of what is considered normal. The experiences of being an outsider and the lack of encounters and the dominance of professional dialogue are also revealed more generally as the young people talk about their varied experiences at school and in residential facilities, or within child protection (Pekkarinen, 2006, p 106).

Both the 'child in need of services' and the 'child in residential care' have attracted interest in Finland, though not so much because of children's rights as because of the purchasing of services and the effectiveness of services. Research is expected to produce methods and classifications, so that both information about the children and information possessed by the children could be smoothly appropriated for administrative uses. The image of the child has begun to change. Industry based on quality assessment favours rapid methods, forms, lists describing the qualities of services and clients, but such methods contrast sharply with several humanistic assumptions on the narration of lives (Plummer, 2001, pp 249-50). Ungar (2001, p 150) proposes that, when studying 'problematic' identities and life paths, we should adopt approaches that identify and give an opportunity for that which is unprecedented and open, for a continuity and a discontinuity of identity and life paths.

So far, the research interest that has developed, evaluated and reflected on social care and child protection has largely bypassed the children and young people in residential care. Therefore, few descriptions, analyses or monitoring exercises concerning childhood and placements in children's homes exist and what does exist is random. In principle, the child's knowledge and his or her participation in the production of information is regarded as important. Nevertheless, mainstream research tends to describe children through characteristics and needs defined from the outside (the 'child in need of services'), and so the angle is that of the body or individual in quest of information rather than that of the child. Naturally, this holds true for other research on children, besides that which concerns child protection facilities (Eskonen et al, 2006; Helavirta, 2007). It is possible that future production of information concerning child protection facilities and children will increasingly study the children from the perspective of the service system (for whom and with what consequences are 'the services of children's homes' provided) in order to implement the interests of the system – the production, marketing and pricing of services.

Residential facilities at the interface of silence and publicity

In this chapter, we have claimed that the debate, research, education and development concerning these facilities are haphazard and fragmented. We are not prepared to accept the justification that the number of children and young people in residential care or the number of facilities themselves is so low that attention would not be justified. On the contrary, judging by the numbers, one would expect the residential facilities to be the object of dynamic education, development and research in Finland.

Residential care is not, of course, the only social practice to remain outside systematic social research and debate. Jorma Sipilä (2003) claims that it is surprisingly late that care has become a research interest internationally. While the research interest was low in the 1980s, it did increase later. According to Sipilä, the low research interest is difficult to justify, especially in light of the human importance of care.

In the same way, one might think that the discussion of special social problems in childhood could have been of interest to Finnish society. In a way, this is actually the case. As an example, Guðný Björk Eydal and Mirja Satka (2006) describe the development of the Nordic welfare states as a process in which the social subsidies, guiding practices and later also the norms and action policies concerning children's participation directed to children and families with children have been present over long periods of time. In child protection as a social institution, an extensive task to support the welfare of children and families has been emphasised (Pringle, 1998; Khoo et al, 2002; Hearn et al, 2004; Pösö, 2007). A strong ideological change took place in Finnish child protection in the 1980s, when reforms in legislation and practices favoured a move from a focus on custodial decisions towards child protection that is more in the nature of community services. In this ideology, foster care and residential care as part of it represent a last-resort intervention. Residential care has fallen outside systematic interest precisely because it is a last resort. The same applies to child protection in a more general sense; because of its last-resort nature, it appears to have been overshadowed by the universal services to children and their families in both social policy and research.

The silence prevailing where debate, research and development concerning residential care should exist may also have other explanations. In Finnish social history, institutions for children have been the topics of visible controversies and policies at two points in time, followed by two different periods of neglect. In the first instance, after the 1918 civil war, Finland was divided into two factions, the White and the Red, and about 20,000 children lost one or all of their caregivers; the share of the Red orphans was nearly 90 per cent. Arranging the care of the war orphans was a substantial social issue and the main topic of the debate during the 1920s was whether to prefer institutional care, fostering or placement in families. The best solution was considered to be to support the homes through public relief so that the children could live in their own homes or foster homes. Opinions on social policy considered a residential placement the last-resort intervention; in particular, it was felt that situations should be avoided where children's homes would become institutions inhabited solely by Red orphans. The division could also be seen in that it was not considered appropriate to solve the problem of widows and orphans on the winning (White) side through public relief, but their condition was improved by pension arrangements (Pulma, 1987, pp 128-30). The opinions voiced during the debate on the Red orphans reflected the social division between the Whites and the Reds. As a generational experience, childhood during the 1920s and 1930s included deprivation, hunger and disease, and for some the death of one or both parents, and in this case a children's home was at least a solution of sorts (Urponen, 1994). The lack of research, debate and reminiscences on children's home could be explained by a generation's long tradition of embarrassment and desire to forget.

The second period of social debate occurred at the turn of the 1960s and 1970s when the widespread social activism also led to a criticism of the weak position and deficient legal protection of people in residential facilities. The criticism concerned mental hospitals and prisons, as well as facilities for people with learning difficulties. As regards child protection, substantial criticism was directed particularly to facilities for young people (Eriksson, 1967; Siren, 1967). This period is still very well remembered. Some of those who worked in the facilities can remember the criticism they faced, while others remember the facilities as somewhere that was primarily out to limit individual rights rather than to support them. This critical period and the resulting ideological preference for community care probably succeeded in demolishing educational programmes specialising in residential care on both the secondary and the tertiary levels, but it failed to eradicate the residential facilities themselves.

The cultural silence over issues of residential care is something that must be examined in relation to the practices, experiences and policies related to the residential facilities. In Finland, a traditional assumption in social policy is that residential facilities will gradually disappear as poverty is eradicated and issues related to orphans are solved. On the other hand, the 1980s' legislation favoured community care and the development of family-focused and preventive work methods, with precisely this end in view. However, instead of disappearing, residential facilities became marketable products. Ian Milligan and Irene Stevens (2006, p 21) emphasise that viewpoints on residential care have a linkage to the children being placed; a childhood in residential care is always a personal experience, but also something linked to society, time and culture. Therefore, the policy of silence must also be examined from the angle of what it means to those who are spending or have spent their childhoods in residential care and to those who have worked there.

Speaking of national memory, alongside what is remembered it is important to become sensitive to what is forgotten and what is bypassed with silence (Misztal, 2003). Increasingly, many are demanding that the national memory must be challenged and reformulated by reintroducing topics that have been silenced. This is what Kjersti Ericsson and Eva Simonsen (2005) did when studying the neglected issue of war children in Norway. Childhoods in residential care and child protection facilities are not likely to be undisputed main topics of national memory anywhere; the other Nordic countries probably have their own waves of forgetting. However, in our opinion, the fact that in Finland it is possible to locate two, or actually three, waves of forgetting in addition to the general, universalistic social political orientation may be an important factor in explaining why there are residential facilities in Finland despite the apparent lack of them as a policy issue. In any case, there are children and young people in residential care, and we should assume responsibility for them despite the fact that "now you don't see them".

ELEVEN

Epilogue: on developing empowering child welfare systems and the welfare research needed to create them

Keith Pringle

Introduction

In this concluding chapter, my aim is not to summarise, or indeed synthesise, what has gone before. Instead, inspired by some of the major themes within the preceding chapters of the book, I will seek to outline what I see as four major future challenges facing research, policy and practice in the field of child and family social work, not only in the Nordic countries but also beyond. These are vital if we wish to create what might be regarded as truly empowering welfare systems for those living within them.

I undertake this task as an 'insider/outsider' within the Nordic countries both as a researcher and as a member of society.[1] Of course intense debates about the possibilities – as well as the potential advantages and disadvantages – of being an insider/outsider in social research have been ongoing at least since Robert Merton's famous article a quarter of a century ago (Merton, 1972). In recent years, the concept of insider/outsider has become central to more postmodern appreciations of the complexities around identity and research (see, for example, Skeggs, 1997) – complexities that cannot be entered into here because of limited space. Suffice to say that there seem to be considerable epistemological advantages – as well as dangers – in exploiting the ever-shifting boundaries of being an insider/outsider. And I intend to use those advantages here.

A Nordic welfare model: developing more complex analyses incorporating 'bodily citizenship'

My first inspiration is derived from Chapters Two and Three in this volume: the interrogation of a Nordic welfare model. These two chapters make a valuable contribution in helping readers – especially those from outside the Nordic countries – appreciate both the dynamic heterogeneities as well as homogeneities of the Nordic countries. The picture is *dynamic* because the complex intermeshing of similarities and dissimilarities between them is made even more complex by the fact that the trajectories of these countries are constantly changing. I would in fact argue for even greater complexity in terms not only of the Nordic welfare systems but also of comparative welfare analysis more generally. For, I have suggested elsewhere (Pringle, 1998, 2005; Hearn and Pringle, 2006a) that comparative assessments of welfare systems must focus far more than they have done hitherto on multiple – and indeed intersecting[2] – dimensions of disadvantage and social exclusion. Most of such assessments – including feminist-inspired ones (see, for example, Sainsbury, 1999) – focus primarily on aspects of welfare associated with work: either in the labour market (including issues of income and income replacement); or in the home (for instance, levels of parental leave, day care provision, parental insurance). They largely ignore how far welfare systems respond to dimensions of marginalisation that may be conceptualised under the rubric of 'bodily integrity or citizenship' (Pringle, 2005, 2008a). Within this concept are included forms of exclusion associated, for example, with violence to women, violence to children, ageism (in relation to younger as well as older age), racism, heterosexism/homophobia, disablism.

This is not to argue against the importance of welfare services that challenge social problems arising from poverty and class differences or inequalities connected with labour issues in the home or at work. It is to argue that the life opportunities of individual human beings can be just as limited or expanded by considerations of bodily citizenship; and that welfare systems should be researched just as closely on these dimensions as on those that are the more 'normal' foci of scholarly attention.

Such considerations make the specific Nordic picture more complex on two particular counts. First of all, it has been argued (Hearn and Pringle, 2006a) that the Nordic societies and welfare systems in general seem to have performed less well when responding to matters of bodily citizenship than they have when dealing with more 'mainstream' social concerns such as poverty alleviation or labour-related issues – and this applies to child welfare as much as any other field (Hearn and Pringle, 2006b). Indeed, it has even been suggested that, with the 1990s and early 21st century in focus, one should consider almost turning Esping-Andersen 'on his head' when it comes to bodily citizenship – with the UK welfare system potentially outperforming the Nordic countries in terms of research, policy and practice on issues such as racism, disablism or gendered violence (Pringle, 2005, 2006a).

However, a second level of complexity is added to the Nordic picture when issues of bodily citizenship are taken fully into account. For, a closer analysis of, for instance, societal responses to gendered violence or racism (Balkmar et al, 2008) suggests that there is not only – once again – considerable heterogeneity between the Nordic countries but also perhaps a growing heterogeneity. Certainly, on these dimensions of social marginalisation a widening gap seems to be developing between, on the one hand, relatively progressive Swedish research, policy and practice responses and, on the other hand, the relatively much more limited responses in the Danish system. In terms of interpersonal violence, this applies both to violence to women and to men's violence to children – especially sexual violence to them (Balkmar and Pringle, 2005; Iovanni and Pringle, 2005).

The studies, both Nordic and European, from which these suggestions have been derived are of course exploratory. What are needed are further studies to open out the issues to further scrutiny. Among the studies required are detailed ones that seek to link social work practice with both the policy domain and the structural/cultural domain. A number of chapters in the present volume make valuable contributions to this enterprise, not least Chapters Three and Four.

Developing methodologies in welfare research

No doubt there are numerous methodological approaches that might be of value from an epistemological point of view in developing such studies. However, I want to bring into focus two approaches that are seriously underdeveloped. One involves focusing on the discursive resources drawn on in welfare research, policy and practice and the power relations associated with the resulting discursive formations. This is an approach that I have sought to deploy (Pringle, 2005, 2006a, 2006b) as a means of critically interrogating the relations of power that permeate not only various welfare systems but also various national welfare research infrastructures in the Nordic countries. For such configurations of power are central to decisions about which social issues are addressed (or not) in different societal contexts; and in what ways they are addressed in terms of research, policy and practice. This is an approach also used to some extent in Chapter Four of the present volume.

The other research approach I want to emphasise centres on including the voices of service users within the analysis of welfare systems. In terms of children and families, the category of 'service users' includes not only parents but also perhaps most crucially children. The active involvement of children as respondents within welfare system research follows directly from the theoretical perspectives within the sociology of childhood (Christensen and James, 2000). Moreover, among its foremost Nordic exponents is in fact one of the co-editors of this volume (Forsberg, 2005). It is also an approach – combined with narrative analysis – which is deployed very successfully in Chapter Nine of the present volume. In fact, such an approach is already developing quite rapidly in terms of studies of welfare, not least in the Nordic countries (Eriksson and Näsman, 2008; Eriksson et al, 2008).

Interrogating and making visible power relations within different welfare systems

The second future challenge – of interrogating power relations within different welfare systems – has also been inspired by several of the chapters in this book: for instance, by Chapters Four, Five, Six, Seven and Eight. This challenge is a vital one in the field of child and family welfare. Let me use as an example a theme in child and family welfare that runs through many of the chapters in this book that I have cited: family support and child protection.

Like several authors in this book, I do not see these two approaches as inevitably hostile to one another. Nevertheless I accept that there are certainly tensions between them – and each of them can also be problematic in themselves in certain contexts. For instance, some time ago (Pringle, 1998) I offered a critique of both the 'child protection' approach – as it had been practised in England in the late 1980s and early 1990s – and also of the family support approach that gained ground in the UK towards the end of the 1990s, heavily inspired by family support models already established in western and northern Europe. The child protection model as it was practised in England seemed (Harder and Pringle, 1997) to 'miss' many cases of child abuse – at least many cases of child sexual abuse – and, at the same time, fail to provide adequate resources for dealing with those cases of child abuse that it did manage to reveal.

However, here I want to focus more on my critique of the broader family support approach that was gaining ground – under direct governmental encouragement – in England at the very end of the 1990s and in the early 2000s. Moreover, I want to link it to more recent critiques of family support approaches in Denmark and Sweden (Pringle and Harder, 1999; Pringle, 2005; 2006a; Balkmar et al, 2008). As some of the chapters in this volume touch on (especially Chapter Five), there are grounds for doubting how well a family support model might sometimes offer protection to children suffering abuse (Pringle and Harder, 1999). Of course, this depends on context. Nevertheless, there are particular concerns about how far some family support models are able to recognise and deal effectively with cases of child sexual abuse if they adopt a primarily family systems understanding of that phenomenon.[3] In an overview of welfare responses to child sexual abuse across Europe (Pringle, 1998), there was evidence that many western and northern European welfare systems (using family support oriented approaches) were recognising child sexual abuse far less effectively than the – at that time – more child protection oriented English approach. I linked this partly to the differential use of family systems thinking in social work and other caring professions. For, even in the late 1990s, it was far less common for welfare professionals in the UK to explain child sexual abuse in terms of balance within the family system than was – and still is – the case in many western and northern European countries (Pringle and Harder, 1999; Pringle, 2005).

However, it was also possible to connect the greater adherence to family systems thinking as well as the more general difficulties in recognising the extent of child sexual abuse in those European countries to broader cultural and societal patterns. Hence, I suggested a connection between family support approaches and the more solidaristic/collectivist discourses that tend to permeate social institutions in western and northern European countries – compared to the far more individualistic ethos permeating many social institutions in England (Pringle, 1998; Pringle and Harder, 1999). At the same time, I suggested that the dynamics of the solidaristic discourses in countries such as France or Germany might well be rather different from those in the Nordic countries.

Since then, I have been involved with various colleagues in assessing more closely the child welfare systems of both Denmark and Sweden (Harder and Pringle, 1997, 2007; Pringle and Harder, 1999; Balkmar and Pringle, 2005; Iovanni and Pringle, 2005; Pringle, 2005, 2006a, 2006b, 2008a; Hearn and Pringle, 2006a, 2006b; Balkmar et al, 2008). This recent work has led to a more differentiated and nuanced understanding of how the cultural contexts of the various Nordic countries impact on their welfare formations and practices. Yet, the earlier focus concerning differential emphases on solidarity and individualism still remain key to the more recent analysis.

As noted in the earlier sections of this chapter, my more recent studies both critique as a whole and yet also make visible the heterogeneity of the Nordic welfare systems in terms of their responses to issues of bodily citizenship. The explanations put forward by myself and colleagues (Balkmar et al, 2008; Pringle, 2008a) for the relative unresponsiveness of the Nordic societies to issues of bodily citizenship compared to England – as well as the differential degree of response between those Nordic societies – are multidimensional: institutional, political and cultural/societal. Having said that, most weight has been placed by us on the cultural and societal domain (Pringle, 2008a). We place emphasis on the different dominant discourses shaping social institutions in Denmark, Sweden and England focused around the two twin concepts of individualism/collectivism and conflict/consensus. In *all three* countries we distinguish contrasts across both sets of twin concepts. We then connect these contrasts with the differential responses to such issues as violence to women or to racism in the welfare research, policy and practice of the three countries. Once again, these explanations are suggestive and tentative requiring further detailed studies to advance our understanding. However, I think the example I have developed here – how debates about family support/child protection must be linked to much broader cultural and societal understandings of dynamic power formations in societies – has illustrated the vital need for more detailed critical studies of welfare systems (individually and comparatively) that focus on making visible the webs of power relations that shape welfare research, policy and practice.

More complex models of power

To achieve the first two objectives set out in this chapter – developing more complex understandings of welfare systems and more effectively interrogating power relations operating within them – we need to adopt more complex and sophisticated understandings of societal power relations in our analyses. That is therefore my third and final pathway forward here.

There are a number of potential directions that might be suggested, of which I focus only on one here. It is the approach to power relations that has been labelled 'intersectionality' (de los Reyes and Mulinari, 2005; Yuval-Davis, 2006).

This is a perspective that seeks to provide a framework within which we can seek to understand the complex and often contradictory ways by which various dimensions of power impact on one another both structurally and in the day-to-day lived experience of individual human beings. The dimensions of power that might be relevant to a situation at any given time and in any given space could be almost limitless. However, among the most frequently salient are those relations of power associated with gender, 'race'/ethnicity, disability/ability, age (younger or older), sexuality, class (or material resources).

In fact almost no scholar actively involved in the current debates around intersectionality is satisfied with that concept. As many commentators have pointed out (for example, West and Fenstermaker, 1995; Brah, 2001), no matter how we conceptualise the processes by way such dimensions of power operate together, it is clearly too simplistic to see them 'intersecting'. For reasons that cannot be explored in the present space, a number of scholars (including myself) prefer a concept such as the 'mutual constitution of power relations' to that of 'intersectionality'. However, here (as in many other discussions of these issues) I will retain the label of 'intersectionality' simply for ease of reference.

Nor is there space here to detail the main principles within an intersectional approach to power relations. Instead, I will focus on just one of the key issues. For, an intersectional approach suggests that it is almost always impossible in any given social situation to understand the processes by which one dimension of power relations operates without taking into account the complex – *and often contradictory* – interaction of that dimension with one or more other dimensions of power. Thus, depending on the specific situation, it will almost always be impossible to understand how gendered and gendering processes are operating without considering how they interact with other processes of power – most frequently 'race'/ethnicity and/or class/access to material resources and/or age and/or ability/disability and/or sexuality (Brah, 2001).

I have emphasised here that intersectional perspectives on power might well involve contradictions or paradoxes because, in many cases where different dimensions of power intersect, they do not necessarily move in the same direction – that is, they might move counter to one another rather than reinforcing each other. For instance, let us take the situation of a woman from a minority ethnic group who is subject to violence from a man partner in her home (Pringle, 1995). Of course, the situation will vary massively depending on the specific circumstances – it is vital not to stereotype here. Nevertheless, there are some contradictory dynamics that one should at least consider as possibilities in a situation like this. For instance, for some women in such a position the home may represent, at the very same time, a place of terrible non-safety in terms of gendered power relations and a place of great safety in terms of racialised power relations – that is, in some cases the home may represent one of the few refuges from racism and ethnic discrimination within a broader society where such racism and discrimination are common. Conversely, some shelters for women in some countries might represent places of desperately needed safety in terms of gendered power relations and yet places of unsafety in terms of racism and ethnic discrimination.

The application of this kind of approach to welfare contexts – including both practising social work and researching social work – are numerous, as I have recently outlined (Pringle, 2006b, 2008b). For instance, at the most 'micro'[4] level of welfare analysis, an intersectional approach allows us to develop more complex, dynamic – and indeed often paradoxical – understandings of self-identity formation undertaken by both service users and social workers over time and space (Pringle, 2008b). At a 'meso' level of analysis, we can use intersectional approaches to unravel the complex processes by which individuals and various social institutions interact with one another within dynamic and shifting webs of power relations. At a more 'macro' level, the same approaches can be deployed to clarify the complex ways in which different dimensions of power interact more structurally in the formation of social problems. For instance, as I have demonstrated elsewhere (Pringle, 1998, 2005), it is almost always not enough to think about gendered forms of power relations alone in trying to understand the structural processes involved in the commercial sexual exploitation of children (even if such gendered power relations usually predominate). Depending on the specific situation that one is dealing with, one might need to consider oppressive forms of power associated with dimensions such as class, disability/ability, sexuality (often heterosexual), 'race/ethnicity' – and of course age as well as gender.

Moreover, the potential for complexity that intersectionality offers to scholarly social work analysis does not arise only from the greater awareness of the multiplicity of power relations in any given social situation, or from an understanding that those power relations may contradict one another. Nor does it simply arise from the fact that we need to study how these configurations of power vary over space and time. The potential for complexity also derives from the fact that, in any single social situation at any given time, the precise configuration of power relations involved may vary greatly at the different levels of analysis available to us. Then the task may be for us to see how those various configurations at different analytical levels relate to one another.

Like much scholarly social work analysis of power relations in the Nordic countries and elsewhere, many of the analyses in the chapters of this book could be enriched by adopting a more complex power framework, such as the intersectional one I have summarised here. In terms of how the study of child and family social welfare and social work should develop in the future, the broader usage of such a framework is essential – not only in itself but also because it will facilitate the other two ways forward that I have outlined in this chapter.

Conclusion

Many of the contributions in the present volume advocate one or more of the following: first, the need to make links between social welfare practice and broader cultural/societal contexts; second, the need for multidimensional and complex understandings of welfare systems; and, third, the need for more detailed studies of welfare systems, including the use of more innovative theoretical and methodological approaches such as discourse or narrative analysis. I would fully endorse such directions in the future. Indeed, the author's own work in recent years has developed some of these directions in the context of welfare system analysis, not least in the field of child and family welfare.

Moreover, in this chapter I have highlighted the urgent need for: first, a more complex picture of welfare systems both individually and comparatively incorporating issues of bodily citizenship into mainstream studies; second, developing methodologies in welfare research including more incorporation of voices of service users, not least those of children; and, third, further studies adopting more complex and more diverse understandings of how power relations permeate societies and how these formations of power change over time and space.

The Nordic countries – as states with some common features and many heterogeneities – face massive social, political and economic challenges now and in the future, as do most countries in the world in one way or another. At the same time, these Nordic countries have a particular empirical and symbolic meaning for other welfare systems because of their previous welfare achievements. Those achievements have been in many ways real, even though, as I have suggested above, they were never as comprehensive as the rest of the world – or indeed the Nordic countries themselves – may have wanted to believe. Even so, for good reasons, and for less good reasons, the world to some extent still looks to the Nordic countries for a 'lead' on how to meet current and future social welfare challenges in a way that it does not look to many other countries – and not least in the field of child and family social work. Consequently, there is a special pressure on the Nordic countries to deploy the best possible welfare research strategies to enable them to understand and therefore meet such challenges. This book – and I hope this chapter as well – goes some way in assisting with this major task in terms of child and family welfare.

As a part outsider, there are a number of important aspects that deeply dissatisfy me about welfare practice, policy and research in the Nordic countries. Nevertheless, as I have argued elsewhere (Pringle, 2005, 2006a, 2006b, 2008a), if any place in the world has a chance of developing what might be regarded as a genuinely empowering welfare system – combining breadth of welfare assistance with a deep appreciation of the positive qualities of 'difference' in society – then it is still probably one of the Nordic countries. None of them is there yet, largely because of their relatively poor performance in relation to valuing intrasocietal difference. But I have hopes – particularly for Sweden. And so I will remain an insider/outsider.

Notes

[1] My citizenship is British. I grew up in the North East of England and was employed in the UK until 2003. Having held various visiting professorships over several previous years in a number of Swedish universities, my main academic position from 2003 became professor of social work at Aalborg University in Denmark; at which time I also became a formal Danish resident. From November 2006 my main academic positions have been in Sweden (at Mälardalen and then Uppsala Universities). From late 2006 I have also held formal Swedish residency. Currently my main position – and my residency – remains in Sweden but I also hold a 50% research chair at a British university.

[2] See the final sections of this chapter for more on 'intersectionality'.

[3] Of course, family systems approaches may be highly effective in understanding and dealing with many social issues – as discussed, for instance, in Chapter Eleven of this volume. The point I am making here is that they are not suitable for understanding the dynamics underpinning child sexual abuse – nor for dealing with the problem as a whole.

[4] I use the terms 'micro', 'meso' and 'macro' here merely for illustrative purposes. I fully recognise their vast oversimplicity and reductionism. In fact, I believe that most social situations can be understood at an almost a limitless number of analytical 'levels'.

References

Aamodt, L. (1996) *Den gode relasjonen* [The good relation], Oslo: Ad Notam Gyldendal.

Abrahamson, P. (2000) 'The welfare modelling business', in N. Manning and I. Shaw (eds) *New risks, new welfare: Signposts for social policy,* Oxford: Blackwell, pp 57-78.

Ackerman, N. (1937) 'The family as a social and emotional unit', *Bulletin of the Kansas Mental Hygiene Society*, October.

Adams, C.M. (2006) 'The consequences of witnessing family violence on children and implications for family counsellors', *The Family Journal: Counselling and Therapy for Couples and Families*, vol 14, no 4, pp 334-41.

Adamson, P. (2007) *Child poverty in perspective: An overview of child well-being in rich countries* (Innocenti Report Card no 7), Florence: UNICEF Innocenti Research Centre.

Addams, J. (1902) *Democracy and social ethics*, Urbana and Chicago, IL: University of Illinois Press.

Addams, J. (1910) *Twenty years at Hull House*, New York: Macmillan.

Adorno, T.W., Frenkel-Brunswik, E., Levinsson, D. and Sanford, R. (1964/50) *The authoritarian personality: Studies in prejudice*, New York: John Wiley and Sons.

Ahrons, C.R. (1994) *The good divorce: Keeping your family together when your marriage comes apart*, New York: Harper Collins.

Airikka, S. (2003) *Parisuhteen roolikartta* [Role map of pair relationship], Helsinki: Kuntaliitto.

Aitamurto, T. (2004) '"Hyvien perheiden pojat murhasivat kylmästi – Miksi?". Syylliset ja syyttömät Heinojen surmaa seuranneen moraalisen myrskyn pyörteissä kolmessa sanomalehdessä' [Guys from good families murdered coldly – why?], master thesis, Jyväskylä: Jyväskylän yliopisto.

Alanen, L. (2000) 'Visions of a social theory of childhood', *Childhood*, vol 7, no 4, pp 493-500.

Alanen, L., Sauli, H. and Strandell, H. (2006) 'Children and childhood in a welfare state: the case of Finland', in A.-M. Jensen, C. Ben-Arieh Asher, D. Cinzia Kutsar, M. Nic Ghiolla Phádraig and H. Warming Nielsen (eds) *Children's welfare in aging Europe*, Trondheim: Norwegian Centre for Child Research, pp 145-209.

Andersson, B. (2007) *Diversity in residential care and treatment for young people in Sweden*, Göteborg: Göteborg University, Department of Psychology.

Angel, B.Ø. (2003) 'Evidensbaserte programmer – kunnskapsformer og menneskesyn i sosialt arbeid' [Evidence-based programmes: forms of knowledge and ideas of human beings in social work], *Nordisk Sosialt Arbeid*, vol 23, no 2, pp 66-71.

Anglin, J.P. (2002) *Pain, normality, and the struggle for congruence: Reinterpreting residential care for children and youth*, New York: Haworth Press.

Anttonen, A. and Sipilä, J. (1996) 'European social care services: is it possible to identify models?', *Journal of European Social Policy*, vol 6, no 2, pp 87-100.

Artaraz, K., Thurston, M. and Davies, S. (2007) 'Understanding family support provision within the context of prevention: a critical analysis of a local voluntary sector project', *Child and Family Social Work*, vol 12, no 4, pp 306-15.

Arter, D. (1999) *Scandinavian politics today*, Manchester: Manchester University Press.

Auta lasta ajoissa (2004) Lasten ja lapsiperheiden sosiaalipalvelujen arvioinnin erillisraportti Etelä-Suomen läänissä 2003 [Help the child on time: evaluation report of social services for children and families in the Region of Southern Finland 2003], Etelä-Suomen lääninhallituksen julkaisuja 87.

Backe-Hansen, E. (2004) *Barn og unges håndtering av vanskelige livsvilkår* [How children and young people cope with difficult life conditions] (NOVA-report 12-04), Oslo: Norsk institutt for forskning om oppvekst, velferd og aldring.

Bäck-Wiklund, M. (2000) '"Den demokratiska familjen" – det postmoderna samhällets grundbult?' ["The democratic family": foundation pillar of the postmodern society?], *Socialvetenskaplig tidskrift*, vol 7, nos 1-2, pp 44-56.

Bae, B. (1988) 'Voksnes definisjonsmakt og barns selvopplevelse' [Definitional power of the adults and self-exprience of the child], *Norsk Pedagogisk tidsskrift*, no 4.

Balkmar, D. and Pringle, K. (2005) *A review of academic studies relating to men's practices in Sweden*, Critical Research on Men in Europe (CROME), www.cromenet.org.

Balkmar, D., Iovanni, L. and Pringle, K. (2008) 'A reconsideration of two "welfare paradises": research and policy responses to men's violence in Denmark and Sweden', *Men and Masculinities*, vol 11 [online].

Bardy, M. (2001) 'Pikkulapsen sijoitus oman kodin ulkopuolelle – syrjäytymisen ja liittymisen risteytyskohta' [The placement of small children outside their homes – a juncture of exlusion and inclusion], in I. Järventie and H. Sauli (eds) *Eriarvoinen lapsuus*, Helsinki: WSOY, pp 47-82.

Bardy, M. (2006) 'Mitä meille ja meissä tapahtuu?' [What happens fo us and inside us?], in T. Helne and M. Laatu (eds) *Vääryyskirja*, Helsinki: Kelan tutkimusosasto, pp 241-53.

Bardy, M. and Känkänen, P. (2005) *Omat ja muiden tarinat: ihmisyyttä vaalimassa* [The stories of our own and others], Helsinki: Stakes.

Bardy, M., Salmi, M. and Heino, T. (2001) *Mikä lapsiamme uhkaa? Suuntaviivoja 2000-luvun lapsipoliittiseen keskusteluun* [What threatens our children? Guidelines for child politics of the 21st century] (Raportteja 263), Helsinki: Stakes.

Barth, R.P. (1994) *From child abuse to permanency planning: Child welfare services pathways and placements*, New York: Aldine de Gruyter.

Basaglia, F (1972) *Kumous laitosmaailmassa* [A revolution among the institutions], Helsinki: Tammi.

Bateson, G. (1972) *Steps to an ecology of mind*, New York: Ballantine Books.

Bauman, Z. (1991/95) *Modernity and ambivalence*, Cambridge: Polity Press.

Bauman, Z. (2000) *Liquid modernity*, Cambridge: Polity Press.

Bauman, Z. (2003/04) *Liquid love*, Cambridge: Polity Press.

Bauman, Z. (2004) *Identity*, Cambridge: Polity Press.

Beck, U. and Beck-Gernsheim, E. (2002) 'Individualisering i det moderne samfund – en subjektorienteret sociologis perspektiver og kontroverser' [Individualisation in the modern society: perspectives and controversies of a subject-oriented sociology], *Slagmark: Tidskrift for idéhistorie*, no 34, pp 13-38.

Beck, U., Giddens, A. and Lash, S. (1994) 'Living in the post-traditional society', in U. Beck, A. Giddens and S. Lash: *Reflexive modernization: Politics, tradition and aesthetics in the modern order*, Oxford: Blackwell, pp 56-110.

Beck-Gernsheim, E. (2002) *Reinventing the family: In search of new lifestyles*, Cambridge: Polity Press.

Bengtsson, M. and Persson, K. (2005) *Svenskt och norskt barnavårdsarbete. En jämförande studie av socialtjänstens konkreta barnavårdsarbete* [Swedish and Norwegian child welfare services: a comparative study of the specific child welfare work performed by social services], Lund: Lund University, School of Social Work.

Bergman, H. and Hobson, B. (2002) 'Compulsory fatherhood: the coding of fatherhood in the Swedish welfare state', in B. Hobson (ed) *Making men into fathers: Men, masculinities and the social politics of fatherhood*, Cambridge: Cambridge University Press, pp 92-124.

Best, J. (1990) *Threatened children: Rhetoric and concern about child-victims*, Chicago and London: University of Chicago Press.

Best, J. (2001) 'Telling the truth about damned lies and statistics: chronicle of higher education', *Education Research Complete*, vol 47, no 34, pp B7-B9.

Best, J. (2004) *More damned lies and statistics: How numbers confuse public issues*, Berkeley, CA, Los Angeles, CA and London: University of California Press.

Björklund, L. (2008) 'Kannustaminen ja moraali: Kannustamisen idea suomalaisessa yhteiskuntapolitiikassa 1990-luvulta alkaen' ['Incentives and morality: the Finnish activation policy since the 1990s'], PhD thesis, Department of Systematic Theology, Helsinki: University of Helsinki.

Björnberg, U. (1999) 'Familjens pligter og ansvar: Skandinaviske familier i Europea' [Family duties and responsibilities: Scandinavian families in Europe], in L. Dencik and P. Schultz Jørgensen (eds) *Børn og familie i det postmoderne samfund*, Copenhagen: Hans Reitzels Førlag, pp 503-30.

Björnberg, U. (2001) 'Cohabitation and marriage in Sweden: does family form matter?', *International Journal of Law, Policy and the Family*, vol 15, no 3, pp 350-62.

Björnberg, U. and Dahlgren. L. (2003) 'Policy: the case of Sweden', report for the project 'Welfare policy and employment in the context of family change', www.york.ac.uk/inst/spru/research/nordic/swedenpoli.pdf.

Björnberg, U. and Kollind, A.-K. (eds) (1996) *Men's family relations*, Stockholm: Almqvist and Wiksell.

Björnberg, U. and Latta, M. (2007) 'The roles of the family and welfare state: the relationship between public and private financial support in Sweden', *Current Sociology*, vol 55, no 3, pp 415-45.

Björnberg, U., Ólafsson, S. and Eydal, G.B. (2006) 'Education, employment and family formation: differing patterns', in J. Bradshaw and A. Hatland (eds) *Social policy, employment and family change in comparative perspective*, Cheltenham: Edward Elgar, pp 199-220.

Børnerådet i Danmark, Ombudsmandur på Island, Barneombudet i Norge, Barneombudsmannen i Sverige (1999) 'Barns beste i vår samtid. Et debattopplegg om barnas beste i et nordisk perspektiv' [The best interests of the child in our time – a discussion paper on the concept of the best interests of the child from a Nordic perspective], 22 September, www.barneombudet.no/sfiles/1/51/9/file/barns_beste_1999.pdf

Boszormenyi-Nagy, I. and Spark, G. (1973) *Invisible loyalties: Reciprocity of intergenerational family therapy*, London: Harper and Row.

Botnen Eide, S. (2001) 'Hvordan opplever barnevernets barn at barnevernet ser på dem?' [How do children experience the attention to them from child welfare?], in P. Repstad and A. Ryen (eds) *Verneverdig: barnevern, forskning og etikk*, Oslo: Fagbokforlaget, pp 197-216.

Bourdieu, P. (1996) 'On the family as a realized category', *Theory, Culture and Society*, vol 13, no 3, pp 19-26.

Bowen, M. (1978) *Family therapy in clinical practice*, New York: Jason Aronson.

Bradley, D. (1996) *Family law and political culture: Scandinavian laws in comparative perspective*, London: Sweet & Maxwell.

Bradshaw, J. and Hatland, A. (eds) (2006) *Social policy, employment and family change in comparative perspective*, Cheltenham: Edward Elgar.

Bradshaw, J. and Terum, J.I. (1997) 'How Nordic is the Nordic model? Social assistance in a comparative perspective', *Scandinavian Journal of Social Welfare*, vol 6, no 4, pp 247-56.

Bradshaw, J., Hoelscher, P. and Richardson, D. (2007) 'An index of child well-being in the European Union', *Social Indicators Research*, vol 80, no 1, pp 133-77.

Brah, A. (2001) 'Re-framing Europe: gendered racisms, ethnicities and nationalisms in contemporary Western Europe', in J. Fink, G. Lewis and J. Clarke (eds) *Rethinking European welfare: Transformations of Europe and social policy*, London: Sage, pp 207-30.

Brauns, H.-J. and Kramer, D. (1986) *Social work education in Europe: A comprehensive description of social work education in 21 European countries*, Frankfurt am Main: Eigenverlag des Deutsche Vereins für öffentliche unt private Fürsorge.

Brembeck, H., Johansson, B. and Kampmann, J. (eds) (2004) *Beyond the competent child: Exploring contemporary childhoods in the Nordic welfare societies*, Fredriksberg: Roskilde University Press.

Bremberg, S. (ed) (2004) *Nya verktyg för föräldrar – förslag till nya former av föräldrastöd* [New tools for parents: proposal for new forms of parent support] (R 2004:49), Stockholm: Statens folkhälsoinstitut, www.fhi.se/sv/Publikationer/Alla-publikationer/Nya-verktyg-for-foraldrar/

Bruner, J. (1990) *Acts of meaning*, London: Harvard University Press.

Bunkholdt, V. and Sandbæk, M. (1993) *Praktisk barnevernsarbeid* [Practical child welfare work], Oslo: Universitetsforlaget.

Bunkholdt, V. (2006) 'Barnets beste – mellom kontinuitet og stabilitet' [The best interest of the child: between continuity and stability], in R. Follesø (ed) *Sammen om barnevern Enestående fortellinger, felles utfordringer*, Oslo: Universitetsforlaget, pp 100-16.

Burr, V. (2004) *Social constructionism* (2nd edn), London: Routledge.

Calgraft, R. (2004) 'Children left home alone: the construction of a social problem', PhD thesis, Nottingham: University of Nottingham.

Castles, F.G. (ed) (1993) *Families of nations: Patterns of public policy in western democracies*, Aldershot: Dartmouth.

Chambon, A.S., Irving, A. and Epstein, L. (eds) (1999) *Reading Foucault for social work*, New York: Columbia University Press.

Christensen, P.M. and James, A. (2000) *Research with children: Perspectives and practices*, Brighton: Falmer.

Circular Q-0982 (1998) Guidelines on relief measure, cf the Child Welfare Act § 4-4, Oslo: Ministry of Children and Equality.

Clare, B. and Mevik, K. (2008) 'Inclusive education: teaching social work students to work with children', *Journal of Social Work*, vol 8, no 1, pp 28-44.

Claussen, C.J. and Tiller, P.O. (1997) 'Barnevern og barns ytringsfrihet' [Child protection and children's freedom of expression], *Norges barnevern*, vol 74, no 4, pp 5-13.

Cocozza, M. (2003) *Anmälningsplikten som instrument för att identifiera barn som behöver samhällets skydd* [Mandatory reporting as a means for identifying children in need of society's protection] (Rapport nr 26), Linköping: Hälsouniversitetet, Barn- och ungdomspsykiatriska klinikens vetenskapliga rapportserie.

Cocozza, M., Gustafsson, P.Å. and Sydsjö, G. (2007) 'Who suspects and reports child maltreatment to Social Services in Sweden? Is there a reliable mandatory reporting process?', *European Journal of Social Work*, vol 10, no 2, pp 209-23.

Cohen, S. (1972) *Folk devils and moral panics: The creation of the mods and rockers*, Oxford: Basil Blackwell.

Cooper, D. (1971) *Död åt familjen* [The death of the family], Stockholm: Bokförlaget Aldus/Bonniers.

Coppock, V. (1997) '"Mad", "bad" or "misunderstood"?', in P. Scraton (ed) *'Childhood' in 'crisis'?*, London and Bristol: UCL Press, pp 146-62.

Corsaro, W.A. (1997) *The sociology of childhood*, Thousand Oaks, CA: Pine Forge Press.

Crimmens, D. and Milligan, I. (eds) (2005) *Facing forward: Residential child care in the 21st century*, Lyme Regis: Russell House.

Danielsen, S. (2005) 'Foreldreansvar, innhold og beslutningsmulighet ved felles forerldreansvar – felles foreldreansvar i konfliktfylte familier' [Parental responsibility, contents and decision-making opportunities within joint custody: joint custody in conflict-full families], in *Nordiskt seminar om barnerett* (Tema Nord 2005:581), Copenhagen: Nordic Council of Ministers, pp 27-31.

Davis, A.F. (1973) *American heroine: The life and legend of Jane Addams*, New York: Oxford Unversity Press.

de los Reyes, P. and Mulinari, D. (2005) *Intersektionalitet* [Intersectionality], Malmö: Liber.

DfES (Department for Education and Skills) (2003) *Every child matters*, Green Paper, summary, Nottingham: DfES Publications, http://publications.everychildmatters.gov.uk/eOrderingDownload/ECM-Summary.pdf

Dolan, P., Canavan, J. and Pinkerton, J. (eds) (2006) *Family support as reflective practice*, London: Jessica Kingsley Publishers.

Draft UN Guidelines (2007) *For the appropriate use and conditions of alternative care for children*, 18 June, www.crin.org/docs/DRAFT_UN_Guidelines.pdf

Eder, D. and Fingerson, L. (2002) 'Interviewing children and adolescents', in J. Gubrium and J. Holstein (eds) *Handbook of interview research*, Thousand Oaks, CA: Sage, pp 181-201.

Edleson, J.F. (1999) 'Children's witnessing of adult domestic violence', *Journal of Interpersonal Violence*, vol 14, no 8, pp 839-70.

Einarsdóttir, H.R. and Ólafsdóttir, I.B. (2007) 'Greiðslur til foreldra ungra barna í Kópavogi og Reykjanesbæ' [Home care allowances to parents of young children in Kopavogur and Reykjanesbær], unpublished BA thesis, Reykjavík: University of Iceland, Department of Social Work.

Ejrnaes, M. and Kristiansen, S. (2002) 'Perspektiv på sociala problem i USA och Skandinavien' [Perspectives on social problems in the US and Scandinavia], in A. Meeuwisse and H. Swärd (eds) *Perspektiv på sociala problem*, Stockholm: Natur och Kultur, pp 73-93.

Ekeland, T.J. (2007) 'Evidensbasert toalettrening' [Evidence-based toilet cleaning], *Morgenbladet*, 21-27 September.

Ellingsæter, A.L. and Leira, A. (eds) (2006) *Politicising parenthood in Scandinavia: Gender relations in welfare states*, Bristol: Policy Press.

Elliot, J. (2005) *Using narrative in social research: Qualitative and quantitative research*, London: Sage.

Ericsson, K. (1996) *Barnevern som samfunnsspeil* [Child welfare as a society game], Oslo: Pax Forlag A/S.

Ericsson, K. and Simonsen, E. (eds) (2005) *Children of World War II: The hidden enemy legacy*, Oxford and New York: Berg.

Eriksson, L.D. (ed) (1967) *Pakkoauttajat* [The coersive helpers], Helsinki: Tammi.

Eriksson, M. and Näsman, E. (2008) 'Participation in family law proceedings for children whose father is violent to their mother', *Childhood*, vol 15, no 2, pp 259-75.

Eriksson, M., Cater, Å.K., Dahlkild-Öhman, G. and Näsman, E. (eds) (2008) *Barns röster om våld – att tolka och förstå* [Children's voices concerning violence: interpretation and understanding], Malmö: Gleerups.

Eriksson, M., Hester, M., Keskinen, S. and Pringle, K. (eds) (2005) *Tackling men's violence in families: Nordic issues and dilemmas*, Bristol: Policy Press.

Eronen, T. (2004) 'Kiusatut, etsijät, tyytyväiset ja rikkaat – erilaista häpeästä selviytymistä lastensuojelun asiakkaiden omaelämäkerroissa' [The bullied, the searchers, the satisfied and the rich: different coping strategies of shame in child protection clients autobiographies], *Janus*, vol 12, no 4, pp 359-78.

Eronen,T. (2007) *Katsaus 2000-luvulla julkaistuun suomalaiseen lastensuojelututkimukseen* [A review of the Finnish research on child protection], Sosiaalialan kehittämishanke, Lastensuojelun kehittämisohjelma, www.sosiaaliportti.fi/fi-FI/lastensuojelunkasikirja/tuke/lastensuojeluntutkimuskatsaus/.

Eronen, T. and Laakso, R. (2006) '"The ordinary": preliminary findings and conceptualisation of "the ordinary" in children's homes', in A. Oksanen, E. Paavilainen and T. Pösö (eds) (2006) *Comparing children, families and risks* (Childhood and Family Research Unit Net Series 2/2006),Tampere:Tampere University Press, pp 76-87.

Eskonen, I., Korpinen, J. and Raitakari, S. (2006) 'Vallan määrittämät lapsi–ja asiantuntijapuhujat: faktaa, selontekoja ja kokemuksia' [Child and expert speakers defined by power: facts, accounts and experiences], in H. Forsberg, A. Ritala-Koskinen and M. Törrönen (eds) *Lapset ja sosiaalityö*, Jyväskylä: PS-kustannus, pp 21-44.

Esping-Andersen, G. (1990) *Three worlds of welfare capitalism*, Cambridge: Polity Press.

Eurostat (2008) *Population and social conditions*, www.epp.eurostat.ec.europa.eu.

Eydal, G.B. (2005) 'Childcare policies of the Nordic welfare states: different paths to enable parents to earn and care?', in B. Pfau-Effinger and B. Geissler (eds) *Care and social integration in European societies*, Bristol: Policy Press, pp 153-72.

Eydal, G.B. and Gislason, I. (eds) (2008) *Equal rights to earn and care: Parental leave in Iceland*. Reykjavik: Felagsvisindastofnun Haskola Islands.

Eydal, G.B. and Ólafsson, S. (2008) 'Family policy in Iceland: an overview', in I. Ostner and C. Schmitt (eds) *Family policies in the context of family change:The Nordic countries in comparative perspective*,Wiesbaden:Verlag fur Sozialwissenschaften, pp 109-27.

Eydal, G.B. and Jeans, C.L. (2006) 'Children, consumption and poverty', in *Child and teen consumption 2006*, Copenhagen: Copenhagen Business School, www.cbs.dk/forskning_viden/konferencer/ctc2006/menu/papers.

Eydal, G.B. and Satka M. (2006) 'Social work and Nordic welfare policies for children – present challenges in the light of the past', *European Journal of Social Work*, vol 9, no 3, pp 305-22.

Fantuzzo, J. and Mohr, W. (1999) 'Prevalence and effects of child exposure to domestic violence', *The Future of Children*, vol 9, no 3, pp 21-32.

Featherstone, B. (2001) 'Putting fathers on the child welfare agenda', *Child and Family Social Work*, vol 6, no 2, pp 179-86.

Featherstone, B. (2004) *Family life and family support: A feminist analysis*, London: Palgrave/Macmillan.

Featherstone, B. (2006) 'Rethinking family support in the current policy context', *British Journal of Social Work*, vol 36, no 1, pp 5-19.

Finch, N. (2006) 'Childcare and parental leave', in J. Bradshaw and A. Hatland (eds) *Social policy, employment and family change in comparative perspective*, Cheltenham: Edward Elgar, pp 119-42.

Flaquer, L. (2007) *Family change and child poverty in comparative perspective* (Wellchi Working Paper Series no 1/2007), Barcelona: Children's Well-being International Documentation Centre.

Follesø, R. (ed) (2006) *Sammen om barnevern. Enestående fortellinger, felles utfordringer* [Together about child welfare: unique stories, shared challenges], Oslo: Universitetsforlaget.

Forsberg, H. (1994) *Yksi ja monta perhettä. Tutkimus sosiaalityöntekijöiden perhetulkinnoista sosiaalitoimistotyössä* [One and many families: a study about social workers' family interpretations] (Tutkimuksia 42), Helsinki: Stakes.

Forsberg, H. (1995) 'Sosiaalitoimiston isä: kaivattu, toivoton ja uhkaava' [A father in the social work office: missing, hopeless and threatening], in L. Eräsaari, R. Julkunen and H. Silius (eds) *Naiset yksityisen ja julkisen rajalla*, Tampere: Vastapaino, pp 132-49.

Forsberg, H. (1998) *Perheen ja lapsen tähden. Etnografia kahdesta lastensuojelun asiantuntijakulttuurista* [For the sake of the family and the child: an ethnography of two expert cultures within child welfare], Helsinki: Lastensuojelun keskusliitto.

Forsberg, H. (2002) 'Children's feedback on helping practices of shelters', in *Gender and violence in the Nordic countries* (TemaNord 2002:545), Copenhagen: Nordic Council of Ministers, pp 307-20.

Forsberg, H. (2005) '"Talking feels like you wouldn't love dad anymore": children's emotions, close relations', in M. Eriksson, M. Hester, S. Keskinen, and K Pringle (eds) *Tackling men's violence in families: Nordic issues and dilemmas*, Bristol: Policy Press, pp 49-65.

Forsberg, H. (2006) 'Tunteet työssä: esimerkkinä sosiaalityönä tehtävä ihmissuhdetyö' [Emotions in work: social work as an example], in K. Määttä (ed) *Tunteet ja tunteiden tulkit,* Helsinki: Finn Lectura, pp 27-44.

Forsberg, H. and Vagli, Å. (2006) 'The social construction of emotions in child protection case-talk', *Qualitative Social Work*, vol 5, no 1, pp 9-31.

Forsberg, H., Kuronen, M., Pösö, T. and Ritala-Koskinen, A. (1994) 'Perheongelmat ja asiantuntijakäytännöt' [Family problems and professional practices] in M. Heikkilä and K. Vähätalo (eds) *Huono-osaisuus ja hyvinvointivaltion muutos*, Helsinki: Gaudeamus,, pp 212-26.

Forssén, K. (1991) *Asiakasperheet lastensuojelun sosiaalityössä* [Client families in social work of child protection] (sarja A:31), Turku: Turun yliopisto, Sosiaalipolitiikan julkaisuja.

Forssén, K. (2006) 'Lapsiperheiden hyvinvoinnin muutossuunnat 2000-luvun Suomessa' [The changing trends of welfare for families with young children in the 2000s], in L. Hokkanen and M. Sauvola (eds) *Puhumattomat paikat. Puheenvuoroja perheestä* (Pohjois-Suomen sosiaalialan osaamiskeskuksen julkaisusarja 22), Oulu: Pohjois-Suomen sosiaalialan osaamiskeskus, pp 101-14.

Forssén K., Laukkanen, A.-M. and Ritakallio, V.M. (2003) 'Policy: the case of Finland', report for the project 'Welfare policy and employment in the context of family change', www.york.ac.uk/inst/spru/research/nordic/finlandpoli.pdf.

Foucault, M. (1972) *The archaeology of knowledge,* London: Tavistock.

Foucault, M. (1973) *The birth of the clinic*, London: Tavistock Publications.

Fox Harding, L. (1996) *Family, state and social policy*, London: Macmillan.

Fox Piven, F. and Cloward, R.A. (1971) *Regulating the poor: The functions of public welfare*, New York: Vintage Books.

Francis, J., Kendrick, A. and Pösö, T. (2007) 'On the margin? Residential care in Scotland and Finland', *European Journal of Social Work*, vol 10, no 3, pp 337-72.

Frankfurt, H.G. (2005) *On bullshit,* Princeton, NJ: Princeton University Press.

Freire, P. (2003) *Pedagogy of the oppressed*, New York: Continuum.

Frønes, I. (1995) *Among peers: On the meaning of peers in the process of socialization,* Oslo: Scandinavian University Press.

Garbarino, J. (1992) *Children and families in the social environment*, New York: Aldine de Gruyter.

Gaskin, K. and Smith, J.D. (1995) *A new civic Europe? A study of the extent and role of volunteering*, London: Volunteer Centre.

Gergen, K.J. (1991) *The saturated self: Dilemmas of identity in contemporary life*, New York: Basic Books.

Gergen, K.J. (2001) *Social construction in context*, London: Sage.

Gilbert, N. (ed) (1997) *Combating child abuse: International perspectives and trends*, New York and Oxford: Oxford University Press.

Gillies, V. (2005) 'Meeting parents' needs? Discourses of "support" and "inclusion" in family policy', *Critical Social Policy*, vol 25, no 1, pp 70-90.

Gisholt, M.A. (2007) *Barns rett til å bli hørt ved omsorgsovertakelse* [Children's right to be heard in taking the child into care], Oslo: Universitetet i Oslo, Juridisk fakultet, Spesialoppgave.

Goffman, E. (1961) *Asylums: Essays on the social situation of mental patients and other inmates*, New York: Doubleday Anchor.

Goldson, B. (1997) '"Childhood": an introduction to historical and theoretical analyses', in P. Scraton (ed) *'Childhood' in 'crisis'?*, London and Bristol: UCL Press, pp 1-27.

Gómez de León del Río, J. and Guzmán, J.V. (2006) 'The impact of absence: families, migration, and family therapy in Ocotepec, Mexico', in G. Bacigalupe and J. Roberts (eds) *Immigrant families and immigration: Therapeutic work*, Washington DC: AFTA.

Gould, A. (1988) *Control and conflict in welfare policy: The Swedish experience*, London: Longman.

Grinde, T.V. (1989) *Barn og barnevern i Norden* [Children and child welfare in the Nordic countries], Oslo: Nordisk Ministerråd.

Grinde, T.V. (2007) 'Nordic child welfare services: variations in norms, attitudes and practice', *Journal of Children's Services*, vol 2, no 4, pp 44-58.

Guðbrandsson, B. (2006) *Rights of children at risk and in care: Report*, Strasbourg: Council of Europe.

Gulbrandsen, L. and Langsether, A. (2002) 'Svekkes familjesolidariteten?' [Is family solidarity breaking down?], paper presented at the Nordic Sociological Conference, Reykjavík, 15-17 August.

Haaland, T., Clausen, S.-E. and Schei, B. (2005) *Vold i parforhold – ulike perspektiver. Resultater fra den förste landsdekkende undersökelsen i Norge* [Violence in couples: different perspectives. Results from the first national study in Norway], Oslo: Norsk institutt for by-og regionforskning (NIBR).

Haas, L. and Hwang, P. (1999) 'Parental leave in Sweden', in P. Moss and F. Deven (eds) *Parental leave: Progress or pitfall? Research and policy issues in Europe* (vol 35), Hague and Brussels: NIDI CBGS Publications, pp 45-68.

Haavind, H. and Magnusson, E. (2005) 'The Nordic countries: welfare paradises for women and children?', *Feminism and Psychology*, vol 15, no 2, pp 227-35.

Habermas, J. (1963/1973) *Theory and practice*, Boston, MA: Beacon Press.

Hagen, G. (2001) *Barnevernets historie – om makt og avmakt i det 20. århundre* [History of child welfare: about power and powerlessness during the 20th century], Oslo: Akribe.

Hänninen, S., Karjalainen, J. and Lahti, T. (2005) (eds) *Toinen tieto. Kirjoituksia huono-osaisuuden tunnistamisesta* [The other knowledge: writings about recognising marginalisation], Helsinki: Stakes.

Hansson, K., Hedenbro, M., Lundblad, A.-M., Sundelin, J. and Wirtberg, I. (2001) *Familjebehandling på goda grunder: En forskningsbaserad översikt* [Well-grounded family programmes: a research-based overview], Stockholm: Gothia.

Harder, M. and Pringle, K. (eds) (1997) *Protecting children in Europe: Towards a new millennium*, Aalborg: Aalborg University Press.

Harder, M. and Pringle, K. (2007) 'De velfaerdsstatslige betingelser for empowerment i England og Danmark' [The characteristics of welfare empowerment in England and Denmark], in M.A. Nissen, K. Pringle and L. Uggerhöj (eds) *Magt og forandra i socialt arbejde*, Copenhagen: Akademisk Forlag, pp 116-29.

Hårtveit, H. and Jensen, P. (1999) *Familien – pluss én. Innføring i familieterapi* [The family: plus one. An introduction in family therapy], Oslo: Tano Ascheoug.

Havnen, K., Christiansen, Ø. and Havik, T. (1998) *Når gir barneverntjenesten hjelp? Kartlegging av barneverntjenesta sine beslutningar i meldings- og undersøkelsessaker* [When do child welfare services provide help? A survey of the decisions of child welfare services concerning referrals and inquiries] (Rapport no 2/98), Bergen: Barnevernets Utviklingssenter på Vestlandet.

HE 252/2006 vp (2006) *Hallituksen esitys Eduskunnalle lastensuojelulaiksi ja eräiksi siihen liittyviksi laeiksi* [The government's legislative proposal for a child welfare act put before the parliament], www.finlex.fi/fi/esitykset/he/2006/20060252

Healy, K. (2005) *Social work theories in context: Creating frameworks for practice*, Basingstoke: Palgrave Macmillan.

Healy, K. (undated) 'Participatory knowledge creation in social work: recognising diversity, promoting collaboration', unpublished paper.

Hearn, J. and Pringle, K. with members of Critical Research on Men in Europe (2006a) *European perspectives on men and masculinities*, Houndmills: Palgrave.

Hearn, J. and Pringle, K. (2006b) 'Men, masculinities and children: some European perspectives', *Critical Social Policy*, vol 26, no 2, pp 365-89.

Hearn, J., Pösö, T., Korpinen, J., Smith, C. and Whyte, S. (2004) 'What is child protection/lastensuojelu? Historical and methodological issues in comparative research on lastensuojelu/child protection', *International Journal of Social Welfare*, vol 13, no 1, pp 28-41.

Heinämäki, L. (2005) *Varhaista tukea lapselle - työvälineenä kehittämisvalikko* [Early support for a child] (Oppaita 62), Helsinki: Stakes.

Heino, T. (1999) 'Laitoskyselyaineisto. Perhetyö ja perhekuntoutus, alustavia tuloksia. Lastensuojelun työkalupakki perhetyön ja perhekuntoutuksen osalta' [A survey on residential care, preliminary results. A seminar paper], Stakes, Huostaanottoprojekti 1997-2001, Työkokous Helsinki, 28 May.

Heino, T. (ed) (2001) *Familjerådslag - den nya metoden inom socialt arbete* [Family group conference: a new method in social work] (Handböcker 42), Helsingfors: Stakes.

Heino, T. (2006) Voiko hyvän nimissä tehdä pahaa? Miten tämä todennetaan? Entä miten paha vältetään? [Is it possible to do evil in the name of good? How do you document it? How do you avoid it?], paper presented at 42 Valtakunnalliset lastensuojelupäivät, Aulanko, Hämeenlinna, 19 October.

Heino, T. (2007) *Ketkä ovat uudet lastensuojelun asiakkaat? Tutkimus lapsista ja perheistä tilastolukujen takana* [Who are the new clients of child welfare? A study of the children and families behind the statistics] (Työpapereita 30/2007), Helsinki: Stakes.

Heino, T. (2008) *Lastensuojelun avohuolto ja perhetyö: kehitys, nykytila, haasteet ja kehittämisehdotukset* [Child welfare and family work: development, the state of art, challenges and suggestions] (Työpapereita 9/2008), Helsinki: Stakes.

Heino, T. and Pösö, T. (2003) 'Tilastot ja tarinat lastensuojelun tietolähteinä' [Statistics and narratives as sources of child welfare knowledge], *Yhteiskuntapolitiikka*, vol 68, no 6, pp 584-96.

Heino,T., Berg, K. and Hurtig, J. (2000) *Perhetyön ilo ja hämmennys. Lastensuojelun perhetyömuotojen esittelyä ja jäsennyksiä* [Joy and confusion in family work] (Aiheita 14/2000), Helsinki: Stakes.

Heino,T., Kuoppala,T. and Säkkinen, S. (2005) *Lastensuojelun avohuollon tilaston haasteet; kuntakyselyn yhteenveto* [Challenges for the statistics of open care child welfare] (Työpapereita 5/2005), Helsinki: Stakes.

Helavirta, S. (2007) 'Lapset, survey ja hyvinvointi: metodologisia haasteita ja mahdollisuuksia' [Children, survey and welfare: methodological challenges and options], *Janus*, vol 15, no 1, pp 19-34.

Helminen, M.-L. and Iso-Heiniemi, M. (1999) *Vanhemmuuden roolikartta* [Role map of parenthood], Helsinki: Suomen kuntaliitto.

Hendrick, H. (2003) *Child welfare: Historical dimensions, contemporary debate*, Bristol: Policy Press.

Henning, K., Leitenberg, H., Coffey, P.,Turner,T. and Bennett, R.T. (1996) 'Long-term psychological and social impact of witnessing physical conflict between parents', *Journal of Interpersonal Violence*, vol 11, no 1, pp 35-51.

Hessle, S. and Vinnerljung, B. (1999) *Child welfare in Sweden: An overview* (Stockholm Studies in Social Work no 14), Stockholm: Stockholm University, Department of Social Work.

Hetherington, R. (2002) 'Learning from difference: comparing child welfare systems', keynote address at the 'Positive systems of child welfare conference', Waterloo, 20-21 June, www.wlu.ca/pcfproject.

Hiilamo, H. (2002) *The rise and fall of Nordic family policy? Historical development and changes during the 1990s in Sweden and Denmark*, Helsinki: Stakes.

Hiilamo, H. (2007) 'Promoting children's welfare in the Nordic countries', report presented at 'Seminarium om skapandet av en sund utvecklingsmiljö för barn och unga', 8-9 November, Esbo, Finland.

Hiilamo, H. (2008) *Promoting children's welfare in the Nordic countries* (Reports 2008:15), Helsinki: Ministry of Social Affairs and Health.

Hjelmtveit, V. (2004) *Barn og unge i familier med langvarig økonomisk sosialhjelp* [Children and young people in families with long-term financial welfare assistance] (Report no 43-04), Oslo: Oslo University College.

Hochschild, A. (2003) *The commercialization of intimate life: Notes from home and work*, Berkeley, CA: University of California Press.

Hoffman, L. (1981) *Foundations of family therapy*, New York: Basic Books.

Holden, G.A., Geffner, R. and Jouriles, E.N. (1998) *Children exposed to marital violence:Theory, research and applied issues*,Washington, DC:American Psychological Association.

Holland, S. (2004) *Child and family assessment in social work practice*, London, Thousand Oaks, CA and New Delhi: Sage.

Home Office and Voluntary and Community Unit (1998) *Supporting families: A consultation document*, London:The Stationery Office, www.nationalarchives.gov.uk/ERORecords/HO/421/2/acu/sfpages.pdf

Hort, S.E. and McMurphy S.C. (1997) 'Sweden', in N.S. Mayadas, T.D. Watts and D. Elliott (eds) *International handbook on social work theory and practice*, Westport, CT and London: Greenwood Press.

Huhtanen, P., Rintala, T. and Karvonen, S. (2005) 'Sosiaali-ja terveysmenojen alueelliset erot ja hyvinvointi kunnassa' [Regional differences in social and health expenditure and welfare in local municipalities], *Yhteiskuntapolitiikka*, vol 70, no 2, pp 132-42.

Hukkanen, R. (2002) *Psychosocial problems of children placed in children's homes*, Turku: Turun yliopisto.

Hurtig, J. (2003) *Lasta suojelemassa. Etnografia lasten paikan rakentumisesta lastensuojelun perhetyön käytännöissä* [Protecting children: an ethnography of the place of the child constructed in family work practices] (Acta Universitas Lapponisensis 60), Rovaniemi: Lapin yliopisto.

Husby, I.S.D. (2000) '"og så må jeg treffe barnet" – en kvalitativ studie av klientarbeid med barn ved undersøkelser ["and then I have to meet the child" – a qualitative study of social work with children in child protection investigations], master thesis, Trondheim: Norwegian University of Science and Technology (NTNU), Department of Social Work.

Hussain, M.A. (2003) *Børnefattigdom i de danske kommuner 1984-2001* [Child poverty in Danish municipalities 1984-2001], Copenhagen: Socialforskningsinstituttet/ Red Barnet.

Hydén, M. (1994) *Woman battering as marital act: The construction of a violent marriage*, Oslo: Scandinavian University Press.

Hydén, M. (2000) 'Forskningsintervjun som relationell praktik' [Research interview as relational practice], in H. Haavind (ed) *Kjönn og fortolkende metode. Metodiske muligheter i kvalitativ forskning*, Oslo: Gyldendal Norsk Forlag, pp 220-59.

Hydén, M. (2005) '"I must have been an idiot to let it go on": agency and positioning in battered women's narratives of leaving', *Feminism and Psychology*, vol 15, no 2, pp 171-90.

Hydén, M. (2008) 'Narrating sensitive topics', in M. Andrews, C. Squire and M. Tamboukou (eds) *Doing narrative research*, London: Sage, pp 121-36.

Hyytiäinen, T. and Ouni, A. (2000) *Ihmisenä ihmiselle. Asiakasperheiden kokemuksia perhetyöstä* [From person to person: experiences of service user families in family work], Jyväskylä: Jyväskylän ammattikorkeakoulu, Opinnäytetyö, Sosiaalialan koulutusohjelma.

Illich, I. (1972) *Deschooling society*, New York: Harper and Row.

Iovanni, L. and Pringle, K. (2005) *A review of academic studies relating to men's practices in Denmark*, Critical Research on Men in Europe (Crome), www.cromenet.org.

Jacobs, L. and Wachs, C. (2002) *Parent therapy: A relational alternative to working with children*, New York: Jason Aronson.

Jaffe, P.G., Wolfe, D.A. and Wilson, S.K. (1990) *Children of battered women*, Newsbury Park, CA: Sage.

Jallinoja, R. (2006) *Perheen vastaisku. Familistista käännettä jäljittämässä* [The backlash of the family: tracking down the familistic turn], Helsinki: Gaudeamus.

James, A. and James, A. (2004) *Constructing childhood: Theory, policy and social practice*, Basingstoke: Palgrave Macmillan.

James, A. and James, A. (2008) *European childhoods: Cultures, politics and childhoods in Europe*, Basingstoke: Palgrave Macmillan.

James, A., Jenks, C. and Prout, A. (1998) *Theorizing childhood*, Cambridge: Polity.

Jamieson, L. (1988) *Intimacy: Personal relationships in modern societies*, Cambridge, Polity.

Jenks, C. (1996) 'The Postmodern Child', in J. Brannen and M. O'Brien (eds) *Children in families*, London: Falmer Press, pp 13-25.

Jensen A.M. (1999) 'Fra faderkontroll til moderansvar' [From paternal control to maternal responsibility], in A.M. Jensen, E. Backe-Hansen, H. Bache-Wiig, H. and K. Heggen (eds) *Oppvekst i barnets århundre*, Oslo: adNotam Gyldendal, pp 63-78.

Johansson, J. (2007) *Residential care for young people in Sweden: Home, staff and residents*, Göteborg: Göteborg University, Department of Psychology.

Jonsdottir, A.O. and Snaebjornsdottir, S.L. (2005) 'Family values in Iceland: a discourse analysis', Reykjavik, unpublished report.

Júlíusdóttir, S. (1993) 'Den kapabla familjen i det isländska samhället' [The capable family in the Icelandic society], doctoral thesis, Göteborg and Reykjavík: Göteborgs Universitet and Félagsvísindastofnun Háskóla Íslands.

Júlíusdóttir, S. (1997) 'An Icelandic study of five parental life styles: conditions of fathers without custody and mothers with custody', *Journal of Divorce and Remarriage*, vol 26, nos 3/4, pp 87-103.

Júlíusdóttir, S. (1999) 'Humanism – voluntarism - professionalism. Om frivilligt arbete i Island' [Humanism, voluntarism, professionalism: about voluntary work in Iceland], in *Frivilligt socialt arbete, forskning och förmedling* (1999/13), Göteborg: NopusRapport, pp 11-7.

Júlíusdóttir, S. (2004) 'Theorizing practice: target and tools in the transformation process', *SSKH Notat*, vol 20, no 1, pp 31-46.

Júlíusdóttir, S. (2007) 'Young people and changing families: young adults' experiences, expectations, views and values. Extended and extending families', paper presented at CRFR International Conference, Edinburgh, June.

Júlíusdóttir, S. (2008) 'Young people and intergenerational relationships: experiences, views and values. Cultures, generations and family interactions', paper presented at 4th Congress of the European Society on Family Relations (ESFR), September, Jyväskylä.

Júlíusdóttir, S. and Karlsson, T. (2007) 'Some indications for professional development in social work: a study of theoretical interest and attitudes towards research among Icelandic social workers', *European Journal of Social Work*, vol 10, no 1, pp 21-39.

Júlíusdóttir, S. and Peterson, J. (2004) 'Nordic standards revisited', *Social Work Education*, vol 23, no 5, pp 567-79.

Júlíusdóttir, S. and Sigurðardóttir, S. (1997) *Hvers vegna sjálfboðastörf? Um sjálfboðastarf, félagsmálastefnu og félagsráðgjöf* [Why volunteering? Perspectives on social policy and social work practice], Reykjavík: Háskólaútgáfan.

Júlíusdóttir, S. and Sigurðardóttir, N.K. (2000) *Áfram foreldrar. Rannsókn um sameiginlega forsjá og velferð barna við skilnað foreldra* [Still parents: research on joint custody and welfare of children after parental divorce], Reykjavík: Háskólaútgáfan.

Júlíusdóttir, S. and Sigurðardóttir, N.K. (2005) 'Réttur barna og velferð við skilnað foreldra − Um lýðræðishugsun og hagsmuni' [Rights and welfare of children when parents divorce: democratical thinking and interests], *Tímarit lögfræðinga*, vol 55, no 2, pp 183-96.

Julkunen, R. (2001) *Suunnanmuutos. 1990-luvun sosiaalipoliittinen reformi Suomessa* [Change of direction: the social policy reform of the 1990s in Finland], Tampere: Vastapaino.

Julkunen, R. (2006) 'Perhe, työ, hoiva ja valtio − oma ja yhteinen, yksityinen ja julkinen hoivavastuu' [Family, work, caring and the state: own and shared, private and public care responsibility], in L. Hokkanen and M. Sauvola (eds) *Puhumattomat paikat. Puheenvuoroja perheestä*, (Pohjois-Suomen sosiaalialan osaamiskeskuksen julkaisusarja 22) Oulu: Pohjois-Suomen sosiaalialan osaamiskeskus, pp 15-45.

Juul, R. (2004) 'Barnevernarbeideres barneperspektiv og praksiser i møte med barn og unge i vanskelige livssituasjoner' [Child protection workers' child perspectives and practices with children and young people in difficult life situations], *Norges barnevern*, vol 81, no 1, pp 11-22.

Juul, S. (2002) 'Modernitet, velfærd og solidaritet. En studie om moderne danskeres solidaritet i tanke og i handling' [Modernity, welfare and solidarity: a study on solidarity in thought and action of modern Danes], *Politiken*, 29 April.

Kaikko, K. (2004) *Lastensuojelun avoperhetyön kuntoutumista tukevat elementit* [Supportive elements of rehabilitation in child welfare family work], Kuopio: Kuopion yliopisto, Lapsi-ja nuorisososiaalityön ammatillinen lisensiaattityö.

Kaipio, K.(1977) *Antakaa meille mahdollisuus. Johdatus nuorten yhteisökasvatukseen* [Give us a chance: an introduction to community-based education for young people], Jyväskylä: Gummerus.

Kallinen-Kräkin, S. (ed) (2008) *Sosiaalialan kehittämishanke 2003-2007. Loppuraportti* [Final report of the national development programme on social welfare] (2008:6), Helsinki: Sosiaali- ja terveysministeriön selvityksiä.

Känkänen P. and Laaksonen S. (2006) *Selvitys sijaishuollon ja jälkihuollon nykytilasta ja kehittämistarpeista* [Report of current situation and developmental needs in substitute care and leaving care], www.sosiaaliportti.fi/File/7d9702b1-7343-49cf-a3e8-36d4ceb9ead1/Loppuraportti.pdf.

Kemppainen, S.-L. (2006) 'Itseltään huostaan otetut: huumetaustaiset pojat lastensuojelulaitoksessa' [In care: boys with drug-abuse background in a children's home'], licentiate thesis, Rovaniemi: University of Lapland, Department of Social Work.

Kendrick, A. (2008) 'Introduction: residential child care', in A. Kendrick (ed) *Residential child care: Prospects and challenges,* London:Jessica Kingsley, pp 7-18.

Khan, P. and Dominelli, L. (2000) 'The impact of globalization on social work in the UK', *European Journal of Social Work,* vol 3, no 2, pp 95-108.

Khoo, E. (2004) 'Protecting our children: a comparative study of the dynamics of structure, intervention and their interplay in Swedish child welfare and Canadian child protection', doctoral thesis, Umeå: University of Umeå: Department of Social Work.

Khoo, E.G., Hyvönen, U. and Nygren, L. (2002) 'Child welfare and child protection. uncovering Swedish and Canadian orientations to social intervention in child maltreatment', *Qualitative Social Work,* vol 1, no 4, pp 451-71.

Killén, K. (1991) *Sveket* [Betrayed], Oslo: Kommuneforlaget.

Kilpatrick, K.L. and Williams, L.M. (1998) 'Potential mediators of post-traumatic stress disorder in child witnesses to domestic violence', *Child Abuse and Neglect,* vol 22, no 4, pp 319-30.

Kitinoja, M. (2005) *Kujan päässä koulukoti. Tutkimus koulukoteihin sijoitettujen lasten lastensuojeluasiakkuudesta ja kouluhistoriasta* [At the end of the road, a reform school: a study of child welfare clienting and school history of children placed in reform schools] (Report 150), Helsinki: Stakes.

Kjørholt, A.T. and Lidén, H. (2004) 'Children and youth as citizens: symbolic participants or political actors?', in H. Brembeck, B. Johansson and J. Kampmann (eds) *Beyond the competent child: Exploring contemporary childhoods in the Nordic welfare societies,* Fredriksberg: Roskilde University Press, pp 63-88.

Kliman, J. (2001/02) 'In search of Tikkun Olam: after September 11', *AFTA Newsletter,* winter, pp 35-6.

Korkiakangas, M. (2005) *Perheen voimavaroja etsimässä. Tapaustutkimus asiakaslähtöisistä orientaatioista lastensuojelun perhetyössä* [Searching for the strengths of families: a case study of user-centred orientation in child welfare family work], Rovaniemi: Lapin yliopisto, Lapsi- ja nuorisososiaalityön lisensiaattityö.

Kristmundsson, O.H. and Hrafnsdottir, S. (eds) (2008) *Stjórnun og rekstur félagasamtaka* [Managing nonprofit organizations], Reykjavík: Háskólaútgáfan.

Kuhn, T. (1962/80) *The structure of scientific revolutions,* Chicago: University of Chicago Press.

Kuronen, M. (1999) 'The social organisation of motherhood: advice giving in maternity and child health care in Scotland and Finland', PhD thesis, Stirling: University of Stirling.

Kyrönseppä, U. and Rautiainen, J.-M. (1993) *Lapsi laitoksessa* [A child in an institution], Porvoo: WSOY.

Laakso, R. (2008) 'Lasten suojelutyö lastenkodissa – etnografia lastenkotityön sisällöstä' [Doing child protection work in a children's home: an ethnographic study], University of Tampere, Department of Social Work, unpublished manuscript.

Lääninhallitusten keskeiset arviot peruspalvelujen tilasta 2003 (2004) [Estimates of the regional councils concerning the state of basic services in 2003] (Sisäasiainministeriön julkaisu 27/2004), Helsinki: Sisäasianministeriö.

Labov, W. and Waletzky, J. (1967) 'Narrative analysis: oral versions of personal experience', in J. Helm (ed) *Essays on the verbal and visual arts*, Seattle, WA: University of Washington Press, pp 12-44.

Lahtinen, P. (2008) *Perhetyön menetelmät opiskelijoiden teksteissä. Tutkimus perhetyön opiskelijoiden menetelmäkuvauksista* [Methods of family work in student texts], Jyväskylä: Jyväskylän yliopisto, Lapsi- ja nuorisososiaalityön erityisalan lisensiaatintyö.

Laing, R.D. (1972) *The politics of the family and other essays*, New York: Vintage Books.

Laki lapsen huollosta ja tapaamisoikeudesta (1983) [Child Custody and Right of Access Act], Finland, 361/1983.

Laki sosiaalihuollon ammatillisen henkilöstön kelpoisuusvaatimuksista (2005) [Act on Qualification Requirements for Social Welfare Professionals], Finland, 272/2005.

Lapsi- ja nuorisopolitiikan kehittämisohjelma 2007-2011 (2007) [Childhood and youth policy development programme] Opetusministeriön julkaisuja 2007:41, Helsinki: Opetusministeriö.

Larsson, S. (2000) 'Det sociala arbetets intresseorganisationer' [The interest organisations within social work], in A. Meeuwisse, S. Sunesson and H. Swärd (eds) *Socialt arbete. En grundbok* [Social work: A reader], Stockholm: Natur och Kultur, pp 47-61.

Lastensuojelu 2005 (2006) [Child welfare 2005] (Statistical summary 14/2006), Helsinki: Stakes, www.stakes.fi/FI/tilastot/aiheittain/Lapsuusjaperhe/lastensuojelu.htm.

Lastensuojelu 2007 (2008) [Child welfare 2007] (Statistical summary 23/2008), Helsinki: Stakes, www.stakes.fi/FI/tilastot/aiheittain/Lapsuusjaperhe/lastensuojelu.htm.

Lastensuojelulain kokonaisuudistustyöryhmän muistio (2006) [Memorandum of the reform working group on the Child Welfare Act] (Selvityksiä 2006: 25), Helsinki: Sosiaali- ja terveysministeriö.

Lastensuojelulaki (1983) [Child Welfare Act], Finland, 683/1983.

Lastensuojelulaki (2007) [Child Welfare Act], Finland, 417/2007, www.finlex.fi/fi/laki/alkup/2007/20070417.

Laurila, A. (2008) *Barnskyddsanmälningar och interventioner – En studie om barnskyddsanmälningarnas innehåll och barnskyddsarbetarnas interventioner i Björkby* [Child welfare reports and interventions: a study of the content of child welfare reports and the social workers' interventions in Björkby], Helsinki: University of Helsinki, Swedish School of Social Science, Notat.

Lee, N. (2001) *Childhood and society: Growing up in an age of uncertainty*, Maidenhead: Open University Press.

Leinonen, A. (2003) 'Kodinhoitaja perhetyössä: universaalista sosiaalipalvelusta kohdennettuun täsmätyöhön avohuollon lastensuojeluperheissä' [The home helper in family work: from universal social service to targeted work in child welfare families], master thesis in social policy, Jyväskylä: Jyväskylän yliopisto.

Leira, A. (1999) 'Cash-for-child care and daddy leave', in P. Moss and F. Deven (eds) *Parental leave: Progress or pitfall? Research and policy issues in Europe* (CBGS Publications, vol 35), Hague and Brussels: NIDI, pp 267-92.

Leira, A. (2006) 'Parenthood change and policy reform in Scandinavia', in A.L. Ellingsæter and A. Leira (eds) *Politicising parenthood in Scandinavia: Gender relations in welfare states*, Bristol: Policy Press, pp 27-52.

Litmala, M. (2001) *Avioeroprosessin piirteet* [Features of divorce proceedings] Tutkimustiedonantoja 55, Helsinki: Oikeuspoliittinen tutkimuslaitos.

Litrownik, A.J., Newton, R., Hunter, W.H., English, D., and Everson, M.D. (2003) 'Exposure to family violence in young at-risk children: a longitudinal look after the effects of victimization and witnessed physical and psychological aggression', *Journal of Family Violence*, vol 18, no 1, pp 59-73.

Lodrup, P., Agell, A. and Singer, A. (2003) *Nordisk borneret I. Farskap, morskap og underhall till barn* [Nordic child legislation I: fatherhood, motherhood and maintenance of children] (Nord 2003:4), Copenhagen: Nordic Council of Ministers.

Lorenz, W. (1994) *Social work in a changing Europe*, London: Routledge.

Lorentzen, G. (1994) 'Sosialt arbeid – et fargerikt fellesskap' [Social work: a colourful coexistence], *Nordisk Sosialt Arbeid*, vol 14, no 2, pp 83-92.

Løvlie Schibbye, A.L. (1988) *Familien – tvang og mulighet* [The family: an obligation and an opportunity], Oslo: Universitetsforlaget.

Lov om barneverntjenester (1992) [Act on Child Welfare Services], Norway.

Luostarinen, H. and Uskali, T. (2006) 'Suomalainen journalismi ja yhteiskunnan muutos' [Finnish journalism and the change of society], in R. Heiskala and E. Luhtakallio (eds) *Uusjako*, Helsinki: Gaudeamus, pp 179-201.

Lurie, J. (2001) 'Barns rettigheter i barnevern etter innføring av lov om barneverntjenester: er dagens praksis i samsvar med lovens intensjoner?' [Children's rights in child protection after enactment of the law on child protection services: is today's practice in accordance with the intentions of the law?], in I.M. Tronvoll and E. Marthinsen (eds) *Sosialt arbeid – Refleksjoner og nyere forskning*, Trondheim: Tapir, pp 167-84.

Määttä, P. (1999) *Perhe asiantuntijana. Erityiskasvatus ja kuntoutuksen käytännöt* [Family as an expert: special education and rehabilitation practices], Jyväskylä: Atena.

McAlister Groves, B. (2001) 'When home isn't safe: children and domestic violence', *Smith College Studies in Social Work*, vol 71, no 2, pp 183-207.

McGee, C. (2000) *Children's experiences of domestic violence*, London: Jessica Kingsley.

McKie, L. and Cunningham-Burley, S. (2005) *Families in society: Boundaries and relationships*, Bristol: Policy Press/CRFR.

McNamee, S. and Gergen, K.J. (eds) (1993/2004) *Therapy as social construction*, London: Sage.

Månsson, S.A. (2000) 'Kunnskapsutväcklingen inom socialtjänsten och den akademiske forskningen – drar vi åt samme hold?' [Knowledge development within social services and academic research: are we aiming at the same direction?] *Socionomen*, no 8, pp 4-9.

Mapping the number and characteristics of children under three in institutions across europe at risk of harm: Executive summary (2005) Research project Daphne Programme in collaboration with WHO regional Office for Europe and the University of Birmingham, www.childcentre.info/projects/institutions/dbaFile12260.doc.

Marthinsen, E. and Røe, M. (2004) *Fattig eller rik? Slik ungdom ser det* [Poor or rich? As young people see it], Trondheim: Save the Children/NTNU, Department of Social Work and Health Science.

Marthinsen, E. and Tjelflaat, T. (2003) 'Introduksjon til debatten om evidensbasert forskning' [Introduction to a debate on evidence-based research], presentation at Utviklingssentrenes landssamling, Holmen, 22 August.

Meeuwisse, A. and Swärd, H. (2007) 'Cross-national comparisons of social work – a question of initial assumptions and levels of analysis', *European Journal of Social Work*, vol 10, no 4, pp 481-96.

Melby, K., Pylkkänen, A. and Rosenbeck, B. (1999) 'Inledning' [Introduction], in K. Melby, A. Pylkkänen and B. Rosenbeck (eds) *Ægteskab i Norden fra Saxo til i dag*, (Nord 1999:14), Copenhagen: Nordisk Ministerråd, pp 9-17.

Merton, R. (1972) 'Insiders and outsiders: a chapter in the sociology of knowledge', *The American Journal of Sociology*, vol 78, no 1, pp 9-47.

Midgley, J. (1981) *Professional imperialism: Social work in the Third World*, London: Heinemann.

Millar, J. and Warman, A. (eds) (1996) *Defining family obligations in Europe* (Bath Social Policy Papers no 23), Bath: University of Bath, Centre for the Analysis of Social Policy.

Millar, M. (2005) 'A comparative perspective: exploring the space for family support', in P. Dolan, J. Canavan and J. Pinkerton (eds) *Family support as reflective practice*, London: Jessica Kingsley, pp 88-99.

Miller, J. and Garran, A.M. (2007) *Racism in the United States: Implications for the helping professions*, Belmont, CA: Thomson Brooks.

Milligan, I. and Stevens, I. (2006) *Residential child care: Collaborative practice*, London, Thousand Oaks, CA and Delhi: Sage.

Mishler, E. (1995) 'Models of narrative analysis: a typology', *Journal of Narrative and Life History*, vol 5, no 2, pp 69-73.

Mishler, E. (1999) *Storylines: Craftsartists' narratives of identity*, Cambridge, MA: Harvard University Press.

Misztal, B.A. (2003) *Theories of social remembering*, Maidenhead and Philadelphia, PA: Open University Press.

Möller, S. (2004) *Sattumista suunnitelmallisuuteen. Lapsen elämäntilanteen kartoitus lastensuojelussa* [From coincidences to orderliness: assessment of the child's life situation in child welfare] (Opas- ja käsikirjat 1/2004), Jyväskylä: Pesäpuu ry.

Morago, P. (2006) 'Evidence-based practice: from medicine to social work', *European Journal of Social Work*, vol 9, no 4, pp 461-77.

Moran, P., Ghate, D. and van der Merwe, A. (2004) *What works in parenting support? A review of the international evidence* (Research Report no 574), London: HMSO, Policy Research Bureau.

Morgan, K. and Zippel, K. (2003) 'Paid to care: the origins and effects of care leave policies in Western Europe', *Social Politics*, vol 10, no 1, pp 49-85.

Moss, P. and Deven, F. (eds) (1999) *Parental leave: Progress or pitfall? Research and policy issues in Europe* (CBGS Publications, vol. 35), Hague and Brussels: NIDI.

Munro, E. (2001) 'Empowering looked-after children', *Child and Family Social Work*, vol 6, no 2, pp 129-37.

Myllärniemi, A. (2006) *Huostaanottojen kriteerit pääkaupunkiseudulla* [The Criteria for taking into care in the capital region], Helsinki: Yliopistopaino, SOCCA Pääkaupunkiseudun sosiaalialan osaamiskeskus.

Myllärniemi, A. (2007) *Lastensuojelun avohuollon perhetyö ammattikäytäntönä – jäsennyksiä perhetyöstä toimintatutkimuksen valossa* [Family work in child welfare as professional practice] (Soccan ja Heikki Waris -instituutin julkaisusarja 6/2007), Helsinki: Heikki Waris-instituutti.

Näsman, E. (1995) 'Vuxnas interesse av att se med barns ögon' [Adults' interest to see with children's eyes], in L. Dahlgren and K. Hultqvist (eds) *Seendet och seendets villkor. En bok om barn og unges välfärd*, Stockholm: HLS Förlag, pp 279-304.

Nätkin, R. and Vuori J. (2007) 'Perhetyön tieto ja kritiikki. Johdanto perhetyön muuttuvaan kenttään' [Knowledge and critique of family work: introduction to the changing field of family work] in J. Vuori and R. Nätkin (eds) *Perhetyön tieto*, Tampere: Vastapaino, pp 7-38.

Nelson, K (ed) (1989) *Narratives from the crib*, Cambridge, MA: Harvard University Press.

Nielsen, L. (1997) 'Denmark: the family principle and the individual principle – and recent legislative news', in A. Bainham (ed) *The international survey of family law 1995*, The Hague: Kluwer Law International, pp 127-40.

Nordic statistical Yearbook 2007 (2007) (Nord 2007:001), Copenhagen: Nordic Council of Ministers.

NOSOSCO (Nordic Social-Statistical Committee) (2005) *Social protection in the Nordic countries, 2003: Scope, expenditure and financing*, Copenhagen: Nordic Social-Statistical Committee.

NOSOSCO (2007) *Social protection in the Nordic countries, 2005: Scope, expenditure and financing*, Copenhagen: Nordic Social-Statistical Committee.

Nupponen, R. and Simonen, L. (1983) *Kodinhoitajan tehostettu perhetyö: valtakunnallisen kokeilun loppuraportti* [Intensive family work of home helpers: final report of the national pilot], Helsinki: Mannerheimin lastensuojeluliitto.

O'Connor, P. (2000) *Speaking of crime: Narratives of prisoners*, Lincoln, NE: University of Nebraska Press.

OECD (Organisation for Economic Co-operation and Development) (2007a) *Babies and bosses: Reconciling work and family life. A synthesis of findings for OECD countries*, Paris: OECD.

OECD (2007b) *Social expenditure database*, www.oecd.org/els/social/expenditure.

OECD (2007c) *Family database*, www.oecd.org/els/social/family.

Ofstad, K. and Skar, R. (1995) *Barnevernloven* [Child Protection Law], Oslo: Juridisk forlag.

Ólafsson, S. (1999) *Íslenska leiðin. Almannatryggingar og velferð í fjölþjóðlegum samanburði* [The Icelandic way: social security and welfare in a comparative perspective], Reykjavík: Tryggingastofnun ríkisins.

Ombudsman for Children in Finland (2008) www.lapsiasia.fi.

Oppedal, M. (1997) 'Blir barn sett og hørt ved akutte vedtak?' [Are children seen and heard before emergency decisions?], in E. Backe-Hansen and T. Havik (eds) (1997) *Barnevern på barns premisser – barn, ungdom og familie*, Oslo: Ad Notam Gyldendal, pp 231-43.

Ottosen, M.H. (2006) 'In the name of the father, the child and the holy genes: constructions of "the child's best interest" in legal disputes over contacts', *Acta Sociologica*, vol 49, no 1, pp 29-46.

Paavola, A. (ed) (2004) *Perhe keskiössä. Ideoita yhteistyöhön perheiden parhaaksi; kokemuksia Ruotsin Leksandista ja useista Suomen kunnista* [Family at the centre: ideas for cooperation for the benefit of families; experiences from Leksand in Sweden and from Finnish municipalities], Helsinki: Lastensuojelun keskusliitto.

Pasanen, T. (2001) *Lastenkodin asiakaskunta. Psykiatrinen tutkimus lastenkotilasten kehityksellisistä riski- ja suojaavista tekijöistä, oirehdinnasta sekä hoidon tarpeesta* [The clients of a children's home: a psychiatric study of the developmental risks and protective factors, symptoms and needs for treatment among the residents of a children's home] (Annales Universitatis Turkuensis C 170), Turku: Turun yliopisto.

Patterson, W. (ed) (2002) *Strategic narrative: New perspectives on the power of personal and cultural stories*, Lanham, MD: Lexington Books.

Payne, M. (1997) *Modern social work theory* (2nd edn), Basingstoke: Macmillan.

Pekkarinen, E. (2006) 'Murrosikäisten tyttöjen kokemukset lastensuojelun ryhmätoiminnasta' [The experiences of teenage girls of group treatment in child protection], in H. Forsberg, A. Ritala-Koskinen and M. Törrönen (eds) *Lapset ja sosiaalityö*, Jyväskylä: PS-kustannus, pp 99-128.

Peled, E. (1993) 'Children who witness women battering: concerns and dilemmas in the construction of a social problem', *Children and Youth Services Review*, vol 15, no 1, pp 43-52.

Peled, E. and Davis, D. (1995) *Groupwork with children of battered women*, Thousand Oaks, CA: Sage.

Penn, H. and Gough, D. (2002) 'The price of a loaf of bread: some conceptions of family support', *Children and Society*, vol 16, no 1, pp 17-32.

Penna, S. Paylor, I. and Washington, J. (2000) 'Globalization, social exclusion and the possibilities for global social work and welfare', *European Journal of Social Work*, vol 3, no 2, pp 109-22.

Petrie, P., Boddy, J., Cameron, C., Wigfall, V. and Simon, A. (2006) *Working with children in care: European perspectives,* Maidenhead: Open University Press.

Pettersson, U. (2001) *Socialt arbete, politik och professionalisering. Den historiska utvecklingen i USA och Sverige* [Social work, politics and professionalisation: the historical development in the US and Sweden], Stockholm: Natur och Kultur.

Phillipson, M. (1989) *In modernity's wake*, London: Routledge.

Piltz, K.G. and Gustavsdottir, K. (1992) *Den osynliga familjen: samarbetspartner eller syndabock,* [The invisible family: partner for co-operation or scapegoat] Göteborg: Ask og Embla.

Pincus, A. and Minahan, A. (1973) *Social work practice: Model and method*, Itasca, IL: Peacock Press.

Plummer, K. (2001) *Documents of life 2: An invitation to a critical humanism*, London: Sage.

Pösö, T. (1990) 'Pahantapaiset perhehoitoon! Laitoshuollon, sen kritiikin ja yhden vaihtoehdon tarkastelua' [Delinquent children into family care! An analysis of institutional care, its criticism and one alternative], in *Suomalainen sosiaalityö*, Sosiaalipolitiikka 1990: 2), Helsinki: Sosiaalipoliittinen yhdistys, pp 185-200.

Pösö, T. (1993) *Kolme koulukotia* [Three reform schools](Acta Universitatis Tamperensis 383), Tampere: Tampereen yliopisto.

Pösö, T. (1996) 'Lastensuojelun kaksi maailmaa: englantilaisen ja suomalaisen järjestelmän vertailua' [The two worlds of child welfare: a comparison between the English and Finnish systems], *Janus*, vol 4, no 2, pp 169-78.

Pösö, T. (2004) *Vakavat silmät ja muita kokemuksia koulukodista* [Serious eyes and other experiences of the reform schools] (Tutkimuksia 133), Helsinki: Stakes.

Pösö, T. (2007) 'Lastensuojelun puuttuva tieto' [The missing knowledge of child protection], in J. Vuori and R. Nätkin (eds) *Perhetyön tieto*, Tampere: Vastapaino, pp 65–82.

Pringle, K. (1995) *Men, masculinities and social welfare*, London: UCL Press.

Pringle, K. (1998) *Children and social welfare in Europe*, Buckingham: Open University Press.

Pringle, K. (2005) 'Neglected issues in Swedish child protection policy and practice: age, ethnicity and gender', in M. Eriksson, M. Hester, S. Keskinen and K. Pringle (eds) *Tackling men's violence in families: Nordic issues and dilemmas*, Bristol: Policy Press. pp 155-70.

Pringle, K. (2006a) 'Swedish welfare responses to ethnicity: intersectional perspectives on the case of children and their families', in P. De los Reyes (ed) *Om välfärdens gränser och det villkorande medborgarskapet* (Rapport av Utredningen om makt, integration och strukturell diskriminering, SOU 2006:37), Stockholm: Fritzes offentliga publikationer, pp 217-48.

Pringle, K. (2006b) 'En fallstudie av bruket och missbruket av intersektionalitet' ['A case study on the uses and misuses of intersectionality'], in K. Sandell and D. Mulinari (eds) *Feministiska interventioner: berättelser om och från en annan värld*, Stockholm: Atlas Akademi, pp 21-53.

Pringle, K. (2008a) 'Studium porownawcze dobrobytu w kategoriach gender, etnicznoinści I koncepcjI "integralnosci cielesnej": Esping-Andersen postawiony na glowie' ['Comparative studies of well-being in terms of gender, ethnicity and the concept of "bodily citizenship": turning Esping-Andersen on his head'], in E. Oleksy (ed) *Tożsamość i obywatelstwo w społeczeństwie wielokulturowym*, Warsaw: Wydawnictwo Naukowe PWN SA, pp 161-75.

Pringle, K. (2008b) 'Intersektionalitet og det sociale arbejdes praksis' [Intersectionality and social work practice], in M.H. Jacobsen and K. Pringle (eds) *At forstå det sociale - kunsten at forbinde teori og praksis* [Understanding the social knowledge connecting theory and practice], Copenhagen: Akademisk Forlag, pp 108-24.

Pringle, K. and Harder, M. (1999) *Through two pairs of eyes: A comparative study of Danish social policy and child welfare practice*, Aalborg: Aalborg University Press.

Pugh, R. and Gould, N. (2000) 'Globalization, social work, and social welfare', *European Journal of Social Work*, vol 3, no 2, pp 123-38.

Pulma, P. (1987) 'Kerjuuluvusta perhekuntoutukseen. Lapsuuden yhteiskunnallistuminen ja lastensuojelun kehitys Suomessa' [From begging to family rehabilitation: the development of child welfare in Finland], in P. Pulma and O. Turpeinen, *Suomen lastensuojelun historia*, Helsinki: Lastensuojelun keskusliitto, pp 7-264.

Rädda Barnen (2006) *'Hur många vuxna tror på en unge egentligen???' En undersökning av ungas upplevelser av våld under uppväxten* ['How many adults actually believe in a youth???' A study on experiences of young people of violence during their development], Stockholm: Rädda Barnen.

Rafferty, M. and O'Sullivan, E. (1999) *Suffer the little children: The inside story of Ireland's industrial schools*, Dublin: New Island.

Raittila, P., Johansson, K., Juntunen, L., Kangasluoma, L., Koljonen, K., Kumpu, V., Pernu, I. and Väliverronen, J. (2008) *Jokelan koulusurmat mediassa* [The school killings of Jokela in the media], Tampere: Tampereen yliopisto, Tiedotusopin laitos, Journalismin tutkimusyksikkö, Julkaisuja A 105.

Raunio, K. (2004) *Olennainen sosiaalityössä* [The essential in social work], Helsinki: Gaudeamus.

Reijonen, M. (2005) 'Mitä työtä se perhetyö oikein on? – ammattina perhetyöntekijä' [What family work actually is? Family work as a profession] in M. Reijonen (ed) *Voimaa perhetyöhön. Arjen tuki ja ammatilliset verkostot*, Jyväskylä: PS-kustannus, pp 7-15.

Richmond, M. (1899) *Friendly visiting among the poor: A handbook for charity workers*, New York: Macmillan.

Ridge, T. (2002) *Childhood poverty and social exclusion: From a child's perspective*, Bristol: Policy Press.

Riessman, C.K. (2008) *Narrative methods for the human sciences*, Thousand Oaks, CA: Sage.

Rimpelä, M., Luopa, P., Räsänen, M. and Jokela, J. (2006) 'Nuorten hyvinvointi 1996-2006. Eriytyvätkö hyvinvoinnin ja pahoinvoinnin kehityssuunnat?' [Well-being of the youth in 1996-2006: do tendencies of well-being and ill-being separate from each other?], in M. Kautto (ed) *Suomalaisten hyvinvointi 2006*, Helsinki: Stakes, pp 57-77.

Ritala-Koskinen, A. (2003) 'Onnistumisia lastensuojelussa' [Going well in child welfare], in M. Satka, A. Pohjola and M. Rajavaara (eds) *Sosiaalityö ja vaikuttaminen*, Jyväskylä: SoPhi, pp 103-24.

Roberto-Forman, L. (2001/02) 'Thinking globally', *AFTA Newsletter*, winter, pp 43-5.

Rojek, C., Peacock, C. and Collins, S. (1988) *Social work and received ideas*, London and New York: Routledge.

Rose, N. (1996) 'The death of the social', *Economy and Society*, vol 25, no 3, pp 327-56.

Rostgaard, T. and Fridberg, T. (1998) *Caring for children and older people: A comparison of European policies and practices*, Copenhagen: The Danish National Institute of Social Research.

Rudberg, M. (1982) *Dydige, sterke, lykkelige barn* [Good, strong and happy children], Oslo: Universitetsforlaget.

Sainsbury, D. (ed) (1999) *Gender and welfare state regimes*, Oxford: Oxford University Press.

Salamon, L.M., Sokolowski, W.S., List, R. (2003) *Global civil society: An overview*, Baltimore, MD: The John Hopkins University, Center for Civil Society Studies, Institute for Policy Studies.

Sallnäs, M. (2000) *Barnavårdens institutioner – framväxt, ideologi och struktur* [Institutions in child welfare: growth, ideology and structure] (Rapport nr 96-2000), Stockholm: Stockholms universitet, Institutionen för socialt arbete.

Salmi, M. (2002) 'Arbete, familj och ömsesidig hjälp mellan generationer' [Work, family and mutual help between generations], paper presented at Nordic Sociological Conference, Reykjavík, 15-17 August.

Salmi, M., Huttunen, J. and Yli-Pietilä, P. (1996) *Lapset ja lama* [Children and the economic recession] (Raportteja 197), Helsinki: Stakes.

Salonen, T. (2003) *Barnfattigdommen i Sverige. Årsrapport 2003* [Child poverty in Sweden: year report 2003], Stockholm: Save the Children.

Salonen, T. (2007) *Barns ekonomiska utsatthet − årsrapport 2006* [Economic vulnerability of children: year report 2006], Stockholm: Rädda Barnen.

Sand, A.B. (2002) 'Vård av hjälpbehövande familjemedlemmar − ett socialt nätverk som fjättrar?' [Care of help-need family members: a social network that enchains?], paper presented at Nordic Sociological Conference, Reykjavík, 15-17 August.

Sandbæk, M. (2002) 'Barn og foreldre som sosiale aktører i møte med hjelpetjenester' [Children and parents as social actors in contact with the helping services], doctoral thesis, Trondheim: NTNU.

Sandbæk, M. (ed) (2004) *Barns levekår − hva betyr familiens inntekt?* [Children's living conditions: what does the family's income mean?] (NOVA-report 11-04), Oslo: Norsk institutt for forskning om oppvekst, velferd og aldring.

Sarvimäki, P. and Siltaniemi, A. (ed) (2007) *Sosiaalihuollon ammatillisen henkilöstön tehtävärakennesuositus* [Recommendations for the task structure of professional social services staff] (Julkaisuja 2007:14.), Helsinki: Sosiaali- ja terveysministeriö.

Satir, V. (1964) *Conjoint family therapy: A guide to theory and practice*, Palo Alto, CA: Science and Behavior Books.

Satka, M. (1994) 'Sosiaalinen työ peräänkatsojamiehestä hoivayrittäjäksi' [Social work from control men to care entrepreneurs], in J. Jaakkola, P. Pulma, M. Satka and K. Urponen, *Armeliaisuus, yhteisöapu, sosiaaliturva. Suomen sosiaaliturvan historia*, Helsinki: Sosiaaliturvan keskusliitto, pp 261-339.

Satka, M. and Eydal, G.B. (2004) 'The history of Nordic welfare policies for children', in H. Brembeck, B. Johansson and J. Kampmann (eds) *Beyond the competent child: Exploring contemporary childhoods in the Nordic welfare societies*, Fredriksberg: Roskilde University Press, pp 33-62.

Savio, A. (1989) *Purkamisen paineet ja potentiaali* [The pressures and potentials for institutional decarceration] (Julkaisuja 13), Helsinki: Sosiaalihallitus.

Schjelderup, L., Omre, C. and Marthinsen, E. (eds) (2005) *Nye metoder i et moderne barnevern* [New methods for modern child welfare], Bergen: Fagbokforlaget.

Seikkula, J. and Arnkil, T.E. (2005) *Dialoginen verkostotyö* [Dialogical network therapy], Helsinki: Tammi.

Seim, S. and Slettebö, T. (eds) (2007) *Brukermedvirkning i barnavernet* [User involvement in child welfare], Oslo: Universitetsforlaget.

Selvini-Palazzoli, M., Boscolo, L., Cecchin, G. and Prata, G. (1978) *Paradox and counterparadox*, New York: Jason Aronson.

Sennett, R. (1998) *The corrosion of character*, London: Norton.

Sennett, R. (2004) *Respect: The formation of character in an age of inequality*, London: Penguin Books.

Shotter, J. (2002) *Conversational realities: Constructing life through language*, London: Sage.

Sihvonen, E. (2005) 'Lasten ja nuorten pahoinvointi. Vastuullinen vanhemmuus julkisuuden valokeilassa' [The illfare of children and young people: responsible parenthood in the limelight of publicity], master thesis in sociology, Helsinki: Helsingin yliopisto.

Simonen, L. (1990) *Contradictions of the welfare state, women and caring* (Acta Universitatis Tamperensis ser A vol 295), Tampere: University of Tampere.

Sinfield, A. and West Pedersen, A. (2006) 'Child poverty: a persisting challenge', *European Journal of Social Security*, vol 8, no 3, 229-34.

Sipilä, J. (2003) 'Hoivan organisointi: vaivaistalosta markkinatavaraksi' [Organising social care: from poorhouse to a market product], *Janus*, vol 11, no 1, pp 23-38.

Sipilä, J. (ed) (1997) *Social care services: The key to the Scandinavian welfare model*, Aldershot: Avebury.

Siren, P. (1967) 'Ei kotia ei koulua' [No home, no school], in L.D. Eriksson (ed) *Pakkoauttajat* [The coercive helpers], Helsinki: Tammi, pp 78-107.

Skeggs, B. (1997) *Formations of class and gender: Becoming respectable*, London: Sage.

Skevik, A. (2005) 'Familier med vedvarende lav inntekt i Norge – har de dårlig råd?' [Low-income families in Norway: how are they doing?], *Barn*, vol 23, no 3, pp 51-66.

Sluzki, C. (2001/02) 'Bridging two continents', *AFTA Newsletter*, winter, pp 50-1.

Smith, D.E. (1987) *The everyday world as problematic: A feminist sociology*, Boston, MA: Northeastern University Press.

Smith, M. (2003) 'Towards a professional identity and knowledge base: is residential child care still social work?', *Journal of Social Work,* vol 3, no 2, pp 235-52.

Smith, M. (2005) 'Rethinking residential child care: a child and youth care approach', in D. Crimmens and I. Milligan (eds) *Facing forward: Residential child care in the 21st century*, Lyme Regis: Russell House, pp 115-25.

Socialstyrelsen (2005) *När mamma blir slagen – Att hjälpa barn som levt med våld i familjen* [When mummy gets beaten – to help children who have experienced domestic violence], Stockholm: Socialstyrelsen.

Somer, E. and Braunstein, A. (1999) 'Are children exposed to interparental violence being psychologically maltreated?', *Aggression and Violent Behavior*, vol 4, no 4, pp 449-56.

Sommer, D. (2003a) *Barndomspsykologi: udvikling i en forandret verden* [Childhood psychology: development in a changed world], Copenhagen: Hans Reitzel forlag.

Sommer, D. (2003b) *Barndomspsykologiske facetter* [Childhood psychology facets], Århus: Systime Academic.

Sosiaali- ja terveydenhuolto vuonna 2005 [Social and health care in 2005] (2006) www.stakes.fi/FI/tilastot/tilastojulkaisut/vuosikirja.htm.

SOTKAnet Indicator Bank (2008) 'Home help, recipient families with children in services funded by municipality, during years 1990-2007', http://uusi.sotkanet. fi.

SOU 1993:82 (1993) *Frivilligt socialt arbete. Kartläggning och kunskapsöversikt* [Voluntary social work: mapping and overview of knowledge], Stockholm: Socialdepartementet, Rapport av Socialtjänstkommittén.

SOU 2001:72 (2001) *Barnmisshandel – att förebygga och åtgärda* [Child abuse: prevention and intervention], Stockholm: Socialdepartementet, Slutbetänkande av Kommittén mot barnmisshandel.

Soydan, H. (1999) *The history of ideas in social work*, London: SWRA/Venture Press.

Spector, M. and Kitsuse, J. (1987) *Constructing social problems*, New York: Aldine de Gruyter.

Stakes (1998) *Lapsen elatus, huolto ja lastensuojelu 1997* [Child support, custody and child welfare 1997] (Tilastoraportti 23/1998), Stakes: Helsinki.

Stakes (2006) *Suomen virallinen tilasto, Sosiaaliturva 2006* [Official statistics of Finland, social welfare 2006] (Tilastotiedote 14/2006), Helsinki: Stakes, www. stakes.fi/FI/tilastot/aiheittain/Lapsuusjaperhe/lastensuojelu.htm.

Stang Dahl, T. (1992) *Barnevern og samfunnsvern: om stat, vitenskap og profesjoner under barnevernets oppkomst i Norge* [Child protection and society protection: about state, science and professions during the development of child protection in Norway], Oslo: Pax forlag.

Statistics Finland (2006) 'EU-maiden työllisyyden erot' [Differences in employment between EU member states], www.stat.fi/tup/verkkokoulu/data/tvt/06/01/ index.

Stevens, I. and Hassett, P. (2007) 'Applying complexity theory to risk in child protection practice', *Childhood*, vol 14, no 1, pp 128-44.

Stierlin, H. (1981) *Separating parents and adolescents: Individuation in the family*, New York: Jason Aronson.

Sullivan, C., Whitehead, P.C., Chiodo, D. and Hurley, D. (2008) 'Perception of risk among child protection workers', *Children and Youth Services Review*, vol 30, no 7, pp 699-704.

Sunesson, S., Blomberg, S., Edebalk, P.-G., Harrysson, L., Magnusson, J., Meeuwisse, A., Petersson, J., Salonen, T. (1998) 'The flight from universalism', *European Journal of Social Work*, vol 1, no 1, pp 19-29.

Sutton, C. (2000) 'Diversity forum: the complexities of compassion', *AFTA Newsletter*, fall, pp 21-4.

Swedner, G. (1993) 'Traditioner som fängslar – en studie av det sociala arbetets motiv och framträdelseformer i Göteborg under tiden 1790-1918' [Capturing traditions: a study on the motives and forms of social work in Gothenburg in 1790-1918], doctoral thesis, Göteborg: Göteborgs universitet.

Szasz, T. (1970) *Psykisk sjukdom – en myt* [Mental illness: a myth], Stockholm: Bokförlaget Aldus/Bonniers.

Taitto, A. (2002) *Päihdeongelma perheessä. Huomaa lapsi. Opas lasten vertaisryhmien vetäjille* [Guidebook for leaders of peer groups for children growing up in families with alcohol problems], Helsinki: Lasten Keskus.

Taylor, C. and White, S. (2006) 'Knowledge and reasoning in social work: educating for humane judgement', *British Journal of Social Work*, vol 36, no 6, pp 937-54.

Tedre, S. (2004) 'Tukisukkahousut sosiaalipolitiikkaan! Inhomaterialistinen hoivatutkimusote' [Support tights to social policy! Distaste-materialist care research approach], in E. Jokinen, M. Kaskisaari and M. Husso (eds) *Ruumis töihin! Käsite ja käytäntö*, Tampere: Vastapaino, pp 41-64.

Tervonen-Arnkil, K. (ed) (1999) *Vaikeahoitoisten lasten ja nuorten hoitomenetelmiä lastensuojelulaitoksissa* [Treatment methods for children and young people with special needs in residential child care] (Sijaishuollon neuvottelukunnan julkaisuja 16), Helsinki: Lastensuojelun keskusliitto.

Therborn, G. (1993) 'Politics of childhood: the rights of children in modern times', in F.G. Castles (ed) *Families of nations: Patterns of public policy in western democracies*, Aldershot: Dartmouth, pp 241-93.

Tilbury, C. (2005) 'Counting family support', *Child and Family Social Work*, vol 10, no 2, pp 149-57.

Tiller, P.O. (1990) *Hverandre: en bok om barneforskning* [Each other: a book on child research], Oslo: Gyldendal.

Titmuss, R. (1974) *Social policy*, London: Allen & Unwin.

Tochluk, S. (2007) *Witnessing whiteness: First steps toward an antiracist practice and culture*, Lanham, MD: Rowman and Littlefield Education.

Törrönen, M. (1999) *Lasten arki laitoksessa – Elämistila lastenkodissa ja sairaalassa* [Children's everyday life in an institution: the life space in a children's home and in a hospital], Helsinki: Yliopistopaino.

Trydegård, G.-B. (2000) *Tradition, change and variation: Past and present trends in public old-age care* (Studies of Social Work 16), Stockholm: Stockholm University: Department of Social Work.

Tuovila, P. (2001) *Eheänä elämään: Lastenkoti korjaavana kokemuksena* [Unbroken into life: children's home as a compensatory experience], Helsinki: Suomen kasvatus- ja perheneuvontaliitto ry.

Tvetene, K.G. (2001) '"Jeg prøver å få det til å bli borte av seg selv" – om barn som lever i familier som over tid har mottatt økonomisk sosialhjelp og deres håndtering av hverdagens møte med økonomiske krav' ["I try to let it disappear by itself": about children living in families who have received financial welfare assistance for longer periods and how they manage to deal with the financial demands of everyday life], master thesis, Oslo: Universitetet i Oslo, Institutt for sosiologi og samfunnsgeografi.

UN Convention on the Rights of the Child (1989) New York: United Nations.

Ungar, M. (2001) 'The social construction of resilience among "problem" youth in out-of-home placement: a study of health-enhancing deviance', *Child and Youth Care Forum*, vol 30, no 3, pp 137-54.

Ungar, M. (2008) 'Resilience across cultures', *British Journal of Social Work*, vol 38, no 2, pp 218-35.

UNICEF (2007) *Child poverty in perspective: An overview of child well-being in rich countries* (Report Card 7), Florence: UNICEF Innocenti Research Centre.

Urponen, K. (1994) 'Huoltoyhteiskunnasta hyvinvointivaltioon' [From the maintenance state towards the welfare state], in J. Jaakkola, P. Pulma, M. Satka and K. Urponen *Armeliaisuus, yhteisöapu ja sosiaaliturva. Suomalaisen sosiaaliturvan historia*, Helsinki: Sosiaaliturvan keskusliitto, pp 163-260.

Uusimäki, M. (2005) *Perhetyötäkö kaikki?* [Is it all family work?], Oulu: Pohjois-Suomen sosiaalialan osaamiskeskus.

Uusitalo, H. (2000) 'Social policy in a deep economic recession and after: the case of Finland', paper presented at the Year 2000 International Research Conference on Social Security, Helsinki, 25-27 Sebtember.

Välivaara C. (2004) *Sijoitettu lapsi tunnepyörässä - menetelmiä ja välineitä lapsilähtöiseen lastensuojeluun* [Methods and tools for child-centred child welfare], Jyväskylä: Pesäpuu ry.

Velstandens paradoks [The paradox of welfare] (2007) Oslo: FAFO and NOVA.

Venkula, J. (2005) *Epävarmuudesta ja varmuudesta* [About certainty and uncertainty], Helsinki: Kirjapaja.

Viittala, K. (2001) *'Kyllä se tommosellaki lapsella on kovempi urakka' – Sikiöaikana alkoholille altistuneiden huostaanotettujen lasten elämäntilanne, riskiprosessit ja suojaavat prosessit* ['It's harder for that kind of child to get along': the life situation of the children exposed to alcohol in utero and taken care of by society, their risk and protective processes] (Jyväskylä Studies in Education, Psychology and Social Research 180), Jyväskylä: University of Jyväskylä.

Virokannas, E. (2004) *Normaalin rajan molemmilla puolilla: tutkimus huumehoitoyksikön nuorten identiteetin rakentumisesta* [On both sides of the normality boundary: a study of identity formation among young people at a drug treatment unit], Helsinki: Stakes

Vleminckx, K. and Smeeding, T.M. (eds) (2001) *Child well-being, child poverty and child policy in modern nations*, Bristol: Policy Press.

von Bertalanffy, L. (1968) *General system theory*, New York: Georg Braziller.

Waaldijk, K. (ed) (2005) *More or less together: Levels of legal consequences of marriage, cohabitation and deregistered partnership for different-sex and same-sex partners. A comparative study of nine European countries*, Paris: INED.

Walsh, F. (2006) *Strengthening family resilience* (2nd edn), New York: Guilford.

Ward, A. (2004) 'Towards a theory of the everyday: the ordinary and the special in daily living in residential care', *Child and Youth Care Forum*, vol 33, no 3, pp 209-25.

Watzlawick, P., Beavin, J.H. and Jackson, D.D. (1967) *Pragmatics of human communication*, New York: Norton.

Watzlawick, P., Weakland, J.H. and Fisch, R. (1974) *Change: Principles of problem formation and problem resolution*, New York: Norton.

Weingarten, K. (2006) 'On hating to hate', *Family Process*, vol 45, no 3, pp 277-88.

Weiss, H. (2001) 'Large systems forum', *AFTA Newsletter*, fall, pp 23-5.

West, C. and Fenstermaker, S. (1995) 'Doing difference', *Gender and Society*, vol 9, no 1, pp 8-37.

Westlund, J. (2007) 'Increased parental choice can lead to reduced gender equality', *NIKKmagasin* 2/2007, pp 8-11.

Westman, R., Haverinen R., Ristikartano, V., Koivisto, J and Malmivaara A. (2005) *Perheinterventioiden vaikuttavuus. Järjestelmällinen kirjallisuuskatsaus* [The effectiveness of family interventions: a systematic literature review on controlled trials] (FinSoc Arviointiraportteja 5/2005), Helsinki: Stakes.

White, S., Fook. J. and Gardner, L. (eds) (2006) *Critical reflection in health and social care*, Maidenhead: Open University.

Whiteford, P. and Adema, W. (2006) 'Combating child poverty in OECD countries: is work the answer?', *European Journal of Social Security*, vol 8, no 3, pp 235-56.

Wiklund, S. (2006) 'Signs of child maltreatment: the extent and nature of referrals to Swedish child welfare agencies', *European Journal of Social Work*, vol 9, no 1, pp 39-58.

Wolfe, D.A., Zak, L., Wilson, S. and Jaffe, P. (1984) 'Child witnesses to violence between parents: critical issues in behavioural and social adjustment', *Journal of Abnormal Child Psychology*, vol 14, no 1, pp 95-104.

Yesilova, K. (2007) 'Perheen puolesta. Perhekasvatus Suomessa 1970-1990 –luvuilla' [For the sake of the family: family education in Finland 1970-1990], in J. Vuori and R. Nätkin (eds) *Perhetyön tieto*, Tampere: Vastapaino, pp 39-64.

Yin, R.K. (1994) *Case study research: Designs and methods*, Thousand Oaks, CA: Sage.

Young, J. (1999) *The exclusive society: Social exclusion, crime and difference in late modernity*, Thousand Oaks, CA, and London: Sage.

Yuval-Davis, N. (2006) 'Intersectionality and feminist politics', *European Journal of Women's Studies*, vol 13, no 3, pp 193-209.

Åberg, Y. (2002) 'Are divorces contagious? The marital status of coworkers and the risk of divorce', paper presented at the Nordic Sociological Conference, Reykjavík, 15-17 August.

Index

Page references for notes are followed by n